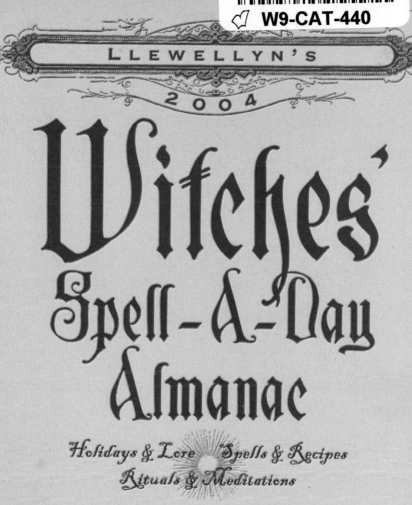

LLEWELLYN'S

2004

Witches'
Spell-A-Day
Almanac

Holidays & Lore ☀ Spells & Recipes
Rituals & Meditations

Copyright © 2003 Llewellyn Worldwide
Editing/Design: Michael Fallon
Cover Design: Lisa Novak; Background Photo: © PhotoDisc
Interior Art: © Claudine Hellmuth (illustrations: pp. 9, 29, 49, 71, 91, 113, 133, 153, 173, 193, 215, 235); © Eris Klein (holiday and day icons)

You can order Llewellyn books and annuals from *New Worlds,* Llewellyn's magazine catalog. To request a free copy of the catalog, call toll-free 1-877-NEW WRLD, or visit our website at http://subscriptions.llewellyn.com.

ISBN 0-7387-0228-5
Llewellyn Worldwide
PO Box 64383, Dept. 0-7387-0228-5
St. Paul, MN 55164

Table of Contents

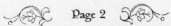

About The Authors

Karri Ann Allrich is an author, artist, and eclectic cook who weaves her Goddess path into all aspects of her life. She shares her Massachusetts home and studio with her husband and two sons. Her published books include: *Recipes From a Vegetarian Goddess, A Witch's Book of Dreams,* and *Cooking by Moonlight.* Ms. Allrich has also written articles for numerous publications.

Elizabeth Barrette is the managing editor of *PanGaia* and assistant editor of *SageWoman.* She has been involved with the Pagan community for more than thirteen years and lives in central Illinois. Her other writing fields include speculative fiction and gender studies. Visit her website at: http://www.worth-link.net/~ysabet/index.html

Denise Dumars is the cofounder of the Iseum of Isis Paedusis, an Isian study group chartered by the Fellowship of Isis, Clonegal Castle, Enniscorthy, Eire. In her professional life she is a college instructor and writer, and in her spiritual life she is an eclectic Isian and Neopagan. She is currently researching the practices of the Gaulish Druids, and she lives in Los Angeles' South Bay.

Ember follows a path of nature-centered spirituality, which inspires her to write poetry and articles about nature and magic. Her writing has appeared in various literary journals and in several Llewellyn annuals. She lives in the Midwest with her husband and two feline companions.

Karen Follett has been practicing witchcraft for over thirty years. She is currently a member of a local Georgian coven. Karen is married and has two teenage sons. She teaches meditation, psychic development, divination, visualization, and working with energy, and she has recently connected with an organization that investigates local paranormal activity.

Therese Francis, Ph.D. is an author, astrologer, folklorist, herbalist, and noted public speaker. Her most recent books are *The Mercury Retrograde Book, 20 herbs to take on a Business Trip,* and *20 Herbs to Take Outdoors* (published by One Spirit). Therese is the author of numerous articles on herbs, astrology, and other New Age topics, and she has written for Llewellyn's annuals for a number of years. An active member of the Sante Fe Astrology Forum, Therese teaches astrology, psychic and intuitive development, self-defense, and the integration of body, mind, heart, and spirit. She currently writes and resides in Sante Fe, New Mexico.

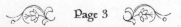

Lily Gardner is a lifelong student of folklore and mythology. She is a priestess in the Daughters of Gaia coven and a member of the Fat Thursday Writers. Lily lives with her husband, two Corgis, and a tuxedo cat in Portland, Oregon. She is currently working on a novel about family.

Magenta Griffith has been a Witch more than twenty-five years, a high priestess for thirteen years, and a founding member of the coven Prodea. She leads rituals and workshops around the Midwest and is currently librarian for the New Alexandria Library, a Pagan and magical resource center; see www.magusbooks.com/newalexandria for more details.

James Kambos is a writer, painter, and herbalist living in Appalachia. He has a degree in history and has had a lifelong interest in folk magic and herbs. He has authored numerous articles on these subjects.

Jonathan Keyes lives in Portland, Oregon, where he likes to fiddle around in the garden and play with his cat. Jon works as an astrologer and herbalist and has written an astrological health book and an herb book. He is at present working on a book titled *Healers,* a series of interviews with various herbalists, *curanderos,* and medicine people from around the United States.

Kristin Madden is a homeschooling mom who was raised in a shamanic home. She is the director of Ardantane's School of Shamanic Studies and is a member of the Druid College of Healing. In her spare time, she writes books, works as an environmental chemist, and rehabilitates wild birds. Visit her cyberhome at http://hometown.aol.com/mamadrum3/kristinshaman.html.

Robert Place is a visionary artist and illustrator whose award-winning works in painting, sculpture, and jewelry have been displayed in galleries and museums in America, Europe, and Japan. He is the creator and coauthor, with Rosemary Ellen Guiley, of *The Alchemical Tarot* and *The Angels Tarot,* published by HarperCollins. He is also the creator and author of *The Tarot of the Saints,* published by Llewellyn. *The Tarot of the Saints* has appeared on the cover of *Publisher's Weekly* and won an award in the interactive sidelines category at the annual International New-Age Trade Show in Denver. He has currently completed his fourth tarot project, *The Tarot of the Buddha,* which will be published by Llewellyn.

Cerridwen Iris Shea is a tarot-reading, horse-playing, hockey-loving kitchen Witch. She writes in several genres under several names. Her plays have been produced in New York, Los Angeles, London, Edinburgh, and Australia. She is working on a website for kitchen Witches, an interesting task for someone as computer-challenged as she.

Susan Sheppard is the author of four books: *Cry of the Banshee,* a book of ghost stories written with Richard Southall; *The Astrological Guide to Seduction & Romance; A Witch's Runes;* and a divination set, *The Phoenix Cards.* Sheppard has worked as a psychic most of her life and investigates hauntings. She runs a popular ghost tour and is a published poet. Her poppets are sold in Laurie Cabot's shop in Salem, Massachusetts.

S. Y. Zenith is three-quarters Chinese and one tad bit Irish. She is a lifelong solitary Pagan who has lived and traveled extensively in Asia for the past two decades. The countries she has visited include India, Nepal, Malaysia, Thailand, Singapore, and Japan. She is currently based in Sydney, Australia, where her time is divided between writing and experimenting with alternative remedies, herb crafts, and culinary delights. She is a member of the Australian Society of Authors.

Introduction

A Note on Magic and Spells

The spells in the *Witches' Spell-A-Day Almanac* evoke everyday magic designed to improve our lives and homes. You needn't be an expert on magic to follow these simple rites and spells; as you will see if you use these spells through the year, magic, once mastered, is easy to perform. The only advanced technique required of you is the art of visualization.

Visualization is an act of controlled imagination. If you can call up in your mind a picture of your best friend's face or a flag flapping in the breeze, you can visualize. In magic, visualizations are used to direct and control magical energies. Basically, the spell-caster creates a visual image of the spell's desired goal, whether it be perfect health, a safe house, or a protected pet.

Visualization is the basis of all good spells, and as such it is a tool that should be properly used. Visualization must be real in the mind of the spell-caster so that it allows him or her to raise, concentrate, and send forth energy to accomplish the spell.

Perhaps when visualizing, you'll find that you're doing everything right, but you don't feel anything. This is common, for we haven't been trained to acknowledge—let alone utilize—our magical abilities. Keep practicing, however, for your spells can "take" even if you're not the most experienced natural magician.

You will notice also that many spells in this collection have a some-what "light" tone. They are seemingly fun and frivolous, filled with rhyme and colloquial speech. This is not to diminish the seriousness of the purpose, but rather to create a relaxed atmosphere for the practitioner. Lightness of spirit helps focus energy; rhyme and common language help the spell-caster remember the words and train the mind where it is needed. The intent of this magic is indeed very serious at times; and magic is never to be trifled with.

Even when your spells are effective, magic won't usually sparkle before your very eyes. The test of magic's success is time, not immediate eye-popping results. But you can feel magic's energy for yourself by rubbing

your palms together briskly for ten seconds, then holding them a few inches apart. Sense the energy passing through them, the warm tingle in your palms. This is the power raised and used in magic. It comes from within and is perfectly natural.

Among the features of the *Witches' Spell-A-Day Almanac* are an easy-to-use "book of days" format; new spells specifically tailored for each day of the year (and its particular magical, astrological, and historical energies); and additional tips and lore for various days throughout the year—including color correspondences based on planetary influences, obscure and forgotten holidays and festivals, and an incense-of-the-day to help you waft magical energies from the ether into your space.

In creating this product, we were inspired by the ancient almanac traditions and the layout of the classic nineteenth-century almanac *Chamber's Book of Days,* which is subtitled *A Miscellany of Popular Antiquities in connection with the Calendar.* As you will see, our fifteen authors this year made history a theme of their spells, and we hope that by knowing something of the magic of past years we may make our current year all the better.

Enjoy your days, and have a magical year!

2004
Year of Spells

January

January is the first month of the year of the Gregorian calendar, and a time of beginnings. Its astrological sign is Capricorn, the goat (Dec 20–Jan 20), a cardinal earth sign ruled by Saturn. The name of the month itself comes from the two-faced Roman god Janus, who rules over gates and doorways. This wintry month is marked by icicles, hoarfrost, and snowdrifts, and by the warmth of the home hearth. Traditionally, handicrafts such as wool-spinning were practiced in January, and the spinning wheel has become a symbol of the season. According to Pagan traditions, even in this frozen time there are signs of new life. The days, for instance, are now slowly growing longer, and a few early flowers, such as the paper-white narcissus and white helle-bore, begin blooming. The Full Moon of January is called the Storm Moon. The main holiday of the month is, of course, New Year's Day, a day that calls for safeguards, augurs, and charms. All over the world, people are eager to see what the new year will bring; they kiss strangers, shoot guns in the air, toll bells, and exchange gifts. In Scotland, people watch the threshold to see what the "firstfooter," or first visitor, augurs for the year. People who make visits on New Year's Day therefore should be sure to bring gifts of herring, bread, and wood for the fire along with them.

January 1
Thursday

New Year's Day – Kwanzaa ends

2nd ♉

☽ → ♉ 12:02 am

Color of the day: Violet
Incense of the day: Chrysanthemum

Luck Lore for the New Year

All ancient religion stems from the same magical impulse. As the Hindu Brahmans say, "We must do what the gods did in the beginning." In all religion and myth, sacred time, or ritual, is a reenactment of the beginning time, the first year, when the gods walked the earth and taught men and women how to live. Knowledge of the beginning is the source of all magical power, and the quest for this knowledge is the reason behind the creation of all myths and rituals. All holidays are a sacred reenactment of the beginning. Many of the holidays that you will find in this almanac are a celebration of this renewal as practiced in its various forms among different the cultures around the world. Chief among these holidays is our current celebration of the New Year. It has not always been celebrated on the same day. In England, the New Year was celebrated on December 25, and then on March 25, before it was moved to the first of January. Despite the confusion, this day is a celebration and reliving of the creation of the world, the wresting of order out of chaos. As we will see, the evening before the New Year is a time when the social order and routines of daily life are suspended to symbolize the world's dissolving into chaos. On New Year's day, thankfully, the order is recreated. This is therefore meant to be a day of serious worship, joyous celebration, and a time to make resolutions—to recreate one's self and to restore one's behavior. Things that are done on this day will affect us for the entire year. It is important to perform a magic ritual to assure our continued good fortune. In popular culture, these magic rituals are often disguised as "good luck" practices. For example, a common practice among some African-Americans is to include a dish called Hoppin' John in the New Year's feast. This dish, made from black-eyed peas, rice, and ham hocks, ensures good luck through the year.

Robert Place

Notes:

oliday lore: New Year's Day calls for safeguards, augurs, charms, and proclamations. All over the world on this day, people kiss strangers, shoot guns into the air, toll bells, and exchange gifts. Preferred gifts are herring, bread, and fuel for the fire.

Notes:

January 2
Friday

2nd ♉

☽ v/c 2:21 pm

Color of the day: Rose
Incense of the day: Nutmeg

Firsts for the New Year Spell

he Japanese have a wonderful custom of honoring the New Year's "firsts," which they call *hatsu.* Among the activities they note on this day are the first day of work, the first visit to temple, and the first practice session for artists. You should note your "firsts" this year, and practice *kakizome* or the act of "first writing." To do so, choose your favorite poem, prayer, or passage of writing. Copy the passage in your best handwriting on to a sheet of the best and whitest paper you can find. The paper symbolizes the pure New Year, a time when much is possible. This practice serves as a good luck charm for a year begun in beauty. And a year begun well, ends well.

Lily Gardner

January 3
Saturday

2nd ♉

☽ → ♊ 12:58 pm

Color of the day: Brown
Incense of the day: Lavender

Lenaia Fruitfulness Spell

ncient Greeks celebrated the god Dionysos on this day. You can prepare a magical Grecian rice dish tonight, and invite love, abundance, and fertility into your life.

- 3 cups cooked long grain rice
- 6 Tbls. extra virgin olive oil
  Juice of one lemon
- 4 green onions, sliced
- 1 Tbl. each: fresh mint, parsley, and dill, chopped
- ½ cup slivered almonds
  Sea salt and pepper, to taste

Drizzle the hot rice with the oil and the lemon juice. Toss the rice with the onions, herbs, and almonds. Add salt and pepper to taste. As you stir your ingredients clockwise, visualize your heart's intentions. Serve this dish warm with a garnish of grape leaves, if you desire. Blessed be prosperity.

Karri Ann Allrich

Notes:

hands as you visualize the blessings you desire. Picture yourself enjoying these blessings in your life. Send this energy into the rice. Release these blessings, through the rice, to the water (or earth) and say: "Make it so!"

Kristin Madden

Notes:

January 4
Sunday

 2nd ♊

Color of the day: Gold
Incense of the day: Poplar

handful of Rice Spell

In some areas of Korea, water and rice are offered to the gods at midnight on this night for good luck and blessings. We can perform a similar ritual to bring blessings into our lives. Go to any local water source with a small handful of rice. If you do not live close to water, go to any place where you will not be disturbed for at least five minutes. Run the rice through your fingers. Pass it back and forth between your

January 5
Monday

2nd ♊
☽ v/c 6:14 pm

Color of the day: Silver
Incense of the day: Maple

Spell to Strengthen Your Bond with Your Pet

Set aside at least one hour to spend with your pet today. While with your pet, create a safe atmosphere and breathe deeply. Then imagine yourself as your pet, and say out loud:

If I were my pet, what would I like best to do? What would I like best to eat? What would be my favorite color?

Listen for the answers, and then take some time to do those things with your pet.

Therese Francis

Notes:

the meal with some hearty bread. Break the bread, and honor each person at the table for being at the dinner. Meals like this will help make your home a more magical and loving place.

Jonathan Keyes

Notes:

January 6
Tuesday

 2nd ♊

☽ → ♋ 1:38 am

Color of the day: Red
Incense of the day: Gardenia

harmony in the home Spell

With the moon in Cancer, now is a good time to make magic and harmony in the home. Bringing joy and cheer to your home life begins by inviting some close friends and family over for dinner. Make a large pot of soup with good Cancerian vegetables such as squash, pumpkin, or cabbage. When the vegetables have cooked down a bit, add Cancerian herbs such as caraway and dill. Stir the ingredients, and add intentions of warmth, love, and nourishment to the pot. When the soup is ready, light some blue candles on the table and serve

Holiday lore: Twelfth night and the night following it are when wassailing used to take place. The word "wassail" comes from the Anglo-Saxon words *waes heil*, meaning "to be whole or healthy." People drank to each other's health from a large bowl filled with drink such as "lamb's wool," which was made of hot ale or cider, nutmeg, and sugar with roasted crab apples. In some parts of Britain, trees and bees are still wassailed to ensure a healthy crop. Having drunk the tree's health, people fire shotguns into the branches. Different regions sing different wassail songs to the tree. Here's one from Worcestershire:

here's to thee, old apple tree,
whence thou mayest bud,
whence thou mayest blow,
whence thou mayest bear
apples enow.

January 7
Wednesday

 2nd ♋

Full Moon 10:40 am

Color of the day: Topaz
Incense of the day: Cedar

Connecting with the Goddess

The month of January is often a time of low energy for many. The hustle of the holidays is over, and another year, full of unknowns, has begun. Even with the slowly lengthening days, we can still feel the effects of limited sunshine on our bodies. When we honor the goddess during this current Full Moon, we can reunite our energies with the divine source. For this reunion, you will need a white or silver candle, jasmine or another herb to represent your spiritual connection, an herb to represent you, charcoal, and a fireproof container. Begin by standing in the goddess salute. State these or similar words:

> Lady of the Moon,
> Mother of night,
> Our energies are one
> within your light.

Light the candle, visualizing your energy blending with the goddess's. Mix the two herbs in your hands, continuing the visualization. Sprinkle the herbs onto the lighted charcoal. As the smoke rises, visualize your energies intertwining with hers. Meditate and listen for her messages of guidance. Thank her, and extinguish the candle.

Karen Follett

Notes:

January 8
Thursday

 3rd ♋

☽ → ♌ 12:38 pm

Color of the day: Crimson
Incense of the day: Evergreen

New Penny Prosperity Spell

To boost your prosperity in the New Year, empty your pockets, purse, wallet—any place where you hoard change. Find as many pennies as you can marked with the year 2004, and put them aside. Take a small, clean jar or box. Cleanse and consecrate it as normal. Gather the pennies, and place them in your receiving hand (left hand if you are right-handed; right hand if you are left-handed). Cup the dominant hand over the receiving hand, and say:

> New year brings new
> wealth. May each penny

symbolize thousandfold abundance.

Feel the energy in your hands. When the heat becomes intense, drop each penny into the jar or box, saying: "New year brings new wealth." Once a week, check your change, and add the 2004 pennies to the jar, speaking the spell. At the end of the year, give half to charity, and use half for yourself.

Cerridwen Iris Shea

Notes:

with handfuls of grain, and the Spitzer who squirts everyone with water. Both bring fertility and abundance. Drive away further winter doldrums with noisemakers and by singing:

Down is up, up is down!

Clown is king, king is clown!

Come feast and dance,
Come laugh and play!
Come one and all, on
Fasching Day!

Elizabeth Barrette

Notes:

January 9
Friday

 3rd ♌

Color of the day: Purple
Incense of the day: Ginger

Celebrate Fasching Spell

Many countries in Europe celebrate Carnival, or Fasching, on this day. Dreary weather can attract pesky spirits who make people feel tired or depressed. When all is cold and dark outside, Fasching encourages us to make merry indoors—that is, to host or attend a party, or to wear colorful costumes. Two favorite characters are the Witch Mother who pelts people

January 10
Saturday

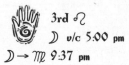 3rd ♌
☽ v/c 5:00 pm
☽ → ♍ 9:37 pm

Color of the day: Gray
Incense of the day: Jasmine

Murphy's Magic

One of the more mundane but useful forms of magic is called "Murphy's magic." Murphy's first law goes: "If anything can go wrong, it will." But the corollary to Murphy's law is that what you don't want to happen will happen. So, you can sort of use Murphy's law to make things happen. For instance, if you wash your car, it will rain (unless you wash your car just to make it rain, in which case, it won't). If you smoke, and you light a cigarette at a bus stop, the bus will come, and you will have to put out the cigarette. When you go to the doctors office, if you don't bring a book you'll have to wait for a long time, and the magazines will be unreadable or nonexistent.

Magenta Griffith

Notes:

January 11
Sunday

3rd ♏

Color of the day: Orange
Incense of the day: Cinnamon

Relax Today Spell

Take some time today to relax. Do what you can to keep stress from overpowering you. To assist you in your efforts, fill a bowl with water and a floating candle. Gaze for a time at the candle flame. Pour your stress into the water, and feel your body relax. Then, imagine the bowl is a deep well, accepting whatever is causing unease, discomfort, or stress in your life. Breathe deeply. Sprinkle dried basil over the water, and then chant softly before the candle flame:

I am calm.

I am at peace with my surroundings.

I am whole and well.

By the powers of earth, air, fire, and water, I am free.

Sit before the bowl for several more moments. When the candle has burned out, pour the water onto the ground, and feel your stress and anxiety going with it. Tell yourself that the earth has taken your stress away. Give thanks.

Ember

Notes:

January 12
Monday

3rd ♏

Color of the day: Ivory
Incense of the day: Lilac

Moon Day Blessing

Named for the Moon, Monday is a time to connect with roots, relatives, the home, and other ancestral powers. Casting spells on Monday brings healing into your domestic sphere. It heals wounds from the past and brings on calm while increasing the creative imagination. Get a new white candle, a flat mirror, some sea salt, and some patchouli oil. Darken the room, and dab oil on your pulse points. Spread salt on your flattened mirror. Light the candle, and repeat these words:

> Dark is the night,
> Light is the Moon.
> Feel her calming energy
> from room to room.
>
> This home is happy,
> Free from stress.
> Children dream and
> parents rest.
>
> Lovers make love,
> Friendships grow,
> Troubles that may come
> now they will go!
> So mote it be.

Susan Sheppard

January 13
Tuesday

3rd ♏

☽ v/c 3:01 am
☽ → ♎ 4:38 am

Color of the day: Black
Incense of the day: Honeysuckle

Air and Fire Energy Spell

Try this air and fire spell to boost both your mental and physical energy. Place a few drops of rosemary oil in a diffuser or on a cotton ball, and inhale, facing east, while saying:

> Winds of intellect,
> attend me.
> My mind is strong and
> alert.
> I retain all I learn.
> I remember all that is
> important.
> Winds of intellect,
> attend me!

Repeat whenever needed, preferably outside on a windy day. Now place black pepper oil or crushed peppercorns in a diffuser or on a cotton

ball and (carefully!) inhale. Facing south, say:

> Fire of strength, attend me.
> I am physically fit and
> strong.
> I perform my work
> energetically.
> I am free of fatigue and
> lassitude.
> Fire of strength, attend
> me!

Repeat whenever necessary, preferably in front of a bonfire or blazing fireplace.

Denise Dumars

Notes:

attract a house spirit, set a small, appealing statue in a special place in your home. Before it, place a small heatproof dish, and burn some of your favorite incense, saying:

> Welcome gentle spirit,
> guard my home.
> Please guard the cradle,
> hearth, and every room.

House spirits love attention. Leave a bit of food or burn some incense in its bowl as an offering. At least once a year, usually in January, pay special tribute by serving your family a meal in your spirit's honor. Pork, wine, and cakes are appropriate items to serve.

James Kambos

Notes:

January 14
Wednesday

 3rd ♎
4th Quarter 3:33 am

☽ v/c 11:46 am

Color of the day: Brown
Incense of the day: Maple

A House Spirit Spell

Ancient Romans honored their guardian house spirits at this time of year. To communicate with or to

January 15
Thursday

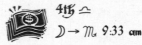 4th ♎
☽ → ♏ 9:33 am

Color of the day: Turquoise
Incense of the day: Vanilla

Carmentalia Spell

Carmentalia is a festival of two calendar days devoted to the worship of Carmentis, the Roman goddess of fertility, childbirth, and prophecy. The first festival day falls on January 11 and the second occurs today. On this day, prayers may be offered to invoke the Carmentes, or the triple aspects of the goddess. Her other two aspects or "sisters" and "attendants" are called Porrima and Postverta. Porrima presides at the birth when a baby emerges headfirst into this world, while Postverta watches over infants who come feet first.

S. Y. Zenith

Notes:

tonight. Pop some fresh popcorn, add butter if desired, and season with love herbs and passionate spices as suggested below. Say as you do so: "Venus, bless us with love and beauty."

> Garlic salt, chili powder, and red pepper—to rekindle your love life.
>
> Parmesan cheese and dried basil—for Italian style romance
>
> Chili powder, garlic, and basil—fiery passion.
>
> A touch of cinnamon, sugar, and vanilla powder—for comfort and warmth.

Karri Ann Allrich

Notes:

January 16
Friday

 4th ♏

Color of the day: Coral
Incense of the day: Parsley

Venus Popcorn Spell

Sharing a bowl of popcorn with someone you love is one of life's simple pleasures. Adding a sprinkle of practical magic may be akin to "gild-ing the lily," but who doesn't like to stir up a little love magic now and then? Rent a favorite romantic movie

January 17
Saturday

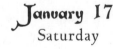 4th ♋

☽ v/c 6:48 am
☽ → ♐ 12:18 pm

Color of the day: Blue
Incense of the day: Violet

Winter Pick–Me–Up Spell

On a dreary winter day, take an orange-colored candle and dress it with carnation oil. Carnation oil is good for courage and energy. Orange is a good color for stamina. Light the candle, and give yourself some quiet time. Watch the flame. Inhale the scent of the oil. As you feel your energy return, ideas will flow. Listen to the ideas, and let the energy of the candle and the scent carry you to your next task. If you can, as you continue your day keep the candle with you until it burns completely.

Cerridwen Iris Shea

Notes:

do only what brings you pleasure. Buy yourself flowers; drink your favorite beverages, and eat your favorite foods. Take a walk into a wilderness area, and fully experience the natural world. Be aware of what the world is like in January, and feel grateful you can be part of it. Return home and have a warm drink. Put on your comfy clothes, and watch your favorite movie. Remind yourself periodically that you deserve this!

Kristin Madden

Notes:

January 19
Monday
Birthday of Martin Luther King, Jr. (observed)

 4th ♐
☽ → ♑ 1:24 pm

Color of the day: Gray
Incense of the day: Coriander

Grounding Spell

During this Capricorn Moon in the middle of winter, you can warm your bones and set strong foundations for your good intentions

January 18
Sunday

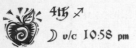 4th ♐
☽ v/c 10:58 pm

Color of the day: Amber
Incense of the day: Sage

Sunday Hedonism Spell

It is Sunday, and the Moon is in hedonistic Sagittarius. Take advantage of this energy by clearing at least part of your day so you can

in the coming year. To prepare for this spell, find a special rock and cleanse and prepare it for magical work. Make a fire, or light a few candles on your altar. Get in touch with your body by stretching out on the floor. When you feel grounded, go to your altar, and place the rock in a spot facing north. Visualize yourself with roots going down into the earth, and say:

> Sacred rock, ground me.
> help me set a course for
> the year ahead.

Jonathan Keyes

Notes:

conversation. Most importantly, do not let anyone kiss you. At bedtime, dress in your best night clothes. Boil an egg until the yolk is hard. Remove the yolk, fill the cavity with salt, and eat it. Walk backward to bed saying:

> Fair St. Agnes,
> play thy part,
> and send to me my own
> sweetheart.
>
> Not in his best or worst
> array,
> but in the clothes he
> wears every day.

You will dream of your future spouse. Tell no one!

Lily Gardner

Notes:

January 20
Tuesday

4th ♑
☉→♒ 12:42 pm
Color of the day: Maroon
Incense of the day: Poplar

A Lover's Divination

January 20 on the Eve of St. Agnes is one of the most famous nights in the whole calendar for love divination. This sure-fire spell dates back hundreds of years. To start, fast all day, and do not engage in any frivolous

January 21
Wednesday

4th ♑
☽ v/c 12:34 pm
☽→♒ 2:11 pm
New Moon 4:05 pm

Color of the day: Yellow
Incense of the day: Pine

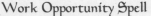

Work Opportunity Spell

Do you want advancement in your current career? Or are you seeking a whole new career? This New Moon can be the beginning of the physical manifestation of your answer to these questions. Therefore, you need to take care now. Keep in mind that the universe may show you it has other plans for you. Plot out the steps that you will need to take to get from point A (where you are now) to Point B (your desired end goal). Be realistic and specific in what you ask for. Light a gold candle, and place a tiger's-eye in front of it. State these or similar words:

> Capricorn's Moon,
> Beginning and new,
> Your wisdom guides me
> in all that I do.

Touch the thumbs and forefingers of both hands together to form a triangle. Center the triangle over the tiger's-eye. Visualize yourself completing the steps necessary to reach your goal. Project your intent into the tiger's-eye. Extinguish the candle. Carry the tiger's-eye until your goal is achieved or you have an answer.

Karen Follett

Notes:

Holiday lore: The lunar new year traditionally celebrates the planet's renewed fertility. In China, during the fifteen-day waxing Moon, celebrants eat food, sing and dance, and promote happiness, health, fertility, and fortune for the year. In the spirit of setting things straight, all debts should be paid off now, and houses cleaned and draped with red flowers, banners, and decorations; red is considered lucky and dispels demons. Celebrants also avoid using swearwords during this season, lest they bring ill fortune to themselves, and parents warn children against blurting out such inauspicious words as "death" or "disaster," or anything of similar sentiment.

January 22
Thursday
Chinese New Year

1st ♍

Color of the day: White
Incense of the day: Sandalwood

Chinese New Year Spell

All that has been said about New Year's celebrations in general applies to the Chinese New Year. We find the world falling into chaos, even as it is reborn. Here chaos takes the form of demons that threaten the well-being of the community. The first duty, then, of celebrants on this day is to expel demons by lighting fireworks and making as much noise as possible. Another weapon in the arsenal against evil is the color red. On this day in China, streets and homes are draped with endless red decorations. This may seem like innocent fun, but at its heart these acts are a magical necessity to protect oneself from chaos. The ritual aspect of this activity is brought to light by the street performance of the dragon with numerous human legs. Once the community is purified, good fortune throughout the year is assured by making offerings to the gods of health and wealth. Offerings can also be given to your ancestors and to monks and priests. The Chinese ginger jar, a ceramic pot with a lid, was originally created for holding gifts of ginger, candy, or tea. Once the contents were used, the jar was returned to the person who gave the gift. Unlike the astrology of the West, which proceeds through all twelve signs of the zodiac each year, the Chinese system aligns each year in a twelve-year cycle with one of the signs. This is the year 4702 on the Chinese calendar, and it is the year of the monkey. All those born in this year will share certain traits. These include cleverness, skillfulness, and success in financial matters. Monkeys are intelligent and good learners with much common sense, but they discourage too easily and may suffer from undue pride. In the spirit of setting things straight for the New Year, all debts should be paid off now. Celebrants also avoid using swearwords during this time, lest they bring ill fortune to themselves, and parents warn children against blurting out such inauspicious words as "death" or "disaster," or anything of similar sentiment.

Robert Place

Notes:

January 23
Friday

1st ≈

☽ v/c 4:33 am

☽ → ♓ 4:29 pm

Color of the day: Pink
Incense of the day: Rose

Tarot Love Spell

The Jewish holiday Rosh Hodesh Shevat begins at sundown. Take the Lovers card from any tarot deck.

Add the Two of Cups. (If you don't have a tarot deck, add the Queen, King, and Two of Hearts from a deck of playing cards.) Get a red candle, or red man and green woman effigy candles from a magic shop. Arrange cards around the candles. Light the wick and repeat:

> heart of my heart,
> mate of my life,
> Dream of me,
> I am your love.
> Stars say "yes" from high above.
> Think of us,
> and be my love.
> So mote it be.

Susan Sheppard

Notes:

Before you go onstage for a public presentation, take a moment. Stand straight, close your eyes, and relax your shoulders. Place your heels close together, but not touching, with your feet at about a right angle. Envision the Full Moon, overhead and slightly in front of you, glowing blue-white and clear. All that you have studied and practiced is within your unconscious. The light of the Moon will free this, and let it flow through your performance. Open your eyes very slowly, and feel this light continuing to flow. Take a slow breath, and let it flow easily out of you as you step on stage.

Therese Francis

Notes:

January 24
Saturday

 1st ♓

Color of the day: Indigo
Incense of the day: Cedar

Before a Performance Spell

In the tarot, the Moon card represents the powers of the unconscious.

January 25
Sunday
Burns' Night in Scotland

1st ♓
☽ v/c 6:09 am
☽ → ♈ 10:06 pm

Color of the day: Gold
Incense of the day: Basil

Rejuvenating the Soul Spell

When you are down and feel life is going nowhere, go to your sacred space or a room where you are comfortable. Light up the surroundings with a multicolored nurturing glow using seven candles of seven different colors. Ensure the candles are placed in secure holders before arranging them in a circle on a bare table. It is essential that all windows are shut and that you keep an eye on the candles once they are lit. Sit or recline near the table, meditate for a few moments, and feel the candlelight replenishing your soul. This ritual can also be used when you feel lonely or worried. Visualize the colors surrounding you with warmth, radiant health, and strength. See yourself overcoming your problems and solving your problems.

S. Y. Zenith

Notes:

Holiday lore: Burns' Night is a key event in Scotland that has been observed for about 200 years in honor of Robert Burns, who was born on this day. One of Scotland's most beloved bards, Burns immortalized in a famous poem the haggis, a Scottish dish of offal boiled in a bag with suet and oatmeal among other ingredients. "Burns' Suppers" are celebrated not only in Scotland but wherever patriotic Scots or those of Scottish descent live.

January 26
Monday

1st ♈

Color of the day: White
Incense of the day: Myrrh

An Inch Will Do Spell

When I was young, I never felt satisfied just making a snowman. I made snow men, women, children, gods, goddesses, and fantastic beasts of all shapes and kinds. If you live in a cold climate, and especially if you have children, you should make the effort now to go play in the snow. Build a fort, throw snowballs, make sculptures. Enjoy the winter wonderland. To make a snow god, first build a snowman and then put branches on his head for antlers. A snow goddess gets a crown of icicles. Big icicles make terrific unicorn or dragon horns. You can "paint" snow sculptures by diluting food dye in water and spraying this on to the snow. If you have not received any snow, try saying:

Spirits of the snow,
we sing to you.

Send us your blessings,
an inch or two will do.

Elizabeth Barrette

Notes:

Let it drift peacefully into the night.
Repeat this spell on Mondays or
Tuesdays if needed.

James Kambos

Notes:

January 27
Tuesday

 1st ♈

☽ v/c 11:59 pm

Color of the day: Gray
Incense of the day: Juniper

A Winter Cleansing Spell

During the winter, negative energies can accumulate in our homes. Protect your home with this spell. At night build a fire, and onto the flames scatter nine whole cloves. As the fire burns say, "Spirits dance, spirits mingle. Bad spirits depart, good spirits linger." Using your ritual fire, light a black candle. Place this candle in front of a window, and surround it with two or three small mirrors, placed facing the window. Now say, "Into the blackness, into the night. Bad spirits take flight." Visualize the candle's flame being reflected by the mirrors through the window, taking with it any negativity.

January 28
Wednesday

 1st ♈

☽ → ♈ 10:06 pm

Color of the day: Topaz
Incense of the day: Neroli

Clearing Up Spell

This is a favorable day for clearing up old business from last year. If you have too many debts from the holiday season, deal with them now. After paying what you can and mailing the checks, make a stack of the portion of your bill receipts. Put a piece of malachite on them, the larger the better. Light a green candle, and say:

Debt flow out,
cash flow in.
Without a doubt,
money I win.

Then blow out the candle. Remember, the extra money that comes to you has to be used to pay your debts or the magic will stop working.

Magenta Griffith

Notes:

Upon the breeze, accept this gift.

Release the feather into a strong wind, or, if necessary, leave it outside where the wind can take it.

Ember

Notes:

January 29
Thursday

 1st ♐
2nd Quarter 1:03 am

☽ v/c 9:04 pm

Color of the day: Green
Incense of the day: Carnation

Feather Ritual for Good Fortune

For this spell, you will need a feather from a wild bird (found, not taken), one drop of pine or juniper oil, a candle, some incense, some salt, and water. First, consecrate the feather with the energies of the four elements. Sprinkle it with salt (earth), pass it through incense smoke (air), pass it quickly near the candle flame (fire), and sprinkle it with water (water). Anoint the feather with a single drop of oil and say:

Fortune, find me.
hear my wish.

January 30
Friday

 2nd ♉
☽ → ♊ 8:18 pm

Color of the day: Rose
Incense of the day: Dill

Waxing Moon Love Spell

For the next seven days, drink rose-petal tea every night at some time between 9 pm and 11 pm. There are several companies that make black tea with rose petals, or else you can add fresh rose petals from your garden to your tea. As you sip, visualize yourself as a loveable person who attracts the kind of person you are looking for. Add honey if you wish to appear especially sweet; cinnamon to appear spicy hot; rosemary to appear brilliant. Go outside at 11 pm on the night of the Full Moon, and seal the spell by saying:

> As my will, so mote it be.

Denise Dumars

Notes:

January 31
Saturday

 2nd ♊

Color of the day: Black
Incense of the day: Patchouli

Spell for Breaking Emotional Bonds
This spell is for when we have outgrown long-standing relationships with certain people and wish to move on without hurting the other persons' feelings. This prevents guilt-trips, emotional blackmail, and other manipulations. To start, carve the person's name on a candle with a pin and imbue it with positive thoughts. Anoint the candle with patchouli oil before putting it in a holder. Trace a pentagram with salt on the altar. Place the candleholder in the middle of the salt pentagram. Visualize the person shifting his or her focus to a joyful new interest, thus relinquishing

reliance upon you. Light the candle, and say:

> Candle light,
> by your might,
> assist in my plight.
> Free me from emotional
> fetter.
> Past bonds now scatter.
> Unchained, I am free
> forever.

S. Y. Zenith

Notes:

February

February is the second month of the Gregorian calendar, and the year's shortest month. Its astrological sign is Aquarius, the water-bearer (Jan 21–Feb 20), a fixed air sign ruled by unpredictable Uranus. The month itself is named for Februa, an ancient festival of purification. As days slowly lengthen, people begin to emerge from their inward state and look outward toward the planting season. There are signs of life as snow begins to recede, buds begin to appear, and some herbs such as thyme and witch hazel begin to grow. February is traditionally a good time for foretelling the future and for purifying oneself. The Full Moon of the month is appropriately called the Chaste Moon. February is also the time for banishing winter, and the main holiday of the month, Imbolc or Candlemas, is a time to gather the greenery used to adorn the house during Yuletide and use it to feed a sabbat fire. A ritual of the season is known as the Bride's Bed, in which a bundle of corn from the harvest is dressed in ribbons and becomes the Corn Bride. At midmonth, we celebrate Valentine's Day, named for the legendary patron saint of love. Images of Cupid, Venus, and the heart are common on this day. Medieval people believed February 14 was the day wild birds chose to couple in order to begin their spring mating.

February 1
Sunday

 2nd ♊

Color of the day: Yellow
Incense of the day: Coriander

Breath and Intention Spell

Our words and thoughts have an impact on the world. This spell helps us focus our minds and words toward healing ends. On this Gemini Moon, go to your sacred altar and light a yellow or white candle. Strike a chime or bell, and listen to the sound as it fades. Breathe deeply until silence returns—this is the unbounded Source. Concentrate on the Source for a few moments, then open your eyes, and set your intentions to speak and think in nourishing and harmonious ways.

Jonathan Keyes

Notes:

February 2
Monday
Imbolc – Groundhog Day

 2nd ♊
☽ v/c 7:56 am
☽ → ♋ 9:03 am

Color of the day: Lavender
Incense of the day: Chrysanthemum

Imbolc Spell

Imbolc is the Celtic holiday that marks the beginning of spring. It is ruled by the goddess of spring, known as Brigit or Brigantia in Ireland, and Bride in Scotland. In Irish myth, the god of the earth Dagda, also known as the "good god," had three daughters, who were all named Brigit. The first Brigit was the goddess of poetry, the second was the goddess of smithcraft, and the third was the goddess of fire and healing. All three are really aspects of one triple goddess who was associated with the Sun and with fire. On this day Brigit used her flame to rekindle the fire in the earth and assure that plants would have the heat that they need to break through the earth and begin to grow. In ancient times, a woman dressed as Brigit would bless the fires in the households and forges across Ireland. On this day, Brigit's snake would come out of its mound, and the snake's behavior would determine how long the remaining frost will last. This is the most likely origin of Groundhog Day. In Christian times, Brigit became a saint associated with the Virgin Mary. Imbolc became the Christian Candlemas, the Feast of the Purification of the Blessed Virgin Mary, which is celebrated by lighting candles. A Brigit's cross is a talisman made of woven reeds that form a cross with a woven square in the center and four equal arms extending out from the center. This design gives the cross a sense of rotation that evokes the wheel of the year. Brigit's cross should be made or bought on this day and used to protect the home throughout the year. Also on this night one can leave a silk ribbon on the doorstep for Brigit to bless. Later it can be used for healing.

Robert Place

Notes:

Brigid Festival

The ancient Irish celebrated Brigantia, a festival of the goddess Brigid, at this time of year. It focused on her aspect as the All-Seeing Eye. People made diamond-shaped goddess eyes and solar crosses out of wheat straw. You can make another type of goddess eye by fastening two dowels into an equal armed cross and then winding different colors of yarn around them to make a diamond shape. Hang these charms on the door to protect your house from harm.

Elizabeth Barrette

Notes:

Holiday lore: On Imbolc, a bundle of corn from the harvest is dressed in ribbons and becomes the Corn Bride. On February 2, the Corn Bride is placed on the hearth or hung on the door to bring prosperity, fertility, and protection to the home.

February 3
Tuesday
St. Blaise's Day

 2nd ♋
Color of the day: White
Incense of the day: Poplar

February 4
Wednesday

2nd ♋
☽ v/c 12:52 pm
☽ → ♌ 7:50 pm

Color of the day: Brown
Incense of the day: Sandalwood

St. Agatha Loaves for Breast Disorders

St. Agatha, patron saint of breast disorders, is celebrated on February

5. The custom on February 4 is to bake loaves of bread called "Agathas" that are shaped like breasts. These loaves are blessed and distributed to friends of an ill woman. Use any bread recipe that will hold its shape when baked. Make as many of these loaves as you can. Hold your friend's good health in your mind and heart as you mix the dough, knead, and shape it. When the Agathas are baked, distribute them to everyone who loves your friend. Tell them to hold her good health in their hearts as they eat.

Lily Gardner

Notes:

finances, paychecks, and bills may preoccupy your thoughts now. Instead of focusing on a financial limitation, however, center yourself in possibility, and open your life to sharing the wealth. Worrying about money inhibits the magic of opportunity. Instead, give away five things today. Donate five food items to a local food bank, or a box of warm hats and gloves to a homeless shelter. Write five five-dollar checks to your favorite charities. Appreciate all that you do have, and invite someone home for dinner tonight. Sharing the wealth creates wealth. An open hand that gives away freely is also ready to receive.

Karri Ann Allrich

Notes:

February 5
Thursday

2nd ♌

Color of the day: Purple
Incense of the day: Carnation

Sharing the Wealth

Today is an auspicious day for all things monetary. Concerns over

February 6
Friday

2nd ♌
Full Moon 3:47 am
☽ v/c 12:38 pm

Color of the day: Coral
Incense of the day: Thyme

Dream Wisdom

Whether you seek the solution to a specific problem or you seek the path to a desired goal, the answers await you in the infinite universe. All too often our days are too busy to allow our brains to be responsive to the messages of the universe. The receptivity of the dreaming mind is the perfect channel for the answers that you seek. Prior to sleep, compose your question to the universe on paper. Anoint it by tracing a "drawing in" spiral in lavender oil. Start with the outer perimeter, tracing deosil (clockwise) until you reach the spiral's inner core. While you trace your spiral, say:

> Creative fire that shines
> as gentle lunar light,
> shine from the universe
> into my dreams tonight.

Slip the paper under your pillow. Within your first thirty waking minutes write down anything that you remember from your dreams. Even if you don't actually remember a dream, write down any words or symbols that pop into your mind. Dream language is symbolic language, so the answer to your question may be encoded in symbols.

Karen Follett

Notes:

February 7
Saturday
Festival of Diana

3rd ♌

☽ → ♍ 4:03 am

Color of the day: Blue
Incense of the day: Lilac

Reality Check Spell

Saturday is named after Saturn, planet of matter, reality, and the shattering of delusions. Saturn is the imposing god who ate his own children, but he is also sower of seeds and bringer of new growth. Saturday is a good time to clear any negativity from our lives and out of our closets. Now is the time to rid ourselves of any "stuff" that has outlived its usefulness. But before casting this spell, ask yourself the following crucial questions.

> Do I really need this?
> Do I have a practical
> application for this?
> Can I not get by without
> it?

If you have answered your questions honestly and still are convinced of your need, get a black candle and light it while chanting:

> Free my life of all that is
> not useful to me.
> I embrace the truth.
> I understand what

works me, and what
does not.
I live my life simply and
effectively.
Goddess, clear my life.
So mote it be.

Susan Sheppard

Notes:

your eating habits. As a reminder of
a healthy lifestyle, create an amulet.
Wrap a piece of either citrine quartz,
carnelian, or pyrite in yellow cloth,
along with six whole sunflower seeds
or cloves, a pinch of dried basil, and
a pinch of dried marigold petals.
Smudge the amulet with incense, and
anoint it with orange or lemon oil.

Ember

Notes:

February 8
Sunday

 3rd ♏

D v/c 7:23 pm

Color of the day: Orange
Incense of the day: Clove

Purify for health

February comes from the Latin
februarius, meaning "to purify."
Spend a day thinking about what you
eat. Go one entire day without eating junk food. Concentrate on raw
fruits and vegetables, and drink lots
of water. At the end of the day, sit
before your altar with a yellow candle,
and meditate on how you feel, identifying the strengths and weaknesses in

Holiday lore: Today is the Buddhist
Needle Memorial. On this day,
as part of the principle of endless
compassion espoused by the Buddhist
faith for all sentient and nonsentient
beings, all the sewing needles that have
been retired during the year are honored. That is, needles are brought to
the shrine and pushed into a slab of
tofu that rests on the second tier of
a three-tiered altar. Priests sing sutras
to comfort the needles and heal their
injured spirit.

February 9
Monday

3rd ♍

☽→♎ 10:12 am

Color of the day: Gray

Incense of the day: Daffodil

Early Spring Cleaning

For an extra dose of spiritual cleansing at this time of year, during early February when the weather first begins to get warm take some fresh lavender buds, and spread them from left to right on the windowsills and door thresholds of your home as you chant:

> Spring is near,
> The light returns.
>
> Bring blessings upon all
> that enter here.

Therese Francis

Notes:

February 10
Tuesday

3rd ♎

Color of the day: Red

Incense of the day: Evergreen

Spell of the Library Goddess

It's natural to want to hibernate during the cold winter months. But instead of sleeping the months away, you can use them to gain knowledge. That is, at this time you can take the time to study a topic in which you are interested. Or you can spend some extra time in your local library, wander the stacks, dig through the older books—the books that no one has checked out in a long time. The winter is perfect for seeking out hidden and forgotten treasure troves of information. After all, you don't feel like going outside, so why not take advantage? Before you begin your searches, ask for the blessing of the library goddess to lead you to what you need, or to even what you don't need but that might simply improve your life in some unexpected way. Then, wander the stacks with an open heart. You will feel the tingle in the air when you begin to close in on what you are meant to find. Think of this as a game of "hotter, colder." When you are finished, thank the library goddess and make offerings. Such offerings include donations of books you no longer need to libraries, schools, or social service programs.

Cerridwen Iris Shea

Notes:

breath as it flows naturally. As your breath deepens, ask the air to carry away your stress and bring you the inspiration you need. Release this prayer with your breath.

Kristin Madden

Notes:

February 11
Wednesday

3rd ♎

☽ v/c 12:42 am

☽ → ♏ 2:58 pm

Color of the day: White
Incense of the day: Coriander

Blessings of Air Spell

Both Sun and Moon are in air signs today. To gain the blessings of inspiration and clarity, go outside and breathe deeply of the air. Focus on your breath, and simply observe it for a moment. Deepen your breath, so that it comes from your diaphragm, then breathe deeply into any areas of tension in your body. Feel them relax. Count as you breathe, and try to exhale for twice as long as you inhale—but only if this feels easy for you. Otherwise, just be with your

February 12
Thursday
Lincoln's Birthday

3rd ♏

Color of the day: Green
Incense of the day: Geranium

Divining Success Spell

Not many people know that Abraham Lincoln was psychic. His wife held seances in the White House, but Lincoln himself did not need a seance in order to see ghosts. He reportedly saw wavering ghostly figures in mirrors, including the ghost of his deceased son and those of former inhabitants of the White House. He sometimes received psychic visions in dreams, and had one that

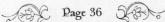

foretold his own death just a few days before his assassination. Since Lincoln's death, many prominent people, including Teddy Roosevelt, have reported seeing Lincoln's ghost in the White House. Today, why not hold a Lincoln-era style seance? This works best with three or more people. Cover a table with a black cloth. Place a crystal ball in the center of the table. Display a picture of Mr. Lincoln if you wish. Participants should sit with each person's hands touching another's on the tabletop. Designate one person as medium. Decide as a group who you will try to contact. You may choose to contact Lincoln himself. The medium should have all participants take three deep breaths before calling on the spirit. Everyone should look intently into the crystal ball until someone sees or feels a presence. Good luck.

Denise Dumars

Notes:

Holiday lore: Lincoln is called the Great Emancipator and is thought of as one of our great presidents.

Know this, however: Lincoln was a rather unknown figure until the age of forty, when he first entered the Illinois state legislature. His later assassination threw the country into widespread mourning, inspiring Walt Whitman to write:

Coffin that passes
through lanes and street,
through day and night
with the great cloud
darkening the land . . .
I mourned, and yet shall
mourn with ever—
returning spring.

February 13
Friday

3rd ♏
4th Quarter 8:39 am
☽ v/c 8:39 am
☽ → ♐ 6:35 pm

Color of the day: Pink
Incense of the day: Sandalwood

Love Divination Spell

In medieval calendars this was a day of love, when all nature found a mate. By the eighteenth century this was called St. Valentine's Day Eve, and was set aside as a time to divine the identity of a future love. Prophecies were sought by inducing dreams or by scrying. To see a possible future mate, try this spell. On a table, place your favorite scrying tool—a sphere, mirror, or bowl of water. Surround this with five dried bay leaves, placed so they will roughly represent the shape of a pentagram. Inhale the scent of the leaves, relax, and say:

> With these leaves of bay,
> let me see the love com—
> ing my way.

Scry for about ten to fifteen minutes. When done, put the leaves in a love charm bag to use again.

James Kambos

Notes:

February 14
Saturday
Valentine's Day

 4th ♐

Color of the day: Indigo
Incense of the day: Juniper

Valentine Love Spell

There is some confusion about which St. Valentine we celebrate on the holiday on February 14. There are two Valentines, both of whom are venerated on the same day. One was a Roman priest martyred in 269, and the other was a bishop of Terni martyred several years earlier. Some have also suggested that the holiday is named after the Gnostic leader Valentinus, who was noted for his sanctification of sexual practices. However, the weight of opinion falls on Valentine the priest. According to the legend, Valentine was a priest in Rome under the reign of Emperor Claudius II. The emperor had ordered that all soldiers should remain unmarried so that they would not create any attachments that would interfere with their duties, especially when they were ordered to leave for war. Valentine, however, defied the emperor and secretly married the soldiers and their brides. He was eventually arrested and sent to prison to await his execution. While in prison, he fell in love with the blind daughter of the jailer, and through his faith he miraculously restored her vision. When he was led away to his death, he signed his farewell message to her with the words: "from your Valentine." The February 14 holiday is most likely a continuation of Lupercalia, a Roman holiday held in honor of Juno in mid-February. On the eve of Lupercalia, young men would draw the name of a suitable mate from a jar and agree to remain faithful to her for a year. It is believed that our modern holiday is a Christianization of this practice. This is an excellent day for love magic, but remember to allow fate to have a hand in your love life. Always avoid trying to manipulate the will of others.

Robert Place

Notes:

pate in the main ritual. They met in a grotto or cave on the Palatine Hill outside of Rome. There, they sacrificed goats and a dog and fashioned whips and loincloths from the skins. They set out wearing the loincloths and brandishing the whips. First, they ran a few circuits around the Palatine Hill to sanctify it, then they ran through Rome. They whipped anyone in their way. Strangely, it was considered lucky to be touched by the whips. Afterward, there were feasts and parties throughout Rome. Lupercalia was one of the most famous of all Roman festivals.

Magenta Griffith

Notes:

February 15
Sunday

 4th ♐
)) v/c 3:20 pm
)) → ♑ 9:14 pm

Color of the day: Amber
Incense of the day: Poplar

Corn Curing Spell

This is the ancient Roman holiday of Lupercalia, a festival in honor of the god Lupercalus, also known as Faunus. He aided the growth of crops and the well-being of animal herds, and he kept wolves away from the livestock. During Lupercalia two groups of young men were chosen to partici-

February 16
Monday

President's Day (observed)

4th ♑
Color of the day: White
Incense of the day: Rose

Celebrate Victoria Spell

Today marks the celebration of the Roman goddess Victoria. As her name suggests, she is a figure who brings victory in all its guises: winning contests or races, getting a raise or a grant, earning success and reputation as a leader, and so forth. On this day, you can make a charm to foster leadership skills by tying a blue ribbon to a brass ring. Charge it with these words:

> With this blue ribbon
> and brass ring,
> bring me the best of
> everything.
>
> Light the darkness and
> lead my day,
> let me always find the
> way.
>
> Show me all that I need
> to see,
> Victoria, so mote it be!

Carry the charm with you, or hang it in your office. Repeat the verse silently whenever you need a boost.

Elizabeth Barrette

Notes:

February 17
Tuesday

4th ♑
☽ v/c 12:00 am
☽ → ♒ 11:27 pm

Color of the day: Black
Incense of the day: Sage

Runic Candle Protection

After an argument or some other negative experience that leaves you feeling engulfed by negative vibes and vulnerable to harm, use a pin to carve the runic symbol of eolh (ᚣ) on a purple candle. This rune represents the antlers of the elk or the splayed fingers of the warding-off hand, and so it confers a good dose of protection. Dress the candle with basil oil, and place it in a secure holder. Light the candle, and sit near the light for a few minutes or for as long as you feel the need to. If you like, close your eyes in the silence of the light, and meditate for a short time by clearing your mind of everything. If any stray thoughts come to mind, observe them and let them pass on their way. Visualize yourself being insulated from all baneful or harmful energies. Know that there is no need to worry. This runic symbol is very potent for defending against all baneful thought-forms and any evil forces both visible and invisible.

S. Y. Zenith

western night, I break any curse. It takes flight." Snuff out the fire, take a breath, and eat the fruit.

Susan Sheppard

Notes:

February 18
Wednesday

4th ≈

Color of the day: Topaz
Incense of the day: Eucalyptus

Spell to Dispel Negativity

This spell, if properly applied, will dispel negativity, break curses, and add protection—and so is essential for sensitive Witches. To start, get a green candle, some real or fake ivy, a green fruit such as pear or apple, and a bell. Cut the fruit in four pieces. Arrange the ivy. Place the slices of fruit in the four directions. Light the flame. Face north and chant: "By the powers of the northern light, I break any negativity in my life." Ring the bell, and allow it to resonate. Face south, and say: "By the powers of the southern side, strong I am. Let my powers rise." Face east, saying: "By the powers of the eastern Sun, I face my fears and watch them run." Face west, and say: "By the powers of the

February 19
Thursday

4th ≈
☉ → ♓ 2:50 am
☽ v/c 12:34 pm

Color of the day: Crimson
Incense of the day: Musk

Spell for Better Community Relations

On this Moon-in-Aquarius day, try this spell for increasing harmony with your community. This is especially helpful if there has been some tension between you and the people you know (at home or in your neighborhood). Find a piece of string the size of a bracelet, and tie it into a loose knot. Place the string on your altar, close your eyes, and imagine all the frustration and tension that has

built up in your relations with the community. Focus on that negative energy, and then open your eyes and untie the knot. Say the words: "May all negative energy dissipate." Now visualize harmonious relations within your community, and tie the string again around your wrist, saying: "This string is a symbol of my good relations with all my community." Keep the string on for at least two weeks, and see if your relations improve.

Jonathan Keyes

Notes:

February 20
Friday

 4th ≈

☽ → ♓ 2:27 am

New Moon 4:18 am

Color of the day: Purple
Incense of the day: Ylang-ylang

Cord of Connection Spell

Whether we describe ourselves as "lone wolves" or "social butter-flies," we are interdependent social pack animals. That is, some degree of social interaction is necessary to maintain physical, mental, emotional, and spiritual harmony. To reinforce this, light a pink candle representing the maiden Moon's aspect of attraction. Cut a length of natural (i.e. hemp or linen) cord. Focus your intent onto the cord. Now pass the cord through the flame's "aura." Hold the cord and focus on the candle. Relax your mind and body. Ask the universe to reveal the actions that will lead to better social connections. Decide on the specific actions that you can take today. Tie a knot in the cord while focusing on your decision. Extinguish the candle. Wind your cord around the remaining candle once it has cooled, and store this in a safe place. Using the same cord and candle, repeat this process daily until the Full Moon. Incorporate a new action into each new day. At the Full Moon, dispose of the cord and the candle according to your intuition. Thank the universe for the connections that you have made.

Karen Follett

Notes:

February 21
Saturday

 1st ♓

☽ v/c 12:34 pm

Color of the day: Brown
Incense of the day: Pine

Tribute to Mother Tongue Spell

In Bangladesh, this is Shaheed Day. Tribute is paid today to one's mother language, and thanks are given for the freedom and gift to speak it. Light a candle today in honor of the freedom you have to use your mother language. Gaze into the candle flame, and give thanks to all those that have fought for this freedom. Give thanks for the many different ways that people fight for freedom around the world. Pause and consider that many of these battles are fought peaceably, while many require sacrifice and blood. Make a pledge to be grateful for all the freedoms that that you have. As you gaze into the flame, consider how you can contribute to the cause of freedom for others who still may lack it, and for future generations whose battles for freedom are still unknown. Ask how you can become a flame for freedom and justice. Make a list of those things that you feel you can honestly do and create a plan to take action.

Kristin Madden

Notes:

February 22
Sunday
Washington's Birthday – Islamic New Year

1st ♓

☽ → ♈ 7:45 am

Color of the day: Gold
Incense of the day: Cinnamon

New Year Moon Spell

The Islamic calendar is purely lunar. It recognizes twelve months, each of which starts at the first sighting of each New Moon. Therefore, the weather can affect the sighting, so in this calendar it is almost impossible to do more than estimate the date of the New Year in advance of the actual day. If the skies are clear today though, it will be the start of the first month of the year 1425 on the Hijri calendar. It is called Hijri because in Islam the calendar starts with the Hijri, the event that marks the beginning of the Islamic religion. This is when Mohammed fled from persecution in Mecca by going to Medina. There he was supported by the local Christian and Jewish population and allowed to develop his religion based on the scriptures that were dictated to him by the archangel Gabriel. In the Gregorian calendar this happened in the year 622. Except in Saudi Arabia and a few other countries, the Islamic calendar is only used for religious purposes. The New Year is not an important holiday, and not everyone chooses to celebrate it. This indifference toward the New Year seems ironic when we realize that the oldest recorded New Year's celebration comes from this area of the world. Four thousand years ago in Babylon, the people began an eleven-day New Year's festival on our March 23 by stripping the king of his clothes and sending him away. For eleven days the people did whatever they liked. On the last day, the king returned wearing splendid robes, and everyone went back to work.

Robert Place

Notes:

Holiday lore: We all know the lore about our first president—cherry tree, silver dollar, wooden teeth—but the truth behind this most legendary of American figures is sometimes more entertaining than the folklore. For instance, did you know that once, when young George went for a dip in the Rappahannock River, two Fredericksburg women stole his clothes? This story was recorded in the Spotsylvania County records. Picture then the young man scampering home flustered and naked, and the icon of the dollar bill becomes just a bit more real.

February 23
Monday

1st ♈

Color of the day: Silver
Incense of the day: Frankincense

Cheery Cherry Spell

Keep the kids happy with this fun day-after-Washington's-birthday activity. Put up an image of Amaterasu, the Japanese Sun goddess. Tell the kids it is Cheery Cherry Blossom Day, and that dinner will be Japanese-style. Sit cross-legged on the floor around the coffee table for dinner. Serve green tea scented with cherry, and Japanese take-out with cherry pie for dessert. Burn Japanese cherry incense and have each family member ask Amaterasu for happiness and sunny days. Encourage the kids to dress Japanese-style for this event. Get library books and learn to write haiku or to make origami animals. Have fun.

Denise Dumars

Notes:

your home against a thief, in a small dish combine the flowers of three crocus flowers, a teaspoon of dried basil, and a generous dash of black pepper. Sprinkle this mixture outside your home, moving around the building in a clockwise direction. Repeat this charm three times as you go:

> Crocus for protection,
> Basil to purify,
> Pepper to sting.
> Let no thief penetrate
> this ring.

Repeat this fair charm again in one year.

James Kambos

Notes:

February 24
Tuesday

Mardi Gras — Fat Tuesday

1st ♈
☽ v/c 1:55 pm
☽ → ♉ 4:30 pm

Color of the day: Maroon
Incense of the day: Musk

Protection Spell Against Theft

Now that the crocuses begin to carpet lawns with their color, it is a good time for a spell to protect against theft. Ancient magicians burned crocus petals, hoping the smoke would reveal the face of thieves. To protect

February 25
Ash Wednesday

Wednesday

1st ♉
☽ v/c 9:55 pm

Color of the day: Yellow
Incense of the day: Cedar

Getaway Spell

Today is the perfect day to pretend you are somewhere else. If you are in the middle of a cold harsh winter, it is time to pretend you are in the tropics. If you are in a warm, sultry place, it's time to pretend to be in the snow. Decorate one room of your home in your chosen motif. Brightly colored fabrics can suggest the tropics; a fleece throw and some chenille cushions suggest a ski lodge. Consume piña coladas and quesadillas for your tropical day, or have a hot toddy and a roast for a wintry meal. Play salsa or Scandinavian music. Dance around the room. Sit in a corner and read a book. Do what you want to do—whatever comes to mind—and imagine you are in the place of your choice. Today is your one-day vacation from the dull, dry routine of your ordinary life.

Cerridwen Iris Shea

Notes:

February 26
Thursday

1st ♉

Color of the day: Turquoise
Incense of the day: Jasmine

Spell for Pentagram Night

February 26th is Pentagram Night. The pentagram, symbol of our Pagan beliefs, is a five-pointed star encircled by a Full Moon. The five points of the star symbolize many concepts in our faith: spirit and the four elements, our four limbs and head, our five senses, and the five stages of life. In a tarot reading, the pentagram corresponds with north and the element of earth. To honor our faith, make a paste from holy water and the ashes from your Yule log. At the stroke of midnight, light a red candle, and paint the symbol of the pentagram over your heart with the paste to rededicate yourself to the craft.

Lily Gardner

Notes:

February 27
Friday

 1st ♉
  ☽ → ♊ 4:22 am
2nd Quarter 10:24 pm

Color of the day: Rose
Incense of the day: Nutmeg

Love Strengthening Spell

To strengthen your love with a partner on this Venus day, light a purple candle. Take an amethyst crystal in your left hand and hold a photograph of your loved one in your right hand. Focus on the flame, and see the two of you standing inside it, protected from all outside influences. Slowly raise your hands above the flame, up toward the ceiling. While holding the crystal and photo, blow out the candle, knowing that the flame continues to protect the two of you.

Therese Francis

Notes:

February 28
Saturday

2nd ♊
  Color of the day: Gray
Incense of the day: Lavender

A Simple Meditation

If possible on this day, burn some pure sandalwood incense. This is the best incense for meditation. As your incense smolders, focus on the smoke's rising and billowing movements. After several moments, close your eyes, but do not let your mind wander. If it does, gently return your thoughts to the incense. Inhale the fragrance. Breathe deeply, and clear your mind. To aid meditation, play music or the sounds of water if you like. Being near actual running water is desired, even if you have to use an indoor fountain. Concentrate on the sounds only; nothing else exists or matters. Try this for five minutes each day, gradually increasing the time until you can sit for thirty minutes or an hour.

Ember

Notes:

February 29
Sunday

Leap Day

 2nd ♊
) v/c 5:08 am

) → ♋ 5:12 pm

Color of the day: Orange
Incense of the day: Basil

Do the Unlikely Spell

Leap day comes only once every four years. It is also called Bachelor's Day, or Sadie Hawkins Day, when it was okay for women to propose to men, instead of the other way round. Legend has it that St. Bridget took up the cause of spinsters everywhere with St. Patrick, and he allowed this role reversal to occur once every four years. In 1288, Scotland established this day as the one when a woman could propose marriage to a man; if he refused, he had to pay a fine. And until about 300 years ago, in some places no official business was transacted on February 29th because the day was not part of the regular calendar and so was thought not to have even occurred. Deals made today would not hold up in court. Leap Day is, according to Roman tradition, good for spells for improbable purposes. Try something unlikely today, it just might work.

Magenta Griffith

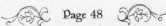

March

March is the third month of the year according to the Gregorian calendar, and the first month of the Roman calendar. Its astrological sign is Pisces, the fish (Feb 21–March 20), a mutable water sign ruled by Neptune. The name of the month itself comes from the Roman god of war, Mars. March heralds the end of winter and coming of spring. It is a transitional time, when warm spring rains and green budding plants return. The robin is a herald of spring, and a symbol of March—along with other migrating birds. Pruning season begins now in the garden, and branches are gathered and bundled together to dry for the coming Beltane Fire on May 1. As trees are still dormant, it is a good time to collect wood for wands now. It is also time to make use of a besom, or a Witches' broom, traditionally made of an ash handle and a bundle of birch twigs. Ritual sweeping is practiced at this time to purify. The main holiday of March is Ostara, or the Vernal Equinox, a time when day and night are equal once again after the dark winter. Seeds saved from the autumn harvest are celebrated and blessed now to ensure a good planting, and the March Full Moon is called the Seed Moon. Eggs are a symbol of the season. They are dyed or painted and used to make talismans, or else they are ritually eaten.

March 1
Monday

 2nd ♋

Color of the day: Lavender
Incense of the day: Peony

Play with a Guardian Angel Spell

By the beginning of March, we are usually starting to get rather stir-crazy. There is a sense of new beginnings stirring at Imbolc, and the excitement we feel for all the new growth is just about unbearable. It's time therefore for a guardian angel day. Mondays are traditional days for guardian angels. As you perform your morning ablutions, ask your guardian angel to play with you this day. Even if you have to go to work or school, you and your angel can create a joyous day together. Wear bright clothing. Look for the positive in everything. Give in to impulse. See where your guardian angel leads you, and play. Find the joy in the minutiae of the day, and watch how it grows with exponential energy.

Cerridwen Iris Shea

Notes:

March 2
Tuesday

2nd ♋
☽ v/c 10:42 am

Color of the day: Red
Incense of the day: Gardenia

Using Bay for Protection Spell

The bay laurel leaf, associated with the element of fire, has long been cherished by Witches as a symbol for consecration, protection, and healing. Kitchen Witches use it whole to season stews, soups, and sauces with prosperity, love, and protection. Note that bay leaves should be removed from the dish before serving; if ingested whole, they cause indigestion. Bay may also be used as an herbal element of protection in dream sachets and medicine bags. Hang a bay laurel wreath in your kitchen or near your back door. Write a protection charm on a large bay leaf, and tuck it beneath your mattress or into your wallet. Evoke the power of bay by saying:

> May the fire of bay
> protect me by love,
> not by fear.

Karri Ann Allrich

Notes:

March 3
Wednesday

2nd ♋
☽ → ♌ 4:18 am

Color of the day: Brown
Incense of the day: Maple

Open heart Sufi Meditation

Find a close friend or partner, and try this heart-opening exercise. Go to an open space in your house where you can gently dance. Then place your palms against your friend's palms, and allow your hands to follow and lead the other's where they spontaneously want to go. Imagine love pouring through your hands into the other person's, and imagine receiving love from the other person's hands. Close your eyes, and visualize this energy flow. After a few minutes, open up your eyes and look directly at your friend and say: "I honor the god (or goddess) in you," and then allow your friend to say the same.

Jonathan Keyes

Notes:

March 4
Thursday

2nd ♌
Color of the day: Green
Incense of the day: Vanilla

Egg Divination Spell

Jack Lindsay writes in *The Origins of Astrology:* "Mother Earth lies in the world's midst rounded like an egg, and all blessings are there inside her." The egg, as a symbol of creativity, fertility, and new beginnings, is a powerful tool for magic. Egg magic is most potent through the month of March. For this divination spell prepare an altar with blue cloth, green candle, athame, egg, and cauldron filled with cold, pure water. Center, and light the candle. Prick the small end of an egg, and let three drops of egg white fall into the water. Stir the water three times with the athame. You can divine the seeker's future from the shapes the egg white assumes.

Lily Gardner

Notes:

March 5
Friday

2nd ♌
☽ v/c 12:13 pm
☽ → ♍ 1:12 pm

Color of the day: Pink
Incense of the day: Ginger

Planting the Seeds of Love Spell

Long ago in Europe, this was the day spring plowing would begin. Using the agricultural theme of today, cast this spell to promote universal love. On your altar, place three candles—one in each of these colors: light blue, yellow, and lavender. Dress each candle with sweet pea oil. In the center of the altar, set a flowerpot of soil and a packet of blue sweet pea seeds. Light each candle, and say: "I light blue for peace, yellow for wisdom, and lavender for love." Press the seeds into the soil saying: "Now I plant the seeds of friendship." Transplant the seedlings into your garden. As they grow, so will your tolerance. Think of this spell when dealing with a difficult person, and you will feel much better.

James Kambos

Notes:

March 6
Saturday

2nd ♍
☽ Full Moon 6:14 pm

Color of the day: Blue
Incense of the day: Patchouli

March Purification and Regeneration Spell

March begins the season of regeneration. Winter has provided the purification by clearing away any "foliage" that is no longer viable. What remains creates the fuel that nourishes the earth's revitalization. The heavens, the Earth, and all of her inhabitants are creations of the same divine energy. Virgo's Full Moon embodies our oneness with the cycles of the universe. Sit under the Full Moon, preferably outside if weather permits. Focus on the pure lunar energy. Take a deep breath in, inviting the energy into your body. Visualize this energy purifying you with each breath. As you exhale, feel this energy release from your body and go into the Earth. Now feel the gentle heartbeat of the planet. Visualize her energy reaching up to you. Take in a deep breath, inviting the Earth's energy into your body. Feel the nourishing warmth as her energy fills you. As you exhale, visualize your energy flowing back to the Earth. Repeat this process of purification and nourishment as needed. Thank the universe for revitalizing your connection with heaven and Earth.

Karen Follett

Notes:

each vase. Put the candles a little distance in front of each of the vases and light them. Sit comfortably in the space between the two tables. Feel the solar energies charging the flowers, the candles, and the beams reflecting between the mirrors. Feel this energy empowering your mind, body, and spirit. Visualize yourself completely revitalized.

S. Y. Zenith

Notes:

March 7
Sunday

Purim — Junoalia

 2nd ♍
☽ v/c 3:49 am

☽ → ♎ 5:31 pm

Color of the day: Yellow
Incense of the day: Parsley

Enhance Well-Being Spell

To bring well-being to your weary soul, select a room in the home where the morning Sun shines most strongly. Make sure windows and doors are shut to keep out any strong breezes. Clean two mirrors, and arrange some orange-colored flowers in two separate vases. Put two gold candles in decorative holders. Place the vases on small tables on opposite sides of the room, and place a mirror behind

Holiday lore: Although the month of June is named for Juno, principal goddess of the Roman pantheon, major festivals dedicated to her are scattered throughout the year. For instance, today marks Junoalia, a festival in honor of Juno celebrated in solemnity by matrons. Two images of Juno made of cypress were borne in procession with twenty-seven girls dressed in long robes, singing a hymn to the goddess composed by the poet Livius. Along the way, the procession would have a dance in the great field of Rome before proceeding ahead to the temple of Juno.

March 8
Monday
International Women's Day

3rd ♎

Color of the day: White
Incense of the day: Lilac

Sanctity of Women Meditation

This is International Women's Day, a holiday recognized by the United Nations. Think about the sanctity of women today, and about the importance of cooperation. As you go about your business today, try to match each woman you see with a goddess. The tall blonde at the bus stop? Freya. The large woman who grins as she hands you your tuna sandwich at lunch? Yemaya. The coworker who always hits the mark? Artemis, of course. Don't forget to look for the goddess in yourself, too. Sit in front of a mirror, light a white candle, and meditate for a while. Wait and see who shows up. And if you're a guy, don't think this spell is not for you too. Every human soul has both masculine and feminine aspects. The goddess lives in all of us.

Elizabeth Barrette

Notes:

Holiday lore: While most holidays across the world celebrate the lives and achievement of men, this is one day wholly dedicated to the achievement and work of women. Originally inspired by a pair of mid-nineteenth-century ladies' garment workers strikes, today the holiday is little known in its country of origin; though this day's legacy is clear in March's designation by the U.S. Congress as Women's History Month. Throughout the month, women's groups in American towns hold celebrations and events, concerts, exhibitions, and rituals that recall heroic and gifted women of every stripe.

March 9
Tuesday

3rd ♎
☽ v/c 7:43 am
☽ → ♏ 9:03 pm

Color of the day: Gray
Incense of the day: Poplar

Burning Barriers Ritual

Tuesday is ruled by Mars, the "motivator," and this is a good time to use his energy in working toward a goal. Invoking Mars can help remove barriers that are preventing you from achieving success. Since the related element is fire, burning and smoldering are actions to take on this day. Prepare a sacred space and create a relaxed atmosphere. Incense smoke is easiest to watch against a dark background, so place a black cloth or board nearby; light as many candles as you desire. Prepare your preferred method of incense and light it. Spend long moments watching the smoke curl and float through the air. Gaze upon the candle flames. Consider the burning process, and invoke the fiery presence of Mars for energy, courage, and success.

Ember

Notes:

hold an almond in your hands before leaving your house in the morning. Visualize yourself having a successful day. Feel wisdom flowing through you. Say to yourself:

> **I am open mental clarity and spirit guidance.**
> **I ask for the blessings of wisdom in all that I do.**
>
> **May I attract prosperity and creativity throughout this day.**

Send this energy into the almond. Carry the almond in your pocket and purse. Repeat your visualization periodically throughout the day, and trust that you are attracting these blessings.

Kristin Madden

Notes:

March 10
Wednesday
Tibet Day

 3rd ♏

Color of the day: Topaz
Incense of the day: Pine

Spell to Find Treasure

It is said that carrying an almond will lead you to treasures. These nuts are associated with wisdom and magic. To use this energy for the benefit of your business or school,

March 11
Thursday

3rd ♏
☽ v/c 11:11 pm
☽ → ♐ 11:57 pm

Color of the day: Purple
Incense of the day: Sandalwood

Quiet Space Spell

To rid yourself of the headaches that a lack of money frequently causes, gather together all your current bills, your checkbook, and any cash or coins you have in the house. Wrap them together in a green velvet cloth, and go to a quiet space, preferably in nature. Lie down on the ground, and place the velvet bag under your head. Close your eyes and slowly chew two fresh leaves of feverfew. Imagine what your life will be like when all your financial obligations are easily met each month. What type of work would you have? What would you eat? What would you do after work? Remember this feeling of freedom whenever you pay a bill or are feeling particularly panicky about money. Do not do this ritual if you are taking prescription medications.

Therese Francis

Notes:

March 12
Friday

3rd ♐

Color of the day: Coral
Incense of the day: Rose

Letting Go Spell

Sometimes it is difficult to let go. You can use this waning Moon to quell the pain of a failed relationship and free yourself from lingering attachments. When the Moon rises, prepare to take a bath by candlelight. Light as many white candles as it takes to fill the room with light. Place a picture or statue of a cat near the candles. You will call on Freya for this ritual, for as the Norse goddess of love she will understand and help take away your pain. Pour a cup of Epsom salts and a few drops of a relaxing essential oil (try lavender, rose, or jasmine) into the bath. Stand before the candles for a few moments. Breathe in the light and energy from the candles. Tell Freya your troubles, slowly and softly, and ask her to release you from the pain. Wait there a few moments while the candles burn and the silence fills the room. Then bathe, visualizing yourself being cleansed of all negativity. After bathing, thank Freya, extinguish the candles, and give your cat a hug and a soft kiss.

Denise Dumars

Notes:

of the traditional seven, a perfectly symmetrical system had to be modified. It was finally decided that Uranus rules the sign of Aquarius, the sign of group and global consciousness. Interestingly enough, soon after the discovery of Uranus, the planet that rules flight, the first manned balloon flight took place.

Magenta Griffith

Notes:

March 13
Saturday

3rd ♐

4th Quarter 4:01 pm

☽ v/c 4:01 pm

Color of the day: Black
Incense of the day: Lilac

Uranus Discovery Day

On this day in 1781, in Bath, England, the astronomer William Herschel discovered the planet Uranus. Uranus means "heaven"; the planet was named after the father of Kronos, also known as Saturn. Uranus was the first planet discovered since ancient times, and the first discovered using a telescope. This discovery required astrologers to rethink their science, and there was considerable confusion about the rulership of this planet. Since there were now eight astrological planets instead

March 14
Sunday

4th ♐

☽ → ♑ 5:06 am

Color of the day: Amber
Incense of the day: Cinnamon

Poppet Magic healing Spell

Toxic emotions can bring on health concerns. It is essential to clear the air after any kind of argument or misunderstanding. One way to clear the air is by using poppet magic. For this, go to a craft store and buy a small rag doll without features or hair. Pin to the doll the name of the person

who has been causing you problems, as well as his or her astrological sign on the doll's chest, near the area of the heart. If you have a picture of the person, all the better; you can scan the image and pin it to the doll's face. Light a white candle, saying:

> Peace we make,
> disquiet friend.
> With this prick our
> troubles end.
>
> Peace is the way.
> Love is the power.
> Our problems flee this
> very hour.
>
> Serenity,
> that is the key.
> heal our love.
>
> So mote it be.

Susan Sheppard

Notes:

March 15
Monday

4th ♐

Color of the day: Blue
Incense of the day: Chrysanthemum

A New Play Affirmation

I view each morning as the opening of a new play. You can charge yourself magically this morning with this new play affirmation. Upon rising, stand in a darkened room facing east. Visualize a white candle burning very steadily, and say:

> Divine power,
> power of perfect protection,
> protect my family, home,
> car, and myself.
> Protect us from accident
> and illness.
> Assure that we will return
> home safely tonight.
> And help us solve any
> problem that may arise,
> calmly, quickly, and for
> the good of all.
>
> So mote it be.

Thank the divine power for listening to you and for the power you raised. Open the curtains and let the morning light in. If you feel threatened during the day, remember the words you spoke. You'll be surprised at how much easier you will be able to deal with stress.

James Kambos

March 16
Tuesday

4th ♑
☽ v/c 12:34 am
☽ → ♒ 6:10 am

Color of the day: Black
Incense of the day: Juniper

Irish Charm for Protection

Winter has weakened its icy grip, yet March winds howl like the Irish Bean Sidhe, the wailing woman of the hills. Known commonly as the banshee, this Celtic death spirit is thought to haunt the fairy hills and knolls, keening her death cry into the wind. Her flowing hair and robes create a formidable image. Hearing her wail portends a death. Make an Irish charm of protection tonight. Gather a green candle, a plate, a four-leaf clover (or its image), and four drops of rosemary oil. Melt the candle wax to make a coin-sized puddle on the plate. As it hardens, press in the clover, add the oil, and shape a charm. As you mold, infuse it with protection energy, saying:

Love conquers fear.

Karri Ann Allrich

Notes:

Holiday lore: Why is March 15 considered so unlucky? On this date in 226 B.C., an earthquake brought the Colossus of Rhodes—one of the seven wonders of the ancient world—to its knees. But a more famous incident probably accounts for the superstition regarding the "Ides of March." Julius Caesar's family may have belonged to the "Peoples' Party," but somewhere along the way he became a tyrant. In February of 44 B.C., Caesar had himself named Dictator Perpetuus Dictator for Life. Brutus assassinated him on March 15, 44 B.C. Caesar's murder was foretold by soothsayers and even by his wife, Calpurnia, who had a nightmare in which Caesar was being butchered like an animal. Caesar chose to ignore these portents and the rest, of course, is history. As for us, well, the Moon is in Capricorn today, so lead with your pragmatism today, not by dictate.

March 17
Wednesday
St. Patrick's Day

4th ≈≈

Color of the day: White
Incense of the day: Neroli

Liberalia Spell

While many people spend today celebrating St. Patrick by getting drunk on green beer, here's an alternative option from the Roman calendar: Liberalia. Today is sacred to Liber, the Roman god of passion, wild nature, fertility, and wine. On this day, women sold cakes on small altars in honor of freedom. To tap into this energy, bake bread or make a cake today. Think about what exactly freedom and liberty mean to you. Decide what action you can take to promote liberty and tolerance in your life and in the lives of those around you. Ruminate on what the concept of freedom means around the world, and how often people struggle to attain it. Once you have thought enough about these concepts, clean up your altar, rearrange it, and take care to rededicate it. Eat the bread or cake you created to symbolize the embodiment of your commitment to freedom and liberty, and to your growing understanding of the responsibility associated with those privileges.

Cerridwen Iris Shea

Holiday lore: Much folklore surrounds St. Patrick's Day. Though originally a Catholic holy day, St. Patrick's Day has evolved into more of a secular holiday today. One traditional icon of the day is the shamrock. This stems from an Irish tale that tells how Patrick used the three-leafed shamrock to explain the Trinity of Christian dogma. His followers adopted the custom of wearing a shamrock on his feast day; though why we wear green on this day is less clear. St. Patrick's Day came to America in 1737, the date of the first public celebration of the holiday in Boston.

March 18
Thursday

 4th ≈

)) v/c 7:15 am

)) → ℋ 10:26 am

Color of the day: Crimson
Incense of the day: Carnation

Sheila-na-gig Day

No one is exactly sure why the Sheila-na-gig is carved over the doorways of Irish churches. It is obviously a Pagan symbol, but it is not something one would think particularly appealing to the average church-goer. After all, her leering face and gaping vagina contrast with a bald head, skeletal body, and wasted flesh. Still, Sheila gives form to the mystery of the elusive and powerful Mother Goddess, from whom all life comes and to whom all life will one day return. Her feast day follows St. Patrick's Day. Patrick is celebrated for driving the snakes, that is to say symbolically speaking the Pagans, out of Ireland. So why did the churchmen carve the Sheila-na-gig over their doorways? We may never know; in this case, the Sheila has the last word—so why question it? Simply decorate your altar with green cloth, green candles, a shamrock plant, and if possible a statue or picture of the Sheila. Play Celtic music all day, and dance to life.

Lily Gardner

Notes:

March 19
Friday

 4th ℋ

Color of the day: Rose
Incense of the day: Dill

Dreamwork Spell

This time of the year is a transitional time between winter and spring in the Northern Hemisphere. Therefore, this is often the time when bears begin to stir and become more active in the world, and the messages we get from dreams can be very profound during these times. During this Pisces Moon, make a cup of mugwort tea and place a few leaves of this herb under the pillow. Ask for messages from your dreams tonight about what you need to do or areas you need to explore in the months ahead. When you awake, write down your dreams and explore their meanings.

Jonathan Keyes

Notes:

March 20
Saturday
Ostara – Spring Equinox –
International Astrology Day

4ħ ♓
☉ → ♈ 1:49 am
☽ v/c 3:57 pm
☽ → ♈ 4:29 pm
New Moon 9:38 pm

Color of the day: Indigo
Incense of the day: Pine

Vernal Equinox Spell
The Vernal or Spring Equinox marks one of the two points during the year when the Sun's path crosses the celestial equator and the day and the night are of equal length. The ancient Celtic calendar only had three months, but in 1752 it was reconstructed with four months and

eight holidays steaming from ancient festivals. In this more modern Celtic calendar, the Vernal Equinox marks the point of mid-spring. In our Gregorian calendar, meanwhile, this day is the first day of spring. And among the Teutonic peoples, this day was the time for a festival of spring called Ostara. Ostara is named after the goddess of spring whose name was Ostèra among the Germans, and Eostre or Eastre among the Anglo-Saxons. This goddess's name is derived from the word for "dawn." It should be obvious at this point that Eastre also lent her name to the major Christian spring holiday that celebrates the rebirth of Christ—Easter. Although Easter eggs are usually said to derive from the egg's use as a symbol of rebirth in ancient Egypt and in the Near East, and from its adoption by Christians as a symbol of Christ's resurrection, clay eggs have been found in prehistoric tombs in Russia and Sweden. That is so say, the symbolism of the egg is universal. Of course, almost all holidays make use of magic; still, one does not often hear it described so plainly, particularly when dealing with Christian holidays. More often, magic acts and symbols are called traditions, or are thought of as things that bring luck. But in reality, the Easter egg is a magic talisman that assures rebirth, renewal, and good fortune. Start painting yours on Ostara, and use lots of red.

Robert Place

Notes:

 Psychic Balance Spell for the New Moon

I have met people who are so grounded in the physical plane that they will never acknowledge what they cannot perceive with their five senses. On the other side of the coin, I have met people who are floating so deeply within the psychic realms they cannot distinguish the physical from the psychical. Any skill, spiritual path, or belief system that is not integrated and balanced is detrimental in a world that demands a kind of balance in order for us to survive and thrive. The interest in the psychic arts is increasing hand in hand with the interest in the occult mysteries. The following spell not only speaks of your intent to further your psychic abilities, but it offers you the opportunity to learn balance. To start,

light a black and a white candle. Focus your mind in between the two flames, and state these words:

Shadows of light,
illumination of night,
I see a balance
between psychic and
mundane sight.

Begin an intuitive journal, and write about how you are integrating your psychic skills into your mundane life.

Karen Follett

Notes:

March 21
Sunday

Ist ♈

Color of the day: Gold
Incense of the day: Sage

Isis healing Ritual

The Egyptian goddess Isis can be called upon in the early spring to enhance your physical and emotional well-being. Cover your altar with white fabric. Decorate it with a vase of white tulips, a white candle, and one white feather, and burn some gardenia incense. Here and there, sprinkle small decorative silver stars. Light the candle. Using the feather, fan the incense about you. Now speak these words:

> Isis, Great Mother,
> hear my words of power.
> Let the season of light
> bring me wellness and
> protection.

End the ritual by brushing your body lightly from head to toe with the feather. If you have a specific problem, mention it as you say your words of power.

James Kambos

Notes:

Negating Any Negative Energies Spell

The refreshing and aromatic properties of essential oils can be used to keep the home and its inhabitants free of negative energies. An air freshener spray is a simple and effective way to perfume the dwelling and disperse the oils. This is also useful for banishing unpleasant vibrations left by unwelcome visitors. Just dissolve 25 drops of eucalyptus oil, 15 drops of gardenia oil, and 10 drops of lemon oil in a cup of vodka. Pour the mixture into a glass pump-spray bottle, and fill the bottle to the top with fresh spring or distilled water. Shake the bottle and give the home and everyone in it a good spritz.

S. Y. Zenith

Notes:

March 22
Monday

1st ♈
☽ v/c 10:14 am
Color of the day: Ivory
Incense of the day: Myrrh

Holiday lore: Cybele was the Great Mother of the gods in Ida, and she was taken to Rome from Phrygia in 204 B.C. She was also considered the Great Mother of all Asia Minor. Her festivals were known as *ludi,* or "games" and were solemnized with various mysterious rites. Along with Hecate and Demeter of Eleusis, Cybele was one of the leading deities of Rome when mystery cults were at their prime. Hila'aria, or "Hilaria," originally seemed to have been a name given to any day or season of rejoicing that was either private or public. Such days were devoted to general rejoicings and people were not allowed to show signs of grief or sorrow. The Hilaria actually falls on March 25 and is the last day of a festival of Cybele that commences today. However, the Hilaria was not mentioned in the Roman calendar or in Ovid's *Fasti*.

March 23
Tuesday

1st ♈
☽ → ♉ 4:29 pm

Color of the day: White
Incense of the day: Honeysuckle

Springcleaning Preparation Spell

Clarify your mind before you attempt to declutter your environment. Do this by taking a hot lemongrass bath. Just place a handful of lemongrass herb in a square linen handkerchief, and tie it shut. Place the sachet under hot, running water to make a herbal bath. Soak yourself in the bath with the sachet

for at least ten minutes. Breathe deeply. Keep your mind as open and clear as you are able.

Therese Francis

Notes:

March 24
Wednesday

1st ♉
☽ v/c 5:29 pm

Color of the day: Yellow
Incense of the day: Coriander

Day of Blood Spell

The Romans ended a nine-day fast on this day, known as the Day of Blood. This would be a good day to partake of a pomegranate. The pomegranate is often used as an alternative for blood or magical ink in spells. This is a delicious fruit that is associated with many things, including luck and wishes. After cracking open your pomegranate, make a wish on the first seed you eat. As you eat the second seed, give thanks for a particular blessing, or send your blessings to another person. Continue to alternate with wishes and thanks or blessings until you have finished the seeds.

Kristin Madden

Notes:

robes a celestial blue. Her floral symbol is the red rose of alchemy. She is the divine feminine who gives birth to the returning light; she is heaven's queen, Isis incarnate. Place a red rose upon your altar today in honor of Mary and of the sacred feminine principle. Meditate today on the hidden strengths of compassion and grace. Reclaim the archetypal virgin within you. Virgin originally signified "a woman unto herself," or a woman complete. Envision yourself complete, and write down your dreams and aspirations.

Karri Ann Allrich

Notes:

March 25
Thursday

1st ♉
☽ → ♊ 12:35 pm

Color of the day: Turquoise
Incense of the day: Evergreen

Queen of the heavens Ritual

On this feast day of Mary's Annunciation, may we look upon the archetypal Virgin Mother as Queen of the Heavens, a modern guise of the goddess returning. Study Mary's image today. She stands upon a crescent Moon, her head crowned with a ring of stars, her

March 26
Friday

1st ♊
Color of the day: Purple
Incense of the day: Almond

Growing Your Love Spell

In order to bring an increasing flow of love your way, obtain seeds (or purchase seedlings) for any plant you wish to grow, along with a small flowerpot and some potting soil. Plant the seeds, or seedlings, and bless them. Imagine that as they grow, so will the love in your life. Visualize yourself giving and receiving love. Nurture the plants by ensuring they have enough water and sunlight, and look upon them each day as a symbol of increasing love in your life. Use words such as this for your visualization:

> Great spirit,
> Bless these gentle plants.
> Allow them to grow in love.
> And as they do, let my
> loving nature increase.
> Help my relationships to
> grow and flourish,
> Seed to flower,
> Minute to hour
> Bring love into my life.

Ember

Notes:

March 27
Saturday

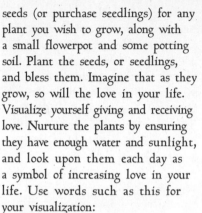 1st ♊
☽ v/c 5:44 pm

Color of the day: Blue
Incense of the day: Lavender

Fairy Invitation Ritual

To invite fairy creatures into your yard, try showing them the way. Choose a smooth surface, like a patch of bare earth or a patio, and lay out a circle of "fairy footprints," that is, make a stencil by cutting tiny footprint shapes in a piece of paper. Lay the paper on the ground, and sprinkle it with sugar or some powdered milk. Then move the paper along, and keep repeating until you have a full circle. Put a few flower petals in the center. As you work be sure to sing appropriate words, such as:

> Little folk of flashing wing,
> little folk of dancing feet,
> hear my words to you
> and bring
> blessings with you when
> we meet.

Fairies love music and flowers. They especially enjoy dancing in circles. Give them this simple hint, and see what happens.

Elizabeth Barrette

Notes:

shells, a crow feather (if you can find one), crystals, and elements you consider sacred. Your items should be odd-numbered—that is, you must use five, seven, nine, or thirteen items in your bag. Place them all on the red flannel. Tie up the cloth into a bag. Wear your gris-gris around your neck or carry it in your hand or pocket, and feel your power surge.

Susan Sheppard

Notes:

March 28
Sunday

1st ♊

☽ → ♋ 1:23 am

2nd Quarter 6:48 pm

Color of the day: Orange

Incense of the day: Basil

Gris—Gris Bag Spell

Today is the birthday of the Chinese goddess Kwan Yin. Use this day to make your own gris-gris bag. In the New Orleans practice of Voudoun, the gris-gris bag is used for not only protection, but also to gain wealth and health. We see parallels to the gris-gris in many more mainstream home remedies, such as pouches with cotton balls dipped in camphor, mint, and ammonia that are worn around the neck until sickness goes away. To create your own gris-gris bag gather the following: a small square of red flannel, a black string, cayenne pepper, cotton balls dipped in oils of mint and eucalyptus, loose herbs,

March 29
Monday

2nd ♋

Color of the day: Gray

Incense of the day: Daffodil

Moon Day Dream Pillows Spell

Prepare for psychic dreams tonight! Make a dream pillow by mixing some or all of the following herbs to make a cupful: (the first two are required) mugwort, lavender, rose petals, catnip, chamomile, jasmine, orange blossoms, and buckwheat hulls. Sew them up in a small rectangle of Moon-and-star printed cloth. Stuff the dream pillow into your pillowcase with your usual pillow. Before sleep, tell yourself that you will remember your dreams. Place a small notebook and pen by the bed so you can record the dreams you remember when you wake up in the morning. Continue using the dream pillow for best results.

Denise Dumars

Notes:

the floor of the most used room in the house—maybe the kitchen, maybe the family room. Cast a circle by sweeping around the supplies with a broom, starting at the east. As you sweep, visualize the house becoming clean, and also everyone in the house becoming happy, cheerful, and healthy. You can use various cleaning implements to cast a more elaborate circle, if you desire. Invoke your favorite goddess of the home—for example, Hestia, the Roman goddess of the hearth—and ask her to bless your work and your house. After you have finished the preparation, get to cleaning. After you're done all the cleaning for the day, thank the goddess before you put away the cleaning equipment.

Magenta Griffith

Notes:

March 30
Tuesday

2nd ♋

☽ v/c 11:00 am
☽ → ♌ 1:07 pm

Color of the day: Scarlet
Incense of the day: Musk

Vernal Purification Spell

Put all of your cleaning supplies, plus your list of chores to do, on

March 31
Wednesday
The Borrowed Days

2nd ♌

Color of the day: Brown
Incense of the day: Sandalwood

The Crone's Cauldron Vision Quest Ritual

The vision quest ritual that follows asks you to seek the advice of the all-knowing crone. To start, find some quiet time alone. Close your eyes, and intone these words:

> Fire and water,
> wind and stone,
> I seek the wisdom of the
> ancient crone.

See yourself walking through the forest. You are surrounded by ferns and trilliums. Then, the Sun begins to filter through the shade. In a small clearing, you see a thatch-roof cottage. An elderly woman in black tends a boiling cauldron near the garden. Smoke and mist conceal her face. She beckons you, and points to the cauldron. To find the answer you are searching for, you must scry into the cauldron. When you do so, your answer is revealed. Now, journey back to your normal daily routine.

James Kambos

Notes:

April

April is the fourth month of the year of the Gregorian calendar, and the first month of the astrological calendar. Its astrological sign is Aries, the ram (Mar 21–Apr 20), a cardinal fire sign ruled by Mars. The name of the month comes from the Latin *aprilis*, which derives from *aper*, or "boar," as April was thought to be the month of the boar. April is the month of burgeoning life force, sunshine, and life returned to the forests. Birds are building nests now; lambs are romping on greening hillsides. Apricot trees are blossoming, and herb gardens are filling out. Now is the time to plant your garden. Potatoes, onions, lettuce, and tomatoes are sacred to various divinities now. It is a good time to create a circle for meditation outside, either of stones or shrubberies. The four cardinal directions should be marked in the circle, and connected by a crossquarter cross. Cut mazes and labyrinths now in turf or in fields. Plant tree saplings too—maples, hawthorn, and holly are sacred in April. Bunnies and hares are symbols of fertility at this time of year, associated with rites of spring. The Full Moon in April is called the Hare Moon. Holidays in April include April Fools' Day, which comes from Roman celebrations of the New Year rebirth. Earth Day on April 22 celebrates the bounty of the planet. April 30 is called May Eve and is celebrated with revels and bonfires.

April 1

Thursday

April Fools' Day

2nd ♌

Color of the day: Gray
Incense of the day: Carnation

Fool's Fish Spell

Because April 1 was the old day for the celebration of the New Year in France, it is often said that the name April's Fool derives from the fact that those who continued to celebrate on this day after the date was changed to January 1 were referred to as fools. However, no one knows for sure how this holiday originated, and in fact, in modern France one who falls victim to an April 1 prank is called *Poisson d'Avril,* or "April Fish." On this day, French children fool their friends by taping a paper fish to their friends' backs. When the "young fool" discovers this trick, the prankster yells "Poisson d'Avril!" It is more likely that this holiday is related to the ancient days of merriment called Hilaria in Latin. In ancient Rome, the popular cult of the mother goddess Cybele and her consort, the vegetation god Attis, were celebrated with several holidays. On each day of these holidays, a part of these figures' myth was retold. On March 15, Cybele was said to find Attis and fall in love with him.

On March 22, because of a love triangle between Attis, a young nymph or another lover, and Cybele, Attis' young lover is lost to him. He is driven mad and emasculates himself under a pine tree. On March 24, "The Day of Blood," Attis was said to die, and his followers would go into morning by fasting and flagellating themselves. On March 25, Attis was reborn and then returned to Cybele. His followers celebrated with Hilaria. There was feasting and cheerfulness, and anything which promoted laughter was permissible. It is easy to see the connection between these ancient fertility cult days and modern April Fools' Day. They are related to the transition from the death that was winter to the new life that is spring. This is a time to renew oneself with meditation and then lightheartedness and fun.

Robert Place

Notes:

April 2
Friday

 2nd ♌

Color of the day: Pink
Incense of the day: Thyme

Spell to Drive out Frost

This spell comes from Germany, where Pagans burned effigies of Old Man Winter in bonfires built on the edge of town to drive out the cold. It was believed that if winter was driven out of the village, this would put an end to the killing frosts for the year. If you're a gardener and are anxious to start your April planting, you can fashion a winter effigy from raffia. Decorate him with old pine cones, dead weeds, and other such symbols of the fading winter. Light a green candle next to your fire, saying:

Old Man Winter's reign
is dead,
to Lady Spring we're
duly led.

The Wheel of Years has
turned again;
storm, ice, and frost be
burned again.

Blessed be.

Throw your effigy into the fire and watch him be consumed by the flames.

Lily Gardner

Notes:

April 3
Saturday

 2nd ♍
☽ v/c 1:23 pm

Color of the day: Indigo
Incense of the day: Jasmine

Purifying Spell

The waxing Virgo Moon at the start of spring is a good time to do some purification. Now is a particularly optimal time to cleanse out any winter toxins that may have accumulated over the past months. Start the day with a glass of clean water with some freshly squeezed lime or lemon juice. Try not to eat until lunch time, and then eat only lightly steamed vegetables and whole grains for the day. In the evening time, bathe yourself and put on fresh clothes. Light a new candle on the altar, and meditate for a while. Afterward, examine the unhealthy aspects of your life that need to be released, and ask what healthy patterns need to be encouraged. State aloud your intentions for making those changes in your life.

Jonathan Keyes

Notes:

also an important part of this celebration, especially when performed on pan pipes, cymbals, or tympanum. Put on CDs of sacred music, or pick up an instrument and create some of your own. Take today to live in your body instead of just in your mind.

Cerridwen Iris Shea

Notes:

April 4
Sunday

Daylight Saving Time Begins 2 am

 2nd ♏
☽ → ♎ 3:52 am

Color of the day: Yellow
Incense of the day: Coriander

Cybele's Games

Today, depending upon how we interpret the calendar, is the start of the seven-day period devoted to Cybele's games. Today, go out and participate in a physical activity. It can be one at which you already excel, or one you've always wanted to try. Enjoy the physicality, use all your senses, and appreciate your body and all its wonders today. Music was

April 5
Monday

 2nd ♎
Full Moon 7:03 am
☽ v/c 5:26 pm

Color of the day: Lavender
Incense of the day: Rose

Love's harmony Spell

Spring heralds the awakening surges of the Earth and all her inhabitants. The desire to love and to be loved is an innate need of our interdependent universe. Since love is both so all-desired and all-encompassing, one wonders why love is so difficult to draw into so many of our lives. One simple word can lend an insight: "intent." Unlike our furry or leafy counterparts, humans generally have more on their minds than propagating their species. We want to bond. We want that love that is in balance and that works in harmony with us. At this time of universal seeking-for-love, place a mirror in front of you, allowing a view of your entire face. Place a small lighted pink candle between you and your mirror. Gaze into the mirror, seeing yourself as the perfect creation of the divine. State these words:

> Mirror, mirror,
> my reflection be
> the perfection of my body
> and soul,
> the perfection of the
> goddess who created me.
>
> I deserve the best
> and will accept nothing
> less than a love that's in
> harmony.

Karen Follett

Notes:

April 6
Tuesday
Passover Begins

 3rd ♎

☽ → ♏ 6:24 am

Color of the day: White
Incense of the day: Gardenia

Liberation Spell for Passover

Passover, called *Pesah* or *Pesach* in Hebrew, is the Jewish holiday that commemorates the ancient liberation of Jews from slavery in Egypt. The story of this liberation and escape, which is told in chapter 12 of the book of Exodus in the Bible, is a dramatization of the escape from confinement and death into freedom and life. This ritual is reworked into all holidays at this time of the year. This is a move from darkness to light. In Exodus, God tells Moses to instruct the congregation of Israel to sacrifice a lamb on this night, and to paint the lamb's blood on their doorposts. During the night, God brought a plague on Egypt and all of their first-born died, but when the angel of death saw the blood of the lamb on a house he passed over the dwelling. Also on this night Moses instructed his people to eat only "unleavened bread and bitter herbs" with the meat of the lamb. On the next morning, the congregation of Israel was freed from bondage by the pharaoh, and they left Egypt for the land of Canaan, bringing their unleavened bread with them for the desert journey. On this day Jews have a ceremonial meal in which they eat lamb, unleavened matzo, and raw vegetables dipped in bitter vinegar. These elements are all derived from the story of Exodus, but the meal also contains the magical hard-boiled egg as a symbol of God's love. The egg talisman reinforces the connection between Passover and the Vernal Equinox celebrations of other cultures. During the meal, the head of the household drinks four cups of wine, but a fifth is left out for the prophet Elijah. By the way, the Bible says that Elijah did not die. Instead, he was taken to heaven in a whirlwind. It is said that when Elijah returns it will mark the true coming of the messiah.

Robert Place

Notes:

April 7
Wednesday

3rd ♏
☽ v/c 7:06 am

Color of the day: Topaz
Incense of the day: Eucalyptus

Safety from Here-to-There Spell

For safety during travel today, carry some comfrey with you. It is said that placing some in suitcases will prevent your bags from being stolen or lost during travel. Before going out for the day, charge a bit of comfrey to take with you. As you chant, see the protective energies of the plant surround you, and say:

> Spirits of this plant,
> I pray.
> Keep me safe throughout
> this day.
>
> Bring me safety and
> security, please.
> Allow me to travel
> where I will with ease.

Place the comfrey in your purse or pocket. You might want to leave some in your car to protect it both on the road and in the parking lot.

Kristin Madden

Notes:

April 8
Thursday

Buddha's Birthday

 3rd ♏

☽ → ♐ 7:50 am

Color of the day: Crimson
Incense of the day: Geranium

Paying Debts Spell

Most everyone has some kind of debt to overcome, whether it's student loans, credit cards, or something more symbolic or spiritual. To help pay off your debts, collect statements or symbols of what you owe, and with black ink, or with an imaginary ink on the tip of your finger, mark an X on them. Then, using scissors, real or imaginary, cut the "bills" into very small pieces, and let the pieces fall in a pile. Visualize the debt being cut until nothing remains—that is, you are free of the financial burdens. Place the paper pieces in the bottom of a heat-proof container, and place a black votive candle on top of them. Light the candle, and allow it to burn completely until cool. The wax will have covered the paper and bound it. Remove the wax and paper and bury the whole where it won't be disturbed. Put the bag out of your mind. Pay the bills, but bury the worry.

Ember

April 9
Friday

Good Friday

3rd ♐

☽ v/c 8:30 am

Color of the day: Purple
Incense of the day: Ylang-ylang

Rediscovering the Maiden Spell

As the days slowly lengthen, Witches celebrate the goddess of spring, the archetypal maiden who is symbolized by the crescent Moon rising in the east. This graceful archetype honors our autonomy, our clarity, and our vitality. Whether we are in partnership or living alone, we must first define who we are before giving ourselves to a relationship. We must honor our maiden within. Light a white candle now, and gaze at the flame. Ask yourself: What are your dreams, your desires, your strengths, your weaknesses? What mistakes have you made in the past that have brought you wisdom and insight? How have you changed from last year's spring? How have you grown? What old skins have you shed and left behind? Record your insights in your Witch's journal.

Karri Ann Allrich

Notes:

April 10
Saturday

3rd ♐
☽ → ♑ 9:33 am

Color of the day: Black
Incense of the day: Violet

Spring Growth Spell

With spring comes gardening. You can use rune magic to help your plants grow tall and strong, protect them from inclement weather, and ward off marauding wildlife. For each row of seeds, you need a stick. Cover the empty seed packet with clear tape to preserve it, and

fasten it to one end of the stick. Along the stick, carve runes. Then post the stick at one end of the row. Consider these runes: feoh (ᚠ) for wealth and nourishment; wynn (ᚹ) for hope, joy, and new energy; nyd (ᚾ) for need; jera (ᛃ) for bounty and fruition; eoh (ᛇ) for resilience; eolh (ᛉ) for luck and protection; sigil (ᛋ) for success; beorc (ᛒ) for healing and renewal; lagu (ᛚ) for protection and growth; and ing (ᛝ) for fertility and energy. As you carve, say this verse:

Knife sharp, wood hard,
Rune strong, rune guard.

Elizabeth Barrette

Notes:

April 11
Sunday

Easter

3rd ♑
4th Quarter 11:46 pm
☽ v/c 11:46 pm

Color of the day: Gold
Incense of the day: Clove

Lucky in Love Spell

Easter is the most important of the Christian holidays. It is the feast of the resurrection of Christ, whose crucifixion and death are now remembered on Good Friday. On Easter, Christ is said to return to life after his death. That the celebration of Christ's triumph over death should come at a time when prechristian peoples were celebrating the seasonal triumph of light over dark, and life over death, is more than coincidental. Easter's connection with the Vernal Equinox is demonstrated by how the date of the holiday is determined. That is, the date of Easter is always on the first Sunday after the first Full Moon following the Vernal Equinox. Also, the name of the holiday is taken from the Germanic equinox festival called Ostara, named after their goddess of spring. The rabbits and eggs associated with Easter are prechristian symbols of fertility and rebirth. Easter also has an obvious connection with the Jewish holiday Passover. The "Last Supper" at which Christ predicted his crucifixion was a Passover feast. At this feast he linked his body with the unleavened bread and his blood with the cup of wine. Further, he took the role of the Passover lamb, whose sacrifice was necessary to save his people. Passover itself was a fusion of two preexisting spring rituals, the spring sacrifice practiced by the nomadic shepherds, and the feast of the unleavened bread practiced by the Canaanite farmers. Easter, then, is a good time to meditate on the underlying connectedness of all religions and customs. When looked at in this light, all religions are one.

Robert Place

Notes:

April 12
Monday

4th ♑

☽ → ♒ 12:33 pm

Color of the day: Silver
Incense of the day: Frankincense

Psyching Up for Taxes Spell

Taxes are due in a few days, and if you've been procrastinating here's an idea for helping you get them done on time. It's simple, and it works. Take a blue or green candle, and find a quiet space. Light the candle, and gaze at the flame. See yourself inside the flame, completely protected by warm, loving energy.

Then slowly repeat nine times:

So much time,
So little to do.

Now, remembering to breathe slowly, turn off the phone, gather your tax papers together, and get started.

Therese Francis

Notes:

istorical note: On 12 April, 1961, Yuri Gagarin piloted the first manned spaceship to leave the pull of our planet's gravity. This achievement is given much less attention than it deserves; part of it is politics, since Gagarin was a cosmonaut for the Soviet Union. Part of it, too, is time; today, space pilots live and work for months aboard space stations, so a simple space flight seems routine. Still, Yuri Gagarin's 108-minute flight in space represented not only a triumph of science and engineering, but also it broke a psychological barrier. It was literally a flight into unknown.

"Am I happy to be setting off on a cosmic flight?" said Yuri Gagarin in an interview before the start. "Of course. In all ages and epochs people have experienced the greatest happiness in embarking upon new voyages of discovery . . . I say 'until we meet again' to you, dear friends, as we always say to each other when setting off on a long journey."

April 13
Tuesday
Thai New Year

4th ♒

Color of the day: Red
Incense of the day: Ginger

Banishing Bad Vibes Spell

his is a spell, written by a friend of mine, to banish evil. He has used it successfully to rid an apartment of very bad vibes. If your home feels like there is something there that shouldn't be, or that someone is thinking ill of you or sending bad vibes your way, try this. Mix salt and water, and bless it. Go through your home, sprinkling the salt water around, and recite in a loud voice:

Dark intruders,
hear my call.

heed my warning,
listen all.

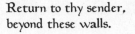

Return to thy sender,
beyond these walls.

Take with thee nothing,
nothing at all.

Magenta Griffith

Notes:

April 14
Wednesday

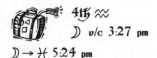 4th ♒
          ☽ v/c 3:27 pm
☽ → ♓ 5:24 pm

Color of the day: White
Incense of the day: Cedar

Spell to Achieve Clarity and Focus

In order for others to meet our needs, we must first know what we want. To initiate this process, get a sky-blue candle and some oil of myrrh. Light the candle and rub your third eye chakra, saying:

By the power of water,
I see clearly and divinely.
I ask and I seek.
My needs are met.

Anoint your throat with the oil, saying:

By the powers of air,
I mean what I say.
I say what I intend.

Daub some oil on your heart chakra (between the breastbone), and say:

By the power of fire,
I know what I desire.
I am led by the heart,
which joins wisdom with love.

Anoint your midsection with the oil, and say:

By the power of earth,
I stick to my dreams.
I remain steadfast.
I understand what it
takes to get me there.
So mote it be.

This spell works best under a clear sky, when the Moon is in an air sign.

Susan Sheppard

Notes:

April 15
Thursday

 4th ♓

Color of the day: Purple

Incense of the day: Musk

Obatala Mercy Spell

Ask for Obatala's mercy on tax day. Obatala is the Yoruban god of purity, goodness, and mercy. Before mailing your tax return, put a little coriander oil on the envelope. You may also anoint your wallet, checkbook, and so on. Take an Epsom salt or milk bath to feel pure, and wear at least one item of white clothing today. Buy an Obatala candle at a botanica, or if unavailable, light a white seven-day candle, anointing it with the oil as well. Ask Obatala to keep you from being one of those unlucky taxpayers who is chosen at random for a tax audit. Offer him a glass of pure spring water, a white rose, and some hard candy. Light the candle every day until it burns down.

Denise Dumars

Notes:

April 16
Friday

4th ♓

☽ v/c 9:43 am

Color of the day: Coral

Incense of the day: Nutmeg

Psychic Improvement Spell

During this Pisces Moon, it is a good time for developing psychic skills. To do this, create an altar that includes some of these Piscean ritual objects: blue and blue-green candles, a bowl of water, and figurines or pictures of otters, salmons, seals, whales, or great blue herons. Place some coral, opal, or labradorite stones on the altar with dried horsetail or sage. Apply some oil of lotus or frankincense, light the candles, and meditate on the water. Gaze deeply into the bowl, and say:

> Water shining,
> water deep,
> bring me answers that I
> seek.

Then ask questions that you do not have the answer for. Watch for images to appear in the water.

Jonathan Keyes

Notes:

April 17
Saturday

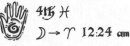

4th ♓
☽ → ♈ 12:24 am

Color of the day: Gray
Incense of the day: Patchouli

Beauty and Magnetism Spell

When invited to a date, party, or social gathering which you feel shy about attending, use this spell to boost your confidence and charge your aura with magnetism. Stand a mirror on a table with your face reflected in full view. (Alternatively prop a full-length mirror against the wall, and stand in front of that.) Gently spray some rosemary infusion all over your hair, face, and body. For a bit of additional zing, add two drops neroli oil to the infusion. Groom and dress yourself before the mirror while saying:

> Mirror, mirror,
> I shall stand tall.
>
> I will today and tonight
> be the fairest of them
> all.

Spray on your favorite perfume and complete all the finishing touches to makeup before adorning yourself with jewelry. Then go out and have a ball.

S. Y. Zenith

April 18
Sunday

4th ♈

Color of the day: Orange
Incense of the day: Poplar

A Creative Playground Ritual

Spring is a time when we feel restless. We want to do something, but we're not sure what. If we are in a rut, we get impatient. We want a way out, but we don't know how to get there. Today, then, is the perfect day to throw caution to the wind and involve yourself in a creative playground. Take large sheets of paper, magazines, glue, glitter, scraps of fabric—anything that you like. Paint, draw, write stories, and create collages. Don't sit and plan it, just let it all flow. Afterward, look back at your creations. Ask yourself what patterns you see? Do you see images of your wishes for the future? What images repeat? What represents pain and parts of your life which need to be released? Create a release ceremony to free yourself of anything that holds you back. When you have

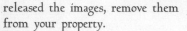

released the images, remove them from your property.

Cerridwen Iris Shea

Notes:

April 19
Monday

4th ♈

New Moon 9:21 am

☽ v/c 9:21 am

☽ → ♉ 9:43 am

☉ → ♉ 1:50 pm

Color of the day: Ivory
Incense of the day: Peony

Seeds of Opportunity Spell

What do you want to achieve before the next Full Moon? Whether it's a new job, new career, or a quick stash of cash, this spell will lead you to your goals. Start by listing the short-term goals that will lead to your long-term aims. All goals need to be specific to time and outcome and take the form of: "I will *blank*." For example, "I will update my resume by April 21." Once you have your goals listed, place a terra cotta pot,

filled with soil, on your working space. Light a gold or a green candle that has been placed in the soil. Allowing a separate line for each, write out your specific goals. Then state these words:

As the earth nourishes
the seeds of spring, so will
these seeds be nourished.

Each time you fulfill a goal, cut off that line, bury the paper in the soil, and repeat the above words. Relight your candle during the Full Moon in celebration of meeting your goal.

Karen Follett

Notes:

April 20
Tuesday

1st ♉

☽ v/c 3:36 pm

Color of the day: Black
Incense of the day: Pine

A Protection Amulet Spell

For this spell, you will need: a smudge or purifying incense, a circle of red or black cloth; a red, black, or white string; some mugwort, rosemary, or sage. Start by smudging yourself, your cloth, and your string. Ask the herbs to work together to bring you security and peace. Place the herbs in the center of the cloth circle, and tie it securely with the string. Ask for the blessings of the god and goddess on this amulet. Ask that only beneficial energies enter your space while you are in the presence of this amulet, and feel the charge of your requests. Thank the spirits of the sacred herbs for their assistance, and wear your amulet with confidence.

Kristin Madden

Notes:

Well, here is a simple spell to help you keep track of your umbrella in this month of wet. Take a short piece of string (natural materials like cotton or wool work best), and tie one end around your wrist. Then tie the other end around the handle of the umbrella. Say this rhyme:

> Keep me covered night
> and day.
> Turn the falling rain
> away.
> Dear umbrella, let me
> know,
> where I leave you when
> I go!

Then break, don't cut, the string. Leave the string tied around the umbrella handle. Take the string off your wrist, and store it in your wallet or purse.

Elizabeth Barrette

Notes:

April 21
Wednesday

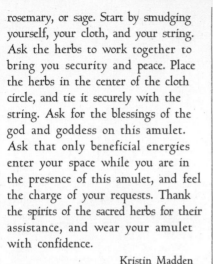 1st ♉

☽ → ♊ 9:10 pm

Color of the day: Brown
Incense of the day: Maple

April Showers Spell

 eware of April showers. Always keep your umbrella close at hand during this rainy month. What's that? You forgot where you left it?

April 22
Thursday

Earth Day

1st ♑

Color of the day: Black
Incense of the day: Sage

Earth Day Ritual

The first Earth Day was proclaimed in 1969 by John McConnell on the Vernal Equinox in San Francisco. This was a day when all people were asked to become conscious of how their actions affected the Earth, and it is appropriate that the holiday began in the city named for St. Francis, the patron saint of ecology. The next year the United Nations declared it the first international holiday and began celebrating it by ringing the Peace Bell and sanctioning two minutes of silence. Although the holiday has been moved to April 22, many people still observe it on the equinox. The Vernal Equinox is the preferred time for the holiday on the official Earth Day website, and it is symbolic of the ancient magical tradition that is at the heart of Earth Day. Although it is a very modern holidays, John McConnell hoped Earth Day would reaffirm our ancient connection to the Earth and the cycles of nature that are at the root of all holidays. It is a modern celebration of the movement from darkness to light that is celebrated in all holidays at this time of the year. For Neopagans this is a time to honor our divine mother Gaia, and to perform magic rituals to thank her and protect her. The ritual can be something as simple as planting vegetables or a tree, or taking a walk instead of a drive.

Robert Place

Notes:

April 23
Friday

 1st ♊
☽ v/c 7:22 pm

Color of the day: White
Incense of the day: Ginger

Conquer Your Demons Spell

April 23 honors St. George, the famous dragon slayer. His Pagan counterparts are Bellerophon and Sigurd the Dragon Slayer of Norse legend. These three heroes are the personification of the Sun that grows very dramatically at this time of year. Use the waxing powers of the Sun now to banish the demons in your life. For this spell, use a gold candle and a picture or statue of a dragon. List the demons plaguing you on a piece of paper. Place the list beneath the dragon. Light the candle, and visualize your problems taking the dragon's shape. Now let the light and heat from the Sun dry up your dragon. Watch its power diminish and ultimately be destroyed by the powers of the Sun.

Lily Gardner

Notes:

April 24
Saturday

1st ♊
☽ → ♋ 9:56 am

Color of the day: Blue
Incense of the day: Lilac

Cutting Down Smoking Spell

Tobacco has significant meaning in many cultures. When you are trying to cut down or quit, add some of the ritual back into smoking. Find a brand that you don't normally smoke—one that has no additives and is preferably organic. These will be your "evening smoke," and shouldn't be touched at any other time. Get a box of wooden matches. Don't light up after dinner until one hour before bedtime. Sit comfortably, outdoors if possible. Light your tobacco with a wooden match. As the cigarette burns, review your day: What went well today? Just acknowledge what happened. When you reach the end of the cigarette, say simply "thanks." Stub it out, brush your teeth, and sleep.

Therese Francis

Notes:

April 25
Sunday

1st ♋

Color of the day: Amber
Incense of the day: Cinnamon

Waxing Moon Tarot Reading

To learn what this waxing Moon has in store for you, pick a significator card (which represents you) from a tarot deck. Think about your questions as you shuffle the deck. Focus on specifics, such as an aspect of your career, love, or health. Pick two cards. Add the significator to the other two and shuffle. Turn cards up. If your card is first, then the other two say where you are headed. If in the middle, then one card explains the past and the other the future. If last, then events that have already taken place with continue to affect you.

Denise Dumars

Notes:

April 26
Monday

1st ♋

☽ v/c 5:56 am

☽ → ♌ 10:14 pm

Color of the day: Gray
Incense of the day: Lavender

Welcoming the Green Man Ritual

As we embark upon our spring-cleaning rituals and sweep away the final cobwebs and clutter of winter, our thoughts turn toward love and the emerging Green Man of the wildwood. His powerful force roams among the sprouting leaves now. Beltane is just around the corner. Witches and wisewomen everywhere awaken to sensuality and desire. Prepare your home or apartment for this time with a thorough cleaning using citrus oil. Open windows and dispel stagnant energies. Lingering negativity inhabits passion. Collect candles in sensuous colors: pink, peach, and lavender. Scent the bedroom and bed linens with rose, sandalwood, and jasmine sachets. Freshen your room with flowers. Buy some good chocolate and set some out in a candy dish, saying:

> Blessed be pleasure, love,
> and laughter.

Karri Ann Allrich

Notes:

April 27
Tuesday

1st ♌

2nd Quarter 1:32 pm

Color of the day: Scarlet
Incense of the day: Juniper

No More Pain in Love Spell

With Beltane fast approaching, you may want to make a charm against being hurt in love. Take a piece of lavender or rose-colored cloth. Put a piece of malachite or jade in the center of the cloth. Add a pinch of lavender, a pinch of thyme, and a pinch of salt (preferably sea salt). Recite:

> Keep my heart
> free from pain.
> Keep my soul
> free from stain.

Then gather the ends of the cloth together in a bundle. Tie it tightly in red thread, and carry the bundle in your pocket or around your neck.

Magenta Griffith

Notes:

reverberate throughout your force field. You should feel better immediately. Repeat the spell as needed.

Susan Sheppard

Notes:

April 28
Wednesday

 2nd ♌
☽ v/c 10:08 pm

Color of the day: Yellow
Incense of the day: Pine

Make Insecurity Fly Away Spell.
Want to rid your life of insecurity and depression? Find a white candle. Get chimes or locate Tibetan *tingsha* cymbals. Tingshas are powerful magical aids that chase away depression and other plagues. Walk outside under the Moon. Light your candle. Put it in a safe spot behind you. Place the cymbals at your feet. Face the Moon. Raise your arms. With a circling hand-motion, imagine pulling the Moon toward you. Chant:

> Powers under the Moon,
> I release insecurity.
> I send you back where
> you belong,
> you have no place in my
> life.

Ring your cymbals. Let the sounds

April 29
Thursday

 2nd ♌
☽ → ♍ 8:00 am

Color of the day: White
Incense of the day: Jasmine

Attracting Wealth Spell
For this spell gather a silver coin (real silver, if possible), some dried basil, a pinch dried sage, one green candle, any combination of malachite, tiger's-eye, pyrite, peridot, or aventurine. Carve a dollar sign into the candle while visualizing your wallet bulging and your bills marked "paid." Place the coin in a heat-proof container beneath the candle. Lay the stones either inside the container or around it, and light the candle. Sprinkle the herbs at the base of the candle, and chant:

> Money, money come to
> me,

As I will so mote it be.
I only wish to fulfill my
need.
I do this out of love, not
greed.

Allow the candle to burn out and cool.
Remove the coin and stones to keep
on your altar as the spell manifests.

Ember

Notes:

April 30
Friday
May Eve

2nd ♍

Color of the day: Rose
Incense of the day: Rose

Daily Devotional for Focus

Daily devotionals help keep your
spiritual path in focus. Some
traditions suggest you attend to these
in the morning when you first wake
up, before meals, at night before bed,
or all of the above. Here is a prayer
suitable for any occasion:

Say a blessing for the
day,
spread good fortune on
the way.

All you do comes back to
you.

Light a blessing for the
night,
make your heart a beacon
bright.
Love will gather round you.

The Law of Returns is not just a
Wiccan concept; it appears in many
other religions as well, under different guises and sometimes with a different number attached. But they all
come down to the same principle:
You get what you give.

Elizabeth Barrette

Notes:

May

May is the fifth month of the year. Its astrological sign is Taurus, the Bull (April 21-May 20), a fixed earth sign ruled by Venus. The month is named for Maia, a Roman goddess and mother of the god Hermes (the word is from the Greek for "mother"). May is a month of full-blown growth and colors of every sort. The main holiday of the month—May Day, or Beltane (May 1)—is a celebration of color and flowers. A traditional part of the May Day celebration is the maypole, which traditionally was cut from a fir tree on May Eve (April 30) by the unmarried men of the village. All its branches, except for the topmost, were removed and then adorned with ribbons and placed in the village square. On May Day, dancers hold the ends of the ribbons attached to the top of the maypole—girls going one way, boys another. As the ribbons wind and shorten, the dance becomes a spiral, symbolizing death and resurrection. Making and exchanging wreaths of flowers is an old tradition in May. In some traditions, the Sacred Marriage—between the May Queen and the May King, also known as Jack-of-the-Green—is important on May Day to ensure a vigorous growth in the crops. The Full Moon of May is called the Dyad Moon, the time when the two become one and all things meet in perfect balance and harmony.

May 1
Saturday
May Day – Beltane

 2nd ♍
) v/c 7:31 am
) → ♎ 2:03 pm

Color of the day: Indigo
Incense of the day: Juniper

Beltane Spell

Beltane, also spelled Beltaine, in the new Celtic calendar marks the end of the first half of the year and the beginning of the summer—the end of the year's dark half and the beginning of the light half. It is dedicated to Belenos, the god of light and healing who in modern British celebrations takes the form of the Green Man—a man with green leaves covering his face and body. The name Beltane means "fire of Bel" or "bright fire." It is believed that the god of light has to be rescued from the god of death or from an earth giant that has kept him prisoner for six months. To accomplish this, in some areas a hawthorn tree, representing the giant, is cut down and used as a maypole. Dancing around the maypole clockwise brings luck throughout the summer. In ancient times, two fires containing nine sacred woods were lit for Belenos. The cattle were passed between the fires to purify and protect them.

Likewise people would jump over the fire for luck. Beltane is essentially a celebration of fertility. At this time, sexual activity is encouraged, and spice cakes, called *barm brack* in Irish and *bannock* in Scottish, are cooked and eaten. As we are between the dark and the light now, the veil between this world and the world of the spirit is thin. It is an excellent time for divination. If you have already received a six-month prediction from the tarot on Halloween, then it is now time to renew your outlook for the next six months. (See the entry on Halloween for more details.) Also, do not forget to leave some barm brack on the doorstep over night for the fairies. If you treat them kindly, you will be assured that they will be kind to you through the year.

Robert Place

Notes:

May 2
Sunday

2nd ♎︎

Color of the day: Orange
Incense of the day: Sage

Sea Salt Protection Spell

People over the world agree that salt has cleansing, restorative, and curative powers. In order to rid yourself of negativity, you can't go wrong using sea salt. Sea salt holds many of the essential healing properties of nature. To increase strength, luck, and fortitude, go to your grocer or health-food store and buy sea salt. Spread the salt on the areas you wish cleansed. Lightly sprinkle sea salt into your bath, saying:

Salt of ocean,
Salt of earth,
From ocean I sprang,
upon my birth.

With Venus I rose above
sea and shell,
The power of salt makes
everything well.
So mote it be.

Susan Sheppard

Notes:

May 3
Monday

2nd ♎︎

☽ v/c 12:49 pm
☽ → ♏︎ 4:38 pm

Color of the day: Lavender
Incense of the day: Coriander

Bona Dea Altar Ritual

Ancient Roman women celebrated the good goddess, Bona Dea, today, with festivities dedicated especially to her. Offerings were made in secret, by women only, to benefit the family and the community at large. Create your own Bona Dea celebration today. Invite your women friends to help you celebrate. Decorate your altar with your favorite images of the goddess. (Traditional rites respectfully veiled images of the gods and goddesses; you may choose to do this too.) Place some freshly cut flowers and vine branches around your sacred space. Set bowls of wine, milk, and honey on the altar. Light some scented candles, and play music that inspires you to dance. Together, invoke blessings upon your family and friends, and have each of your friends make a personal offering for the good of all who have gathered. Form a circle, and light a white candle, saying:

Goddess bring peace to
the family of nations.

Karri Ann Allrich

Notes:

May 4
Tuesday

2nd ♏

Full Moon 4:33 pm

☽ v/c 5:36 pm

Color of the day: Black
Incense of the day: Honeysuckle

Reconnecting to Your Magical Child Spell

Magic is the reaction between the energy of self and the energy of the universe. The energy of self originates with the energy of your inner, or higher, consciousness. The role that your child plays is one of honest, pure belief in the possibility of magic. This child speaks clearly to your inner consciousness, igniting the flame of magical projection. Find a symbol that represents your magical child. This can be a toy, a rock, or any object that connects you to the magic of childhood Place this object on your altar. Relax and meditate on the significance of this object. Allow your mind to drift past your current state of cynical overanalysis to that time when magic was real—when every flower hid a fairy, every crack broke your mother's back, and every found penny or button was a magic talisman. Follow where your child leads. Feel the magic that your child feels. Listen to the messages your magical child sends to you. Keep your magical child symbol in a special place. Periodically reconnect with your magical child, and remind yourself that there are times when cynicism is the delusion and magical possibility is the "real."

Karen Follett

Notes:

May 5
Wednesday
Cinco de Mayo

 3rd ♏

☽ → ♐ 10:42 am

Color of the day: Brown
Incense of the day: Neroli

Transformative Dancing Spell

As the Moon waxes and moves from the sign of Scorpio into the sign of Sagittarius today, now is a good time to do a spell of transformation. Scorpio is a water sign, and Sagittarius is a fire sign. This is a time of bringing emotions, ruled by water, into light, ruled by fire. On this day, make a space in your home where you can dance. Put on some trance-inducing music and slowly dance to the rhythms. That is, imitate the swaying motions of a snake. Check in with your body and see where you are feeling tension or struggle. Bring this tension out in your dancing, through your body. Allow it to exist, and give thanks for its message. Release the tension, and replace it with self-love and acceptance.

Jonathan Keyes

Notes:

Holiday lore: Don't confuse Cinco de Mayo with Mexican Independence Day on September 16. Cinco de Mayo marks the victory of the brave Mexican Army over the French at the Battle of Puebla. Although the Mexican army was eventually defeated, the *Batalla de Puebla* became a symbol of Mexican unity and patriotism. With this victory, Mexico demonstrated to the world that Mexico and all of Latin America were willing to defend themselves against any foreign or imperialist intervention.

May 6
Thursday

 3rd ♐

Color of the day: Green
Incense of the day: Vanilla

Fly The Kite Money Spell for Those Feeling the Pinch

We all need some extra money. To get some buy a red kite. Tie a dollar bill to the end of the kite's tail. Then take the kite out for at least an hour. See how long you can keep the kite in the air; the longer it stays up the better your future financial situation will be. If at the end of the hour, the dollar is no longer on the tail, expect money to arrive to your household within the week.

Therese Francis

Notes:

Notes:

May 7
Friday

 3rd ♐
)) v/c 7:50 am

)) → ♑ 5:17 pm

Color of the day: Pink
Incense of the day: Dill

Be a Good Friend Spell

This day of the week relates to love and relationships. The best way to make friends is to be a good friend yourself. Call or write some of your friends to tell them how much you appreciate them, but don't stop there. Give a smile to a perfect stranger today! Pick up a bouquet of flowers and distribute them one at a time to people you don't know. If anyone asks what you're doing, just explain that you're passing out free smiles. Where is the magic in this? Why, whatever you do returns to you three times over, of course! You spread happy thoughts, and you might just make some new friends this way.

Elizabeth Barrette

May 8
Saturday

3rd ♑
Color of the day: Gray
Incense of the day: Pine

Disperse Nervousness Spell

When you are alone at home feeling nervous and unsettled, don't fret. Just anoint a white candle with patchouli and lavender oils. Light the candle and some fragrant incense. Meditate for a short time, and visualize the house being infused with restful and peaceful vibrations. Feel the candle and incense easing away your anxieties and fears. Hold your favorite crystal in both hands for a few moments. Visualize all your nervousness and forebodings being absorbed by the crystal. Open a window to let some fresh air in. Enter each room with the crystal. Feel it drawing out residues of disturbing vibes from nooks, crannies, and from underneath all the objects. When you are ready, go to the front door and shake the crystal in the air.

Cleanse the crystal in salt water, then dry and keep it for future use.

S. Y. Zenith

Notes:

May 9
Sunday

Mother's Day

 3rd ♑
☽ v/c 9:03 am
☽ → ♒ 6:46 pm

Color of the day: Gold
Incense of the day: Basil

Mothering Sunday Spell

In the seventh century in Britain, servants and apprentices were given the fourth Sunday of Lent off to visit their mothers. This came to be known as mothering Sunday. It was traditional on this day to bring spice cake to your mother. In the nineteenth century, the practice died out, but in the same century in the United States, Anna Reeves Jarvis helped to found a holiday called Mother's Work Day, which promoted her ideas about the importance of sanitation and about a woman's role in this virtuous activity. In 1872, meanwhile, Julia Ward Howe worked to mobilize women in the movement for world peace. She proclaimed June 2 Mother's Day for Peace, and the holiday was observed with annual demonstrations in a handful of American cities for the next thirty-odd years. In 1914, the daughter of Anna Reeves Jarvis, Anna Jarvis, convinced President Wilson and the United States Congress to proclaim Mother's Day a national holiday. In her lifetime the holiday spread to forty other countries. In Spain, the day occurred on December 8, also the Feast of the Immaculate Conception of Mary. This connection with the Christian goddess points out what is ancient and magical about this holiday. The ancient Greeks also held a festival to honor the mother goddess Rhea; the Romans had festivals for Cybele, and the Celts for Brigit. Besides bringing flowers to your mother today, put some out, along with candles of green, blue, white, and red, for the goddess.

Robert Place

Notes:

May 10
Monday

3rd ♒

Color of the day: White
Incense of the day: Chrysanthemum

Renewal Spell

This time of year is traditional for new beginnings. Spring has arrived, graduations are taking place, and as the Moon approaches its phase of newness now is a good time for a new start. Use this current energy to organize family gatherings or as a reminder of freshness and renewal. Fill a decorative glass bowl, jar, or other container with water and place shells, pretty stones, or colorful marbles in the bottom. Select white flowers, such as carnations or mums, and remove the stems so the flower tops can float on the water. This is a symbol of nurturing and growth for your family. Place it in a room where everyone in your home can view it. To light up the evening, float white candles on the water too.

Ember

Notes:

May 11
Tuesday

3rd ♒
4th Quarter 7:04 am
☽ v/c 3:31 pm
☽→♓ 10:52 am

Color of the day: Red
Incense of the day: Evergreen

Cutting It Away Spell

To clear away those things you'd rather not have to deal with now, take a sharp knife, preferably either your athame or a knife that is used only for ritual purposes. Bless it with salt and water, then with fire and air (a candle flame and its smoke usually works well for this). Next, stand facing east, and either use the knife to draw a circle around you three times, or have another person make these gestures in the air (taking care with the sharp knife, of course). Now pause for a moment to visualize all the negative influences in your life, all the unwanted influences and any people in your life who are less than positive, being cut away from you. When the last circuit is finished, touch the point of the knife to the ground or floor, and visualize all the energies being grounded into the earth. Stand here for a brief moment, take a deep breath as you stand, and bless the knife again before you put it away.

Magenta Griffith

Notes:

with my stewartship
please take root.

I wish you health
with all I plant,
frow and thrive
when you hear my chant.

Visualize all your plantings thriving
and healthy.

Lily Gardner

Notes:

May 12
Wednesday

 4℞ ♓

Color of the day: Yellow
Incense of the day: Eucalyptus

A Blessing for Plants

St. Pancras is the middle saint
of the Three Chilly Saints
whose feast days run on May 11, 12,
and 13. The Germans call them the
Iceman months. Folklore has it that
these days are the coldest days in
May. After May 13, finally it is safe
to plant your annuals. Use this occasion as a time to bless your plants
and seeds. Make an altar from your
gardening bench, and arrange everything that is to be planted. Sprinkle
holy water on your plants, and say:

Leaf and bean,
sprig and shoot,

May 13
Thursday

4℞ ♓
☽ v/c 10:14 pm

Color of the day: Turquoise
Incense of the day: Sandalwood

Dream Job Spell

May 13 is the feast day of Our
Lady of Fatima. She can be

petitioned for protection, for help with adversarial relationships, and for release from bondage. When you are in the wrong job, for instance, this is a bondage situation. You are afraid to leave because you are shackled by your need to make a living. However, by remaining in the bad situation, you are drained of everything you need to sustain and nurture the rest of your life. Every day you stay in a negative work environment you lose a piece of yourself. Trust me on this—I know whereof I speak. Thankfully, today is the day to ask Our Lady of Fatima to intervene for help to get yourself back to the path to your dream job. Dress a white candle with uncrossing oil. Ask Our Lady of Fatima to guide you toward the best possible work situation, which will then release you from your current situation. After all, you'd like a bit of an overlap as financial protection. Then, visualize your dream job. Daydream as though you already have the job. Break down the job search into small steps. Do you need to take classes to gain new skills? Where can you network and meet people in the profession that interests you? Is there a volunteer or part-time position in the organization that will help you make this transition? Ask the Lady for her guidance, listen to her response, and

then take action to craft the life you've dreamed about.

Cerridwen Iris Shea

Notes:

May 14
Friday

4th ♓
☽ → ♈ 6:02 am

Color of the day: Purple
Incense of the day: Thyme

Gaulish Wine Wish Spell

Sucellos, or "Good Striker," and Nantosuelta, or "Stream," are the Celtic god and goddess of agriculture. The Gaulish Celts believed it was the Sun god Sucellos who struck the earth with his hammer, thus breaking up the soil for planting. His mate, Nantosuelta, provided water for the crops. Tenders of vineyards especially revered these two deities. To ask for their blessings on a good year for wine, take a glass of French wine and a glass of water outside. Pour each onto the soil, repeating the deities' names and then saying:

> Make us rich in earth
> and water,
> Sun and Moon,
> rain and heat.
>
> Make us rich in grapes
> and grain.
> Strike the earth,
> flow the stream!

Now watch food and wine magazines for their predictions of a great year for wine.

Denise Dumars

Notes:

May 15
Saturday

 4th ♈

Color of the day: Blue
Incense of the day: Lavender

Ides of May Spell

In the original Roman lunar calendar, the Ides, which comes from a word meaning "to divide," marked the center of the month, the time of the Full Moon. When the Romans switched to a solar calendar, the Ides fell out of sync with the Moon. Still, all Ides were still considered sacred to Jupiter, the king of the gods. The Ides of May also marks the Festival of Mercury, who was the son of Jupiter and the nymph Maia. Maia, also spelled Maya, has lent her name in particular to this month. Mercury's festival is called a Mercuralia—or in Greek, a Hermoea. Mercury, the god of travel, luck, skill, wealth, and magic, was worshiped in every culture by a different name. In Greece he was called Hermes, and in Egypt he was equated with Thoth and Anubis. Although he was not worshiped in Rome from the earliest times, there was a temple to him on Aventine Hill overlooking the Circus Maximus. His temple was dedicated on May 15 in 495 B.C. In Gaul and the other Celtic countries, Mercury was the most popular of all the Roman deities. They equated him with the god Lugh, the "master of all arts," and they gave him a female consort called Rosmerta. Any practitioner of magic should not ignore this holiday. Take the day off, and do something special. Light candles to Mercury. He likes candles of every color. If you are using eight-inch glass-enclosed votive candles, you can get one with seven consecutive colors, or with images of St. Christopher, St. Michael, or Christ. As a protector of travelers, Mercury's place in Christianity has been taken by St. Christopher, who in his oldest icons had a dog's head like the Greek-Egyptian Hermanubis. Hermanubis was also associated with the souls of the dead, whom he weighed on his scale. This aspect of the soul-weigher was assumed by St. Michael. And Hermanubis' role as "Good Shepherd" was taken by Christ. During the day, you may receive a gift from Mercury in the form of a windfall or a lucky find. A gift from Mercury is a useful magical tool.

Robert Place

Notes:

May 16
Sunday

4th ♈
☽ v/c 8:17 am
☽ → ♉ 3:57 pm

Color of the day: Amber
Incense of the day: Coriander

A Spell for Pain

No spell will ever take the place of professional medical treatment, especially for serious conditions, but a spell to reduce pain can speed up the healing process. Many years ago, axes or knives were placed beneath the bed of an ill person to "cut" the pain. This spell is based on that old-time remedy. Take three feet of gray yarn made of natural fiber. Knot the yarn three times to capture your pain. With scissors, cut the yarn into small pieces, saying:

No pain will bind me,
I am free.

Cast away the pieces of yarn quickly. Throw them in the trash or in a running body of water, or bury them. Turn and walk away immediately.

James Kambos

Notes:

May 17
Monday

4th ♉

Color of the day: Silver
Incense of the day: Myrrh

Irish Evil Eye Charm

In many cultures, including the Gaelic, it is considered bad luck to compliment a baby or to remark about a child's beauty as bad fairies might take notice. Flattery and envy attracts the evil eye, so wise mothers and crones will speak in reverse, ironically commenting: "How ugly that child is!" Or: "I'm sorry, Mrs. Duffy. Your baby is hideous!" If a stranger has the bad manners to offer a compliment, or a fixed adoring gaze on a babe, the mother can deflect it by asking the person to spit on the child. Returning home, mothers can also perform a simple charm to protect her family by spitting on the children upon entering the house. If she forgets, the grandmother can do it.

Karri Ann Allrich

Notes:

May 18
Tuesday

4th ♉

Color of the day: Gray
Incense of the day: Sage

Review Your Goals Spell

Today is an excellent day to review your goals. Rate your current goals on a scale from one to five. A five means: "yes, absolutely; I want this." Whereas, a one is something you are very ambivalent about. Ask yourself once you have rated your various goals: Does this contribute to my personal evolution? Does it benefit my family, my community, and my world? Does it excite me and create an energy all its own? Adjust the scores on each of your individual goals according to how you respond to the questions. In the upcoming weeks, consult your goals sheet often. Rate your progress on each goal, and adjust your score as you realize that some goals are more easily attained, and others elusive. Ask youself questions such as: How much active time do you spend on this goal each day? How much time do you think about it? How much stress, or joy, does your struggle to attain it create for you? This will give you insight about what you truly desire, and about the best way for you to make a plan to accomplish your goals. Those goals that rate highest consistently through the months are most likely the goals that are most important and most beneficial to you.

Kristin Madden

Notes:

May 19
Wednesday

 4th ♉

New Moon 12:52 am

☽ v/c 12:52 am

☽ → ♊ 3:47 am

Color of the day: White
Incense of the day: Cedar

Love's Ladder Spell

Witches' ladders, also known as Witches' rosaries, are a grouping of beads used for meditation and manifestation. The great rite of Beltane bestows a lusty energy upon the month of May. While thoughts of love and romance abound now, the first love that must be manifested is the love of self. A well-loved and well-nourished self is most likely to attract those who are equally loving and nourishing. For this working, you will need fifteen beads. One bead will represent "you," and the other beads represent the attraction beads of self-nourishment. These beads should be of an attractive material such as rose quartz. You will also need stringing material. Focus the intent of self-nourishment on the "you" bead while you thread it onto the string. Then focus on a particular aspect of your self-nurturing while you string the first attraction bead. You may want to state a positive affirmation, reprogram a negative self-concept, or even plan an act of self-nourishment. Repeat this process daily until the Full Moon. Keep your ladder with your magical tools to occasionally refocus your attention on your self-nourishment.

Karen Follett

Notes:

May 20
Thursday

 1st ♊

☉ → ♊ 12:59 pm

Color of the day: Purple
Incense of the day: Dill

Wash Your Goddess Spell

The Greek festival of Kallyntaria and Plynteria lasted from May 19 through May 28. During this time, people took down the statues of gods and goddesses from their shrines and washed them in the river. Then they adorned the statues with finery and returned them to the shrines in a solemn procession. Now is a good time for spring cleaning. Pay special attention to your altar today. Wash the altar cloth, or dust the tabletop. Throw away any candle stubs or incense ash. Polish your candleholders, athame, chalice, and other tools. Clean divine icons. Then reset the altar, and set out a vase of fresh flowers to welcome the season's new life.

Elizabeth Barrette

Notes:

May 21
Friday

1st ♊

☽ v/c 8:13 am

☽ → ♋ 4:35 pm

Color of the day: Rose
Incense of the day: Ylang-ylang

Spell to heal a Broken heart

Today marks the Egyptian Feast of the Cosmic Twins. Sometimes when romance does not turn out as we hoped, it is better to cut our losses and move on—though this is often much easier said than done. In some cases, we need ritual to remind us it is over. To heal a broken heart, get a black candle. Add dried flowers and a picture of your past love. Cut the picture in four sections. Lay pieces atop the dried flowers. Scratch your lover's name on the side of the candle. Light it, and say:

> You no longer live in me.
> Alas, our love has died.
> Mine as much as yours.
> I hear your voice no
> more.
>
> I see you not in dreams.
> You were not the answer
> to my prayers.
> I pray much wiser now.
> No knot of love still binds
> us.

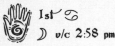

In crowds they will not
find us.
Goodbye, lost love,
You may be good for
someone.
But you are not good for
me.

So mote it be.

Let candle burn down until the name
is entirely melted. Throw the picture
and flowers out the next day.

Susan Sheppard

Notes:

an old-fashioned carousel, you can do
this spell. Carefully choose a horse
to ride, one that goes up and down.
Get on the horse, and as the carousel
moves, and your horse goes up and
down, imagine yourself riding back
in time to your childhood. Ask your
younger self about what it was like
to ride on the merry-go-round back
then, and let yourself become a child
once again for the duration of the
ride. Remember what it was like for
your legs to dangle down from the
horse, and remember how big everything seemed when you were smaller.
Wave to your parents, brothers and
sisters, or other relatives who took
you to the carousel. When the ride
ends, be sure to give yourself plenty
of time to grow up again. Take the
rest of the day if you need to.

Magenta Griffith

Notes:

May 22
Saturday

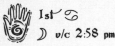 1st ♋
☽ v/c 2:58 pm

Color of the day: Black
Incense of the day: Jasmine

Merry-Go-Round Spell

If you can find an amusement
park or state fair that still has

May 23
Sunday

1st ♋

Color of the day: Yellow
Incense of the day: Parsley

healing the Earth Ritual

For this healing ritual, gather the following to represent the four elements: a container of water, a leaf from a tree, a candle or some incense, and a feather. Find a blue marble, or any other object to symbolize the Earth, and bless it with the four elements. Start by brushing the Earth with the feather, to represent air, then pass the object quickly through a candle flame or incense smoke to represent fire. Next, wrap the Earth in the leaf to represent the element of earth, and finally place the object in the container of water. During this process, focus on letting your energy work to decrease any harm that we do to the Earth. Focus your intentions to drawing humanity's awareness toward hopes and toward efforts to preserve our collective home. Remove the Earth from the leaf, and place it in a location of honor in your home—either on your altar or another place where it can inspire everyone to care for our precious Earth.

Ember

May 24
Monday

1st ♋
☽ → ♌ 5:07 am

Color of the day: Ivory
Incense of the day: Daffodil

Creating a Moon Altar and Goddess Box

In a household space that will not be disturbed, place pictures of family members, pets, and friends. Place three white or clear stones or marbles in the bottom of a clear glass vase. Collect white flowers from your yard or garden, or purchase some at a floral shop. Place the flowers in the vase with water, and add a little sugar and salt. Add a small wooden box, preferably made from white oak or pine. Write down anything that is bothering you and place the paper in the box. Ask the

Goddess to take care of the situation for you, and stop worrying about it. Be sure to remove any wilted flowers immediately, and replace them with fresh flowers. As your problems are resolved, remove them from the box. Thank the Goddess for her help. Bury or burn the paper outside.

Therese Francis

Notes:

May 25
Tuesday

 1st ♌

Color of the day: White
Incense of the day: Musk

Invoke the Corn Maiden Spell

Each May my grandfather would plant corn. After the tasseled stalks grew, I would play among the corn rows with my faithful spaniel at my side. Surrounded by the corn and with a blue Midwestern sky overhead, I felt secure. Using this

ritual will allow you to also draw upon the protective power of the Corn Maiden. On your altar, place three candles—one each of green, yellow, and brown; also place a small dish of yellow cornmeal next to the candles. Light the candles, saying:

> Corn Maiden,
> Mother and Crone,
> Protect my family,
> hearth, and home.

Raise the cornmeal, and continue:

> Please accept this humble
> offering to you.
> I ask for security and
> bounty in all that is yet
> to come.

Conclude by sprinkling the cornmeal outdoors, so the birds and other wild things may share your offering.

James Kambos

Notes:

May 26
Wednesday
Shavuot

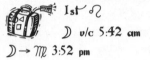 1st ♌

☽ v/c 5:42 am

☽ → ♍ 3:52 pm

Color of the day: Topaz
Incense of the day: Maple

Ancestor Day Ceremony

When one thinks of honoring the ancestors, Samhain and the Days of the Dead are what most often come to mind. However, the veil is also thin at this time—at the opposite spoke of the wheel of the year. That is, many places celebrate Memorial Day at the end of May. And in fact, this is a perfect time to create an Ancestor Day. Further, as Wednesday is good for psychic connection, today is a perfect day for an Ancestor Day ceremony. Cover a table with a purple cloth. Arrange several purple and white candles. Burn a combination of mugwort and sandalwood. Arrange on your altar pictures of your ancestors or items that were handed down to you over the years. Make offerings of favorite food and drink. Meditate at the altar. Communicate with your ancestors. Engage them in conversation. Thank them for the assistance they have given you over the years. And ask them if there is anything that you can do for them. Think of today as a spiritual family reunion. Let the good memories take precedence, and find ways of mutual forgiveness for situations that were hurtful. Celebrate your positive connections to your roots. Use the foundation of family as a starting point for positive changes you wish to make in your life.

Cerridwen Iris Shea

Notes:

May 27
Thursday

 1st ♍

2nd Quarter 3:57 am

Color of the day: Crimson
Incense of the day: Carnation

Being Mindful Spell

As the Moon waxes in Virgo, now is a good time for increasing qualities of mindfulness. Start by going outside and walking to a private backyard or park. Walk around the area very slowly. Deepen and slow down your breath. As you are walking, get in touch with how the wind tickles your arms and face. Breathe in and smell the air. Allow your eyes to take in the surroundings. Surrender to this moment and become aware of your body, your breath, and the world around you. The present moment is a place of joy and serenity. Simply walking and simply breathing can help bring you back to that place of being.

Jonathan Keyes

Notes:

your love. Know that you are lovable. Feel love for yourself. Walk beyond the mirror into a room filled with people. Listen as they speak of what they love best about you. Know that you are loved. Look to an open doorway at your left. It is filled with a blinding pink light, yet you can feel the presence of others approaching. Know you are attracting loving and healthy relationships. Return to the entrance and thank the stone for its blessings.

Kristin Madden

Notes:

May 28
Friday

 2nd ♏
☽ v/c 12:17 pm
☽ → ♎ 11:22 pm

Color of the day: Coral
Incense of the day: Almond

Rose Quartz Meditation
Hold a piece of rose quartz and imagine that you are entering a door into the side of the stone. As you enter, you find a pink mirror. Look into it, and see all your beauty, your strength, your kindness, and

May 29
Saturday

2nd ♎
Color of the day: Indigo
Incense of the day: Violet

Be a Star Tonight Spell
Astarte. Her name evokes the stars, and she is the wickedly sexy side of the goddesses Ishtar, Eostre, Asherah, and Hathor. In the Egyptian myths, she is mistress of bad boy Set, and in any case, she

knows how to be seductive. So girl-friend, why not be a sexy star on the dance floor tonight? Invoke Astarte while bathing in the light of red candles. Put a drop or two of patchouli essential oil in the bath. Dress in black, and if you wear jewelry make it opulent Astarte gold instead of Saturnine silver. Look in the mirror when ready and say: "Goddess Astarte, let all who see me, see you." Blow a kiss to the stars in the heavens before leaving.

Denise Dumars

Notes:

May 30
Sunday
Pentecost

 2nd ♎
☽ v/c 3:09 pm

Color of the day: Gold
Incense of the day: Clove

Renewing the Self Spell

In making fresh beginnings and renewing the self, old wounds must first be healed. Water magic performed on the beach is a potent means of washing away the past to make room for the new to enter. Gather one seashell, a handful of white flowers, and a flask of wine. Take them to the seashore, and wait for the waves to roll up. Hold the shell and flowers in your outstretched hands, and ask for the Sun's blessing. Drink a toast to the ocean and the Sun. If performing this spell at night, toast the Moon and ask for her bless-ing instead. Sit on the sand at the water's edge holding the seashell and flowers as you make a solemn resolu-tion to release past grievances. Hurl the shell and flowers into the ocean while bidding the past goodbye. Pour some wine at the water's edge to honor the guardians of the oceans. Say some words of thanks and walk away without looking back.

S. Y. Zenith

Notes:

Holiday lore: Pentecost Sunday is a day to celebrate the hope of newness, renewal of purpose, and a calling to the divine. It is customary in Italy to scatter rose leaves from the ceiling of churches on this day, and in France trumpets are blown during a divine service. The gentry in England amused themselves with horse races. Those observing Pentecost in Russia, meanwhile, would carry flowers and green branches in their hands.

May 31
Monday
Memorial Day

 2nd ♎

☽ → ♏ 3:08 am

Color of the day: Gray
Incense of the day: Rose

Triple Blessings Spell

The Buddhists celebrate this day as the feast day of the Triple Blessings, honoring the Buddha's birth, his enlightenment, and his passage into nirvana. Interestingly, three is a sacred number in all spiritual faiths. In the Pagan tradition, for instance, we celebrate Maid, Mother, and Crone and the concepts they represent: increase, realization, and decrease, which are, of course, the same concepts we find in the Triple Blessings. Today, decorate your altar in bright flowers and gaily colored cloth. Place either a likeness of the triple goddess or the Buddha at the center of your altar. Make an offering of rice, money, and incense to the deity, and write three wishes on a sheet of fine paper. Ask blessings for the summer ahead.

Lily Gardner

Notes:

June

June is the sixth month of the year. Its astrological sign is Gemini, the twins (May 21-Jan 20), a mutable air sign ruled by Mercury. It is named for Juno, the principal goddess of the Roman pantheon, wife of Jupiter the king of the gods; she is the patroness primarily of marriage and the well-being of women. The warm dry breezes dry the fields now, and the hay is mown. The air is perfumed with the fragrance of honeysuckle and wild rose and filled with the birdsong. Fireflies dance in tall meadow grass. Toads are common in wet areas. Fuchsia, foxglove, and lavender blossom, attracting bees and birds. Culinary herbs are ready for harvesting. Squirrels and chipmunks bicker in the garden over prized plants. Birds are busy feeding hatchlings now. Broken birdshells are to be found cast away from nests under the trees; finding a hatched eggshell is a sign of great fortune and favor. Birds are also molting their old feathers now, which can be used in magic. By mid-June, the weather moves into the full heat of summer. The June Full Moon is the Mead Moon, named for the fermented drink made from honey. June is considered the best month for marriage. The main holiday in June is the Summer Solstice, which marks the time of year when the waxing Sun reaches its zenith and days will begin to shorten again.

June 1
Tuesday

 2nd ♏

☽ v/c 5:15 pm

Color of the day: Black
Incense of the day: Gardenia

Children's Festival Spell

On this day, folks in China observe the Children's Festival. The Chinese enjoy a rich family life with very strong ties through the generations. That is, the Chinese revere their ancestors, and children represent a continuing life for the departed. If you have children, today is a good time to take them for a picnic or a walk in the park. If you don't have children but think you may want some someday, today is a good day to practice. Take a friend's children on an outing, and give the parents a day off. Here is a special blessing you can say silently during the excursion:

Father, mother,
bless each other.

God bless the little boys,
and goddess bless the girls.

They make a joyful noise,
skipping feet, bouncing curls!

Elizabeth Barrette

June 2
Wednesday

2nd ♏

☽ → ♐ 3:52 am

Color of the day: Yellow
Incense of the day: Pine

A Sweet Woodruff Spell for Prosperity

At dusk in my woodland garden, sweet woodruff sends out its fresh haylike scent, and its white flowers glow in the June twilight. In June, sweet woodruff reaches the height of its magical power, and is valuable in attracting prosperity. The prosperity spell which follows should be concluded next month, beneath July's Blessing Moon. On a June evening, just before nightfall, gather some woodruff flowers, leaves, and stems. Cut them all, and put them in a darkened room to dry on a hook or beam. When July's Moon is at its height, and the woodruff has dried, bury it with a dollar and a copper coin. Now, with what you've sown your wealth will increase.

James Kambos

Notes:

June 3
Thursday

2nd ♐

☽ Full Moon 12:20 am

Color of the day: Green
Incense of the day: Geranium

Unveiled Wisdom Spell

Recently a student of the craft commented that she wanted publishers to produce more books that revealed the deeper wisdom of the craft. After a brief period of pondering, I replied to her that you can read to gain knowledge, but you have to seek to gain wisdom. Words are merely mundane symbols that communicate thoughts. Thoughts, however, are doorways across the matrix of time and dimension, providing the path to the wisdom of the ancients. The wisdom has always been in print. But, it is up to you to seek the wisdom behind the word. During this Full Moon take the opportunity to either begin or further this quest. Choose a passage that either inspires or perplexes you. State these words:

> I speak the word,
> I read the line,
> reveal to me the wisdom divine.

Repeat your chosen passage. Meditate on the physical level of this passage. What do the words say to you? Take the passage to the emotional level. What feelings does the passage stir? Take the passage to the mental level. What other meanings can be derived from the passage? Take the passage to the spiritual level. What messages are you receiving about the passage?

Karen Follett

Notes:

June 4
Friday

3rd ♐

☽ → ♑ 3:12 am

Color of the day: White
Incense of the day: Nutmeg

Tending the Garden of Love Spell

What we love, we nurture. If you have recently planted a garden or started herbs in a pot, think of your plants as spiritual helpers. The seeds you have sown this spring reflect the spiritual seeds taking root in your life. As you water and feed, weed and nurture, contemplate your inner life, your intimate soul garden within. Take the time to nourish your blossoming spirit. Cultivate your spiritual needs. Witchcraft is soul work that connects us to the life force and honors the divine within and without. As you lovingly tend your green garden, tune in to your spiritual garden within. Embody the nurturing goddess, love your own emergent spirit, and say:

> Blessed be the soulful
> roots of my self-esteem.

Karri Ann Allrich

Notes:

June 5
Saturday

3rd ♑

☽ v/c 8:47 am

Color of the day: Brown
Incense of the day: Cedar

Oath Day Spell

In the Roman calendar, today is the Nones of June. No legal action could take place on this day. Holidays were announced, and Jupiter was invoked in oaths. Today is a good day then to make oaths. Take thirty minutes or an hour, and write freely about what you like and don't like about your life. Look it over, and divide your list into two columns: the positive and the negative. In a perfect world, the positive column will be longer than the negative one, but don't fret if this is not true. Now, look at the negative column and make another list, this time turning each negative into a positive with suggested action. That is, if you write that your relationship to your parents is not good, add afterward that you intend to take them out to dinner sometime soon. Jupiter is the god of the sky. He protects the state, its laws, and he is associated with abundance and generosity. Light an orange candle. Read your original positive list. Then read the second list, where you turned negatives into positives. Before Jupiter, take an oath to be true to yourself and your dreams, and to spend the next year turning items on the second list from possibilities into realities.

Cerridwen Iris Shea

Notes:

carnation, cedar, chamomile, cinnamon, ginseng, juniper, marigold, olive, orange, rosemary, walnut, and witch hazel. After the herbs of your choice have been inserted into the sachet, sew up the opening. Anoint the four corners of the sachet with sandalwood oil. Consecrate the sachet at your altar, carry it in your pocket or handbag, and tuck under the pillow as you sleep.

S. Y. Zenith

Notes:

June 6
Sunday

3rd ♑
☽ → ♒ 3:10 am

Color of the day: Orange
Incense of the day: Cinnamon

herbal health Sachet

To maintain good health, cut two squares of green cloth measuring three inches each. Make a small sachet by sewing together the two pieces of cloth with orange thread. Leave an opening for inserting some dried herbs. The best herbs for this sachet may include any of the following herbs associated with good health and life-giving properties: angelica, bay,

June 7
Monday

3rd ♒
☽ v/c 2:09 pm

Color of the day: Lavender
Incense of the day: Clove

Dig-Right-In Divination

This is a favorable day for doing divination, especially for the purpose of digging into the past, and in particular for digging into one's own childhood. To do this, you might gather all those old photographs you've had lying around for years and put them at long last into an album. Write down all you can remember about them, then call other family members and ask them for more information about what is happening in the pictures. If you don't have photographs, write down whatever you remember about events in your childhood—including any family stories and jokes, any holiday or vacation recollections. Look at the photos, or stories, and see what else you remember that you have not thought about in years. Our child-hoods are our roots, after all.

Magenta Griffith

Notes:

June 8
Tuesday

3rd ≈

☽ → ♓ 5:38 am

Color of the day: Scarlet
Incense of the day: Ginger

Post-Performance Recovery Spell

If you find yourself having to perform in some intense way—perhaps in a play or at a shareholder meeting or even just in front of a gathering of family members—you will occasionally find that you are more distressed afterward than you were beforehand. You can counterbalance this effect with a touch of solid Saturn energy. To start, stand straight, with feet shoulder-width apart, and relax. Remove your glasses or any other distraction, and allow your eyes to unfocus. Hold your arms out in front of you in a slightly arched posture as if they are draped around a beach ball. Feel your upper back relax. Slowly bring your hands up to your chest, and feel them pass through many successive thin layers of energy. Cross your hands over your lower sternum, draw a slow breath, and hold it for three heartbeats. Then push your breath out, almost in a gasp. You might feel a flush of warmth, but you will be otherwise be ready for your next big performance.

Therese Francis

Notes:

Bless this work and offering!

Prepare your bread dough with reverence. Think of your family and the blessings you wish for them. When the dough is resting in the bowl, say:

> O Vesta grant me thy favor.

Lily Gardner

Notes:

June 9
Wednesday

 3rd ♓
4th Quarter 4:02 pm

☽ v/c 7:37 pm

Color of the day: Brown
Incense of the day: Neroli

Blessing the Family Ritual

June 9 is the festival of Vestalia, honoring Vesta, the goddess of hearth and home. Ovid said of her: "Vesta was fire, and fire was Vestal." In ancient times, barefoot mothers brought offerings of bread to Vesta that they baked in their ovens. To honor Vesta, use your favorite bread recipe. Yeast breads are the best, but if you are short on time make a batter bread instead. Your kitchen table will serve as the altar. Assemble your ingredients, and light a yellow candle, saying:

> Vesta,
> great goddess of hearth and flame,

June 10
Thursday

4th ♓
☽ → ♈ 11:49 am

Color of the day: Turquoise
Incense of the day: Musk

Candle Prosperity Spell

Inscribe your wishes onto a green or gold candle. Be as specific as possible, and clearly visualize your dreams as you do this. Anoint the entire candle with jasmine oil, feeling the energy of prosperity seep into the wax with the oil. Sprinkle some nutmeg over the oil. Light the candle, seeing the flame and its light releasing brilliant green and gold energies. Clearly visualize the wishes and dreams you inscribed on the candle being released to the universe, then, for as long a period as you can, hold the image of your dreams coming to fruition in your mind. When you can no longer hold the image, release it to the flame and allow the candle to burn itself out.

Kristin Madden

Notes:

your romantic partner. Light a pink candle; ground and center. Before you, place the following: the Lovers card from a tarot deck, two yellow yarrow flowers with stems, and one pink ribbon. Gaze deeply at the card. Take note that the angel Raphael's arms are outstretched as he is looking upon the couple. Although the lovers are not touching, they are balanced and comfortable with each other. Next, tie the yarrow stems together with the pink ribbon. Visualize you and your lover united, protected and in harmony with each other. Hang the yarrow to dry near your bed. Yarrow is a strong love herb. Repeat this spell only if absolutely necessary.

James Kambos

Notes:

June 11
Friday

 4th ♈

Color of the day: Pink
Incense of the day: Rose

A healing Love Charm
Use this spell to soothe hurt feelings after you've had a fight with

June 12
Saturday

🖐 4th ♈
☽ v/c 7:31 am
☽ → ♉ 9:37 pm

Color of the day: Blue
Incense of the day: Sandalwood

Releasing Spell

As the Moon wanes in power, now is a good time to do a spell for releasing something in your life that is not serving you. This may be a bad habit, a friendship that is not healthy, or even a way of perceiving the world that is not nourishing to you. Write down what you are releasing onto a piece of paper. Then fold the paper into a small wooden box. Go outside and with a small hand shovel, and dig a small hole. Place the box in the hole, and cover it up. You may want to speak words such as:

> Mother Earth, please
> help me to release that
> which I no longer need.

Jonathan Keyes

Notes:

Healing Light Spell

Create sacred space by sitting outdoors for a few minutes in full sunlight, or in a room with windows allowing sunlight through. Decorate your circle with images and symbols of the Sun, if you desire, or wear jewelry of gold or with an icon that represents the Sun. Enjoy the sensation of sunlight on your skin. Feel your body feeding on the healing light as it destroys all negativity inside you. Know that this light heals and energizes you. This is the same light that is responsible for all life on Earth. Speak these words:

> I feel you, Sun God,
> your fingers in my hair,
> your caresses on my
> shoulders,
> your light within my
> skin.
>
> Fill me,
> Warm me,
> heal me.
> So mote it be.

Ember

Notes:

June 13
Sunday

 4th ♉

Color of the day: Amber
Incense of the day: Basil

June 14
Monday
Flag Day

4th ♉
☽ v/c 10:34 pm

Color of the day: Silver
Incense of the day: Peony

Flag Day Protection Spell

For a good dose of patriotic magic, buy a red, white, and blue uncrossing candle. If you can't find such a tricolor candle, buy a votive in each of the three separate colors. Early in the morning, place them on your altar with a small American flag and with images or statues of Venus, Freya, and Hathor. If using three candles, place Hathor near the red candle, Freya near the white, and Venus near the blue. Breathe deeply, and visualize yourself sending loving protection to each and every on of your fellow countrymen. Continue meditating on this idea until you feel you are sending out a wholly unconditional love. Ask the three love goddesses to assist you in circulating this love. Imagine that you are, with the goddesses' help, surrounding the country with a clear white shield, much like a force field. Thank the goddesses, and hang your flag outdoors until sundown.

Denise Dumars

Notes:

June 15
Tuesday

4th ♉
☽ → ♊ v/c 1:09 am

Color of the day: Gray
Incense of the day: Poplar

Five Points of the Pentagram Protection Spell

Get drawing paper, and draw a large pentagram on it, without drawing a circle around it. Take five votive candles, and place them at each corner of the star. Get your broom, and light each candle saying this:

> With each corner that I light,
> this star of all stars so bright
> will show my way and my path
> to protect loved ones
> from anger and wrath.

Let this path be one of
ease,
as we walk through the
trees
with this fire I com—
mand tonight,
blessings upon those who
walk it right.
So mote it be.

Face outward, and sweep your broom
one full circle counterclockwise around
your pentagram. Finish your pentagram by drawing a circle around it.

Susan Sheppard

Notes:

Wednesday. You'll need a flowerpot,
some soil, and a package of California
poppy seeds. Starting on a Wednesday,
begin filling the flower pot with soil,
bit by bit, each day for six days. As
you do so, think of your business
growing. On the seventh day, fill the
pot completely with soil. Carry the
pot and seeds out to a sunny garden
spot. Spread the soil on the earth,
and press in the seeds. Water the
seeds, then say the following charm:

> With soil and seeds,
> with water and Sun,
> the growth of my business
> has begun.

Nurture the seeds until they can
grow on their own. Then, so shall
your business endeavors thrive.

James Kambos

Notes:

June 16
Wednesday

 4th ♊

Color of the day: White
Incense of the day: Coriander

Increase Your Business Spell
Begin this spell on a Wednesday,
and conclude it on the following

June 17
Thursday

 4th ♊
  New Moon 4:27 pm
☽ v/c 4:27 pm
☽ → ♋ 10:37 pm

Color of the day: Purple
Incense of the day: Sage

Spell for Eloquence

There are times when we need to be at our eloquent "best" in our verbal or written skills. This spell will aid in cutting through any haziness or confusion to produce communication that is concise and clear. Choose a symbol to represent your method of communication. This symbol can be a pen for writing, a lipstick for speaking, or even a gemstone that you associate with clarity and wisdom in communication. Anoint your symbol with peppermint oil. Present this symbol to the directional elements. As you call on these elements, focus the intent of their energies into your symbol: the east brings clarity of thought; the south brings creative passion; the west brings fluidity of thought; and the north brings ideas into action. Hold your symbol, and consider your focused intent. Have confidence in the fact that you have been blessed with eloquence.

Karen Follett

Notes:

June 18
Friday

1st ♋

Color of the day: Rose
Incense of the day: Dill

Passion and Fidelity Spell

To prevent a spouse or lover from straying, take a pair each of your partner's and your underwear. Place them on the bed along with two nutmeg seeds, a length of red ribbon, a red pen, and some superglue. With the red pen, write your partner's name on one of the nutmeg seeds, and yours on the other. Bind the seeds together with superglue. When the glue is dried, wrap them in both pairs of underwear to symbolize passionate fidelity. Place the bundle in a red cloth bag, secure it with red ribbon, and keep it in the wardrobe among your more sensual clothing. The cloth bag may also be placed in between two layers of mattresses.

S. Y. Zenith

Notes:

Set your cares upon the
streams,
watch the flowers,
chase your dreams.
Life is silver water
under you.
Make your boats and let
them go.
See them follow the
current's flow,
just lean back and you
can too.

Meditate on fleeting joys and the power of release.

Elizabeth Barrette

Notes:

June 19
Saturday

 1st ♋

Color of the day: Black
Incense of the day: Maple

Time Turning Spell

Summer days are beautiful, but they never last. Time keeps turning from summer to fall, and then back around to winter and spring. Practice having joy in the moment today. Find a quiet stream in a park and make nature boats. Large fallen leaves work well for this, as do pieces of bark. You can make rafts by tying twigs together too. Fill them with flowers, set them on the water, and watch them sail away. As you do, say this rhyme:

June 20
Sunday

Father's Day – Summer Solstice – Litha

1st ♋
☽ v/c 6:46 am
☽ → ♌ 11:05 am
☉ → ♋ 8:57 pm

Color of the day: Gold
Incense of the day: Parsley

New Start Spell

It is believed that in the Neolithic period the New Year was celebrated on the Summer Solstice. That would seem to make this holiday one of the oldest in the history (or prehistory) of the world. This is the day when the Sun is at its peak, and daylight occupies the greatest possible part of the day. In Ireland it is called Alban Heruin, though many now know it by its Anglo-Saxon name, Litha. The yearly cycle of holidays are strongly colored by the symbolism of the waning and waxing of the Sun's light. Today the Sun, light, health, and strength are at their peak, and by celebrating and sharing these qualities on this day we can increase these powers in ourselves. The traditional way of celebrating is to participate in athletic competitions. In the evening, a bonfire is lit and the participants jump over it for luck and health. In 1909, Sonora Dodd, inspired by a Mother's Day sermon, began to lobby for a similar holiday for fathers. Her father, who was a widower, had brought up Sonora and her five brothers and sisters by himself. As her father was born in June, she held the first Father's Day on Sunday, June 19 in 1910 in Spokane, Washington. In 1966, President Lyndon Johnson proclaimed it a national holiday, which would be held on the third Sunday in June.

This year it fittingly coincides with the Solstice, the pinnacle of the Sun's masculine energy.

Robert Place

Notes:

June 21
Monday

1st ♌

Color of the day: Ivory
Incense of the day: Lavender

Fairy Charm Spell

Fairies are respected and feared in Gaelic culture, accepted as a fact of life by a people acknowledging the mystic realm. Victorian visions of gossamer-winged lovelies are actually a romanticized version of the Sidhe, a fairy spirit-race believed by the Scotch/Irish to have powers to harm and confuse the vulnerable, and influence human fate. According to one charming Irish custom, when a child spills a drink at a picnic or outing, the adult refrains from scolding him or her, saying instead: "Leave it to the fairies!" Fairy lore asserts that fairies abhor a miserly spirit. To appease fairies in your life, leave small gifts of food and drink in your garden, on your doorstep, or any outside place you sense might be a fairy ring or fairy tree.

Karri Ann Allrich

Notes:

visualize yourself surrounded by an egg of energy. See this egg fill with light as it surrounds you completely. In your mind, take a good look at this egg. Inspect the front, the rear, and the sides, and examine the spaces over your head and below your feet. If you notice any holes or anything other than a clear, strong shell, fix it. See the outside of your egg as strong yet flexible. Ask that this shell only allow in the most beneficial energies, while it allows unwanted energy to flow freely out and away from you. If you like, cover the shell with outward-facing mirrors for added protection. Inspect and repair your shell regularly.

Kristin Madden

Notes:

June 22
Tuesday

1st ♌

☽ v/c 3:54 am

☽ → ♍ 10:10 pm

Color of the day: White

Incense of the day: Frankincense

Personal Energy Maintenance Spell

For protection and to maintain your personal energy field,

June 23
Wednesday

1st ♍

Color of the day: Topaz

Incense of the day: Sandalwood

Celebrate Community Ritual

The time around the Summer Solstice is a time to celebrate community. If you can, plan a "Just Because" party for your family, friends, coworkers, and neighbors. Tell them: "I'm having a party just because I'm happy you're in my life." Decorate with bright colors, and serve seasonal foods. Have plenty of music. Take it outside if you can. After the party, plan to spend time volunteering at a local organization. Attend a town meeting. Read your local paper cover to cover, and write a letter to the editor about something positive you observe in the community. Offer to grocery shop for an elderly next-door neighbor who has trouble getting around. Babysit for another neighbor, so the parent can have a few hours of quiet time. Tutor a kid in summer school. Pitch in at a local charity event. See what makes your community special, and then do something to take it to the next level.

Cerridwen Iris Shea

Notes:

June 24
Thursday

 1st ♍

☽ v/c 1:19 pm

Color of the day: Crimson
Incense of the day: Carnation

Financial Picture Meditation

This is an auspicious day for considering your financial picture, starting a budget, or thinking about an investment plan. Why not make a mandala of money today? On a large sheet of paper, draw a large circle that goes nearly out to the edge of the paper. In the middle of the page, draw yourself or something symbolic of yourself—a stick figure or other personal symbol will do. Around it, draw the things that have brought you money in the past: your job, a business, prize winnings, inheritances, and so on. Draw a border of dollar signs or other symbols of money around these symbols. Around that, draw what you have bought with that money, and then around that draw pictures of what you would like to buy in the future. Around the outer edge of these symbols, draw more dollar signs. If you don't feel comfortable trying to draw, you can cut out pictures from magazines and catalogs and paste them on the paper. Or you can paste on play money instead of drawing dollar signs. Use this mandala to gain a clearer understanding of the place of money in your life.

Magenta Griffith

Notes:

your gift infused with good healing energy. Magical gifts like these are ways of strengthening our bonds with and showing our love to our friends. Friendships strengthen our sense of health and well-being.

Jonathan Keyes

Notes:

June 25
Friday

 1st ♍
☽ → ♎ 6:50 am

2nd Quarter 3:08 pm

Color of the day: Coral
Incense of the day: Thyme

Friendship Spell

Often our friendships take a back burner to other priorities and concerns in our life. On this waxing Libra Moon, take a good friend out to dinner. At the dinner, give him or her a simple gift that is from your heart. It may be a stone, a bracelet, a rattle, or something personal. Before the dinner, prepare the gift by smudging it with cedar or sage smoke. Light a candle on your altar space, and visualize your friend enjoying optimal health and happiness. Then visualize

June 26
Saturday

2nd ♎
☽ v/c 7:41 pm

Color of the day: Indigo
Incense of the day: Lilac

Forever Grounding Spell

The technique of grounding brings a sense of calm to otherwise stressed people. Grounding should be done after magical workings, or anytime you need to slow down and relax, to allow excess energy to flow back into the earth. If possible, sit outside and rest your back against a tree. Be sure it is a place you are completely comfortable. Or you can sit inside on the floor, imagining you are outdoors.

Imagine you are a tree. Roots extend from your legs, feet, and the bottom of your torso. These roots spread deep into the ground, releasing anxiety and drawing in nutrients from the earth. Place the palms of your hands on the ground. Feel yourself connected to the land. With each breath, sink more deeply into a relaxed state.

Ember

Notes:

thimble, otherwise known as foxglove. Go to your favorite spot in the woods just before sunset. Make a ring of stones, and build a fire in the ring. When the Sun dips below the horizon, rub the fern seed on your eyelids. Keep your thoughts away from the drudgery of the work-a-day world. Fill your thoughts with the beauty of the plants and trees around you. Dance around the fire. Do you see them?

Lily Gardner

Notes:

June 27
Sunday

 2nd ♎︎
)) → ♏︎ 12:13 pm

Color of the day: Yellow
Incense of the day: Cinnamon

Spell to See the Fairies

Fairies are most often seen on nights between Midsummer, or Litha, and June 29. The best way to see fairies is to gather fern seed on the night of Midsummer. On June 27, make a wreath of fairies'

June 28
Monday

2nd ♏︎
)) v/c 8:57 pm

Color of the day: Gray
Incense of the day: Chrysanthemum

Spell to Find a Lost Cat

For this spell to find a lost cat or other small pet, you'll need the assistance of a tree, rock, or other outdoor entity—preferably one in your yard or very near your home. Take one of your cat's favorite toys and some cat food to the tree. Tell the tree about your pet and that you are concerned because of how long he or she has been missing. Ask the tree if it will help you by providing a beacon for your cat to follow to get home. Leave the cat food near the tree. If a small rock gets your attention, bring it and the cat toy into the house. Keep them near the door. Every time you pass the toy, thank the tree for its help in providing a beacon for your pet.

Therese Francis

Notes:

June 29
Tuesday

2nd ♏

☽ → ♐ 2:15 pm

Color of the day: Red
Incense of the day: Honeysuckle

Blood—Free Battle Spell

Today is the Santería festival of Elleggua, the warrior orisha.

The best battles fought now are the ones fought without bloodshed. It is a good day to cast spells dealing with beginnings, with competition and struggle, and with battles large or small. A good question to ask now is: How do we attempt defensive magic? Get a piece of red cord a foot long. Think of a goal you are struggling to attain. As you knot the red string eleven times, repeat these words:

> With this string I cast.
> A spell to make it last.
> Give to me what should
> have been.
> Bind to me what's
> rightly mine.
>
> I give love,
> and love is divine.
> Grant this wish in all
> due time.
> So mote it be.

Wear or carry the red knotted cord for the next several days. Go after your dream. There is no better time.

Susan Sheppard

Notes:

June 30
Wednesday

2nd ♐

Color of the day: Brown
Incense of the day: Eucalyptus

honor Thy Crones and Thy Cronies Spell

Wednesday is the day of Woden, the father-god of the Norse and Germanic deities. Though an elder, Woden is strong, wise, and protective. Raet is the Egyptian crone goddess, the female Ra. Often shown with a lioness's head, she too is, though aged, strong and fierce. Use today to honor your crones—and cronies. Put down the knitting, and kickstart the Harley. Take the grandkids to some event you both can enjoy—a hockey game, say, or a Rolling Stones concert. Celebrate your age. Refuse to give in to stereotypes. Or, if you are not an elder yourself, find one who is, and take him or her out tonight for an evening of fun. Give your elders a gift depicting lions or lionesses, and let them roar.

Denise Dumars

Notes:

July

July is the seventh month of the year. Its astrological sign is Cancer, the crab (June 21-July 20), a cardinal water sign ruled by the Moon. The month is named for Julius Caesar. The heat of July is oppressive, only occasionally interrupted by sudden summer storms. Leaves wilt on trees and plants suffer in the parched fields. July is the traditional month for visiting the seashore or other body of water as an escape. Sand and seawater are useful in magical rituals at this time; as are shells, particularly cowries, which resemble and symbolize the sexual organs of the Goddess. Snails and shellfish, such as mussels and clams, have magical resonance. A visit to the beach is a perfect time to perform magic; an incoming tide (and waxing Moon) is a time to cast spells of increase, prosperity, and fertility. An outgoing tide (and waning Moon) is a time for spells of banishment. One of the most magical objects you can find on the beach is a stone or pebble with a natural hole in it. July harvest time begins with cabbage, from which one makes sauerkraut for the winter months, followed by all the herbs of the garden. The Full Moon of July is called the Wort Moon; *wort* is old Anglo-Saxon for "herb." Use a white-handled ritual knife to harvest herbs for magical purposes. Give thanks to the spirits that dwell in the herb garden.

July 1
Thursday

2nd ♐

☽ → ♑ 2:01 pm

Color of the day: White
Incense of the day: Geranium

Runic Money Spell

During times when extra money is needed for paying unforeseen bills incurred through no fault of your own, etch the runic symbol feoh (ᚠ) on a green candle. Anoint the candle with bergamot or mint oil before placing it into a candle-holder. Place the candleholder on a round heat-proof dish. Arrange a handful of almonds, bay leaves, cinnamon sticks, and fresh mint leaves around the dish. Scatter a handful of gold or silver coins on the herbs. Light the candle, gaze upon the flame, and visualize monetary blessings coming your way. When your wish comes true, be mindful and pay the bills immediately. If there is extra, donate a portion to charity.

S. Y. Zenith

Notes:

Holiday lore: Today is the first day of the season for climbing Mt. Fuji in Yamabiraki, Japan. Mt. Fuji is the highest peak in Japan and is revered in Japanese culture. Considered the foremother or grandmother of Japan, Fuji is an ancient fire goddess of the indigenous Ainu people. In modern times, the Ainu mostly resided on the northern island of Hokkaido. The name *Fuji* was derived from an Ainu word which means "fire," or "deity of fire." Each year since the Meiji era, a summer festival has been held to proclaim the beginning of the climbing season and to pray for the safety of local inhabitants and visitors or pilgrims to the sacred mountain. The two-month climbing season begins today and ends on August 30.

July 2
Friday

 2nd ♑

Full Moon 7:09 am

Color of the day: Purple
Incense of the day: Sandalwood

You're in the Spotlight Spell

Have you ever been in a situation where you are expected to dazzle those around you? But instead of dazzling, you became a tongue-tied, quivering mess? This spell will uncover your confidence and allow your true inner brilliance to shine.

Light a white candle. Focus your intent on the candle, and on the attributes that you want to project. Know that you already possess these attributes. Draw the vibration of the Earth up through you. With each breath, feel the nourishing confidence of the Earth blend with you. Feel your desired attributes flowing as a brilliant ray of light that originates within you. Focus on your intent, and say:

> I am grounded and
> confident as Mother Earth.
> I shine with the brilliance
> of the Lady of the Sky.

Allow any excess energy to recycle back to the Earth, and enjoy your time in the spotlight.

Karen Follett

Notes:

Fire Release Spell

For a spell to release the energy of fire, you will need a bowl of some type of grain. Build a bonfire outside or a fire in a fireproof container. Taking up a handful of the grain, sit in meditation before the fire. As you gaze into the flames, bring to mind all those issues, patterns, or situations that you want to let go of. Allow all associated feelings, judgments, and concerns to come up as well. Send the feelings into the grain in your hand. When you are ready, throw the grain into the fire. As it burns, see and feel those issues purified and released.

Kristin Madden

Notes:

July 3
Saturday

3rd ♑
☽ v/c 10:25 am
☽ → ♒ 1:22 pm

Color of the day: Black
Incense of the day: Juniper

July 4
Sunday

Independence Day

 3rd ♒
☽ v/c 10:15 am

Color of the day: Orange
Incense of the day: Sage

Independence Now Spell

On July 4 in the year 1776, the Declaration of Independence was approved by the Continental Congress, and the thirteen former English colonies eventually became the United States of America. Many of the men who signed the document belonged to the mystical brotherhood of Freemasons, and in forming this new nation they were realizing an ideal that had been forming in the imaginations of their order for a century. That is, the Freemasons helped to create a new society in which all men were equal under the law, where the people selected their leaders, and where religious freedom was protected by the "separation of church and state." To protect these mystical ideals, a national amulet was created called the Great Seal of the United States. On its front, the national heraldic animal, the bald eagle, clutches thirteen arrows and an olive branch with thirteen leaves and thirteen olives. Above his head are thirteen five-pointed stars, or pentagrams, that are grouped to form one six-pointed star, the mystical seal of Solomon. The olive branch and the arrows show that the eagle is in control of love and peace, strife and war, or the dual forces of the universe that stem from Pythagorean philosophy. The thirteen stars represent the thirteen original American colonies—each a star on its own, but together a greater star,

or a nation, and thus a very potent magical design. That thirteen units in this design emphasize the magical power of a group of thirteen. Further, the unity of these stars is reiterated by the motto, *E pluribus unum,* or "out of many, one is formed." On the reverse of the seal, there is a pyramid with thirteen physical levels and an immaterial capstone formed of a triangle containing the all-seeing eye of God, or the Platonic One. The base of the pyramid is inscribed with the date 1776 in Roman numerals—to indicate when this structure was formed. Again the thirteen units form one structure, and this structure is shown to be patterned after the geometric harmony that is the divine One—a design that again stems from Pythagorean mysticism. All of this is the visual equivalent of the alchemical axiom: "As above, so below." By creating a physical entity that is the manifestation of the divine plan, the founders were achieving an alchemical great work and one of the greatest magical acts of all time. Other mottos read *anuit coeptis,* "he has approved," and *novus ordo seclorum,* "a new order of the ages." Together, these symbols and words indicate that the divine "he" is one with this new "of the ages" creation. We can honor our ideals on this day by exercising our freedom, practicing our religion, and by expressing our opinions.

Robert Place

Notes:

Holiday notes: On July 4, 1776, the Second Continental Congress adopted the Declaration of Independence. Philadelphians were first to mark the anniversary of American independence with a celebration, but Independence Day became commonplace only after the War of 1812. By the 1870s, the Fourth of July was the most important secular holiday in the country, celebrated even in far-flung communities on the western frontier of the country.

bowl. Drizzle them generously with olive oil and balsamic vinegar (or Italian vinaigrette). Add your choice of herbs: basil, rosemary, dill, mint, oregano. Add plenty of chopped fresh garlic, and stir with magical intention. Cover and marinate one hour. Prepare a heart-shaped foil packet for each person by cutting two eight-inch hearts out of aluminum foil. Spoon a serving of vegetables onto one heart, and cover with the second heart. Crimp and seal all the edges. Grill the packets on a medium-hot grill for twenty minutes, until the veggies are tender.

Karri Ann Allrich

Notes:

July 5
Monday

 3rd ♒︎
☽ → ♓︎ 2:26 pm

Color of the day: Ivory
Incense of the day: Myrrh

Grill Magic

Use the backyard grill today to fire up some herbal magic for friends and family. Gather an assortment of summer vegetables in every color. Wash and slice them into bite-size pieces, and place them in a

July 6
Tuesday

 3rd ♓︎

Color of the day: Scarlet
Incense of the day: Evergreen

Talking-to-Ancestors Ritual

As the Moon wanes in Pisces, this is a wonderful time to connect to, and ask for messages from, our ancestors. Begin your work by finding a few pictures of an ancestor you want to contact. Place these pictures on your altar, and light some ceremonial candles. Then make some dream tea (two parts valerian, two parts hops, one part mugwort, and one part licorice). You can find loose herbs at any health food store. After brewing a good cup, drink it while visualizing the qualities and other traits of your ancestors. Then say:

**healing tea, let me sleep.
Bring me messages from
the deep.**

Ask for messages from these relatives, and then lie down to sleep. In the morning write down your dreams. You will likely have had a visitor.

Jonathan Keyes

Notes:

Tanabata Day Spell

In Japan and Korea, people celebrate Tanabata today. Legend tells of two lovers, represented by stars in the sky: a shepherd boy (Vega) and a weaver girl (Aquila). Today, lovers still write each others' names on paper and hang them under the stars. Stars represent hope, our highest aspirations for self and others. Study the names of stars, their history, the constellations, and the accompanying legends from different cultures like Japan and Korea. Go stargazing with your significant other tonight, or visit a planetarium together. Share your dreams of the future. Not partnered yet? Go anyway! Maybe you'll meet someone else out looking at the stars.

Elizabeth Barrette

Notes:

July 7
Wednesday

3rd ♓
☽ v/c 1:30 am

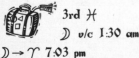

☽ → ♈ 7:03 pm

Color of the day: Yellow
Incense of the day: Cedar

July 8
Thursday

3rd ♈

Color of the day: Green
Incense of the day: Musk

Lucky Money Spell

To encourage the flow of money in your direction, take a dollar coin, and bless it by the four elements, by saying: "I bless this coin by the power of air (and fire, water, and earth, in that order)." Hold the coin to each of the four directions as you say this. Then put the coin where it will be in direct sunlight for a day. Carry the coin in your pocket every day. When it feels right, spend the coin on something magical or otherwise special to you. It's a good idea to let the magic circulate. Then put the charm on another dollar coin.

Magenta Griffith

Notes:

Spell to heal a Broken Connection

To reconnect in a relationship, take a photo or object representative of your loved one, and place it on your altar along with a fresh flower, a crystal, and a bowl of clean water. Change the flower and water each day for seven days. Then leave the flower and water outside, preferably under a healthy tree. Charge the water, add the crystal, and examine the photo, imagining the energy of nature healing your relationship. Be aware that sometimes the healing will come from releasing. Be open for what's best for both of you. Place the crystal and photo back on the altar. Every time you pass your altar, see the energy of nature revealing needed information.

Therese Francis

Notes:

July 9
Friday

 3rd ♈

4th Quarter 4:34 am

☽ v/c 8:52 am

Color of the day: Pink
Incense of the day: Ylang-ylang

July 10
Saturday

Lady Godiva's Ride

4th ♈

☽ → ♉ 3:51 am

Color of the day: Indigo
Incense of the day: Pine

Banish Bad habits Spell

To work on bad habits, gather any combination or amount of obsidian, black onyx, hematite, or smoky quartz. Also gather a piece of cloth, some black ribbon or string, a bowl of water, and some paper and water-soluble ink. Set up the container, and place your selection of stones around it. Think of a bad habit you'd like to be rid of, and write the habit on a slip of paper. Place the paper in the water, visualizing your bad habit ending. Allow the water to dissolve the ink completely from the paper. Bury the paper in the ground, pour the water over the paper, and cover with dirt. Then, collect the stones and wrap them in a piece of cloth. Carry them with you for strength

Ember

Notes:

Historical notes: Lady Godiva's original name was Godgifu, meaning "God-given." She was a Saxon noblewoman who was outraged at a tax levied on the people of Coventry by her mischievous husband Leofric. He offered a deal, though: He would cancel the tax if she rode through the town naked. Godgifu's ride has been commemorated by the grateful townspeople of Coventry for many years on this date with whimsical parades and a festival.

July 11
Sunday

4th ♉
☽ v/c 7:29 pm

Color of the day: Gold
Incense of the day: Clove

Spell to Remove Curses

To most people, it seems impossible to understand why one soul would want to curse another, but still, it happens. Although it is best not to get paranoid about curses, it *is* smart to stay protected. Here's what you can do: With silver gel pen on black paper, write the name and birthday, in backwards writing, of the person you believe is cursing you. Light a black candle, and say:

> hecate, mother of night,
> shield your child from
> curses.
> When enemies direct
> harm,
> make their minds grow
> confused.
>
> No bad thing can ever be
> come of this cursing!
> Mother, shield me.
> So mote it be.

Burn the black paper, and dump the ashes near a graveyard or at a crossroads. Leave an offering of ginger ale and cornbread. Hecate responds well to cakes and ale.

Susan Sheppard

Notes:

time brushing or caressing a pet. Take a bubble bath, or make some cocoa. Get your favorite food for takeout, and be sure to have dessert. Whatever you choose to do, make sure your senses are fully engaged in the luxury and pleasure of the experience. Be fully present and indulge yourself.

Kristin Madden

Notes:

July 12
Monday

 4th ♉
)) → ♊ 3:45 pm
Color of the day: Gray
Incense of the day: Rose

Comfort-of-home Spell
The Moon is in earthy Taurus today. This is an ideal time to relax with the comforts of home and family after the first day of the work week. Burn some sandalwood or myrhh incense, and put on your favorite music. Surround yourself with beauty as you change into your most beautiful and comfortable clothes. Trade back or foot massages with someone dear to you. Spend

July 13
Tuesday

 4th ♊
Color of the day: Black
Incense of the day: Sage

Spell for Scathach
Today is the feast day of Scathach, when the traditional Scottish games begin. Generally, the games are held around the second week of July, and feature games of skill, strength, and artistry. They are watched over by the goddess Scathach, she who bestows strength and endurance. Check your local events listings to see if any groups are sponsoring upcoming Highland

games and meetings of the clans. Tonight, hoist a jigger of good Scotch and toast Scathach, asking her for health and strength. If you are related to any of the Scottish clans, wear your clan's tartan today.

Denise Dumars

Notes:

French film. Write letters for Amnesty International, or send an e-mail to your government representatives with suggestions. You have the power to influence decisions that affect your life. Most importantly, pick an area in your life that needs some liberation. Let today be the first step in self-liberation.

Cerridwen Iris Shea

Notes:

July 14
Wednesday
Bastille Day

4th ♊
☽ v/c 8:33 am

Color of the day: Brown
Incense of the day: Maple

First Step to Self-Liberation Spell

On July 14, 1789, the people of France stormed the Bastille prison. It was the start of the French Revolution, and proof that the power to make decisions resides with the people. Bastille Day is still celebrated in France, and in communities influenced by France. Have fun today. Wear the colors red, white, and blue. Eat French food, and drink French wine. Read a French novel, and watch a

July 15
Thursday

4th ♊
☽ → ♋ 4:40 am

Color of the day: Purple
Incense of the day: Jasmine

St. Swithin's Simplicity Spell

As the saying goes: "St. Swithin's Day, if thou dost rain, full forty days it will remain." This is because the rain fell for forty days when priests moved St. Swithin's remains from a humble churchyard to a fancy tomb inside the church. He was the model of simplicity. The truth is the more you simplify, the more free time you have. On your altar place a black candle, a cauldron, and pen and paper. Place objects that represent those things you can rid yourself of. Write on a sheet of paper: "What obstructs my free time melts away." Visualize yourself with more free time. Burn the paper. From now until the Full Moon in August, remove items you no longer need.

Lily Gardner

Notes:

½ cup flour

½ cup yellow cornmeal

Salt and pepper to taste

½ tsp. brown sugar

3 medium-sized green tomatoes, thinly sliced

¼ cup butter

With a fork mix the flour, cornmeal, salt, pepper, and sugar in a shallow bowl. Coat the sliced tomatoes well with this mixture. Melt the butter in a frying pan until it sizzles. Fry the tomato slices until brown on each side. Serve as a warm side dish. Your romantic partner will love you for it.

James Kambos

Notes:

July 16
Friday

 4th ♋

Color of the day: White
Incense of the day: Nutmeg

Fried Green Tomatoes Spell

In July, most of us eagerly await the first garden-ripened tomato. Until then, we can satisfy ourselves with the following recipe for fried green tomatoes. Surprisingly, fried green tomatoes are a perfect dish to serve your lover. All the main ingredients are ruled by Venus, the planet of love.

July 17
Saturday

 4th ♋

New Moon 7:24 am

☽ v/c 7:24 am

☽ → ♌ 4:56 pm

Color of the day: Blue
Incense of the day: Lavender

Spell for the higher Self

*T*he best piece of advice that I can pass on about developing psychic ability is to strengthen the communication with your higher self on a continuous basis. We may be inherent receivers of psychic perceptions, but the higher self connects with spirit and acts as a sender of perceptions. To encourage this, sit in a comfortable position, relaxing your mind and body. State these words: "Spirit who guides me, I wish to connect with thee." Visualize a gentle flow of energy reaching from your crown to the realms of your higher self. Allow the images to guide you. Your higher self may be revealed in many different ways. Listen for any messages. Ask your higher self to give you a sensation, such as a tingle on the back of your neck, to signal when he or she wants to communicate with you. Thank your guide, and visualize the flow of energy returning back to you.

Karen Follett

Notes:

July 18
Sunday

1st ♌

Color of the day: Amber
Incense of the day: Basil

Swim for health Spell

*S*unday is the day of health, and for focusing on the needs of body and soul. Swimming offers a wonderful way to do both. First, you get to exercise without jarring your skeleton. Second, you immerse yourself in the intuitive and spiritual element of water. So find a pool near you, and take a swim today. Here is a verse to say before you go:

> Give me the grace of
> falling rain.
> Give me the strength of
> running tide.
>
> Give me the power of
> water's force.
> Make me healthy,
> outside and inside.

Afterward, remember to thank the spirits of water for supporting you and for sharing their power.

Elizabeth Barrette

Notes:

July 19
Monday

1st ♌

☽ v/c 2:50 pm

Color of the day: Silver
Incense of the day: Poplar

New Dwelling Spell

July 19 marks the anniversary of the death of Rebecca Nurse, Sarah Good, and Susanna Martin—all found guilty of witchcraft in 1692. Today is a good day to focus on all working together to halt religious intolerance. Place on your altar as many images of the God and Goddess as you can. Light a new purple candle. As it flickers, gaze at the gods and goddesses. Meditate on how different civilizations have imagined the divine in many guises. Search your heart for any anger you harbor toward any other faith or religious system. Say:

> hatred is banished,
> may love now reside.

Feel a new tolerance growing within you. Exhale that feeling into the world.

Magenta Griffith

Notes:

July 20
Tuesday

1st ♌

☽ → ♍ 3:44 am

Color of the day: Gray
Incense of the day: Musk

Spell to Rid Yourself of an Unwanted Lover

St. Uncumber is famed throughout Europe for helping men and women rid themselves of unwanted spouses or suitors. St. Uncumber was a celibate princess who prayed her suitor would not want her. She woke the next day with a full beard, and this did the trick. Since the fourteenth century, women wanting to rid themselves of unwanted husbands have placed oats on her shrine. The oats are in hopes that a horse will carry the husband away. Place a small plate of oats on your altar. Take a picture of a woman, and draw a beard on her, saying: "St. Uncumber, set me free. With your grace, unencumber me." Visualize the unwanted person happy and well, but no longer interested in you. If possible, leave a few of the oats in his or her car or shoe.

Lily Gardner

Notes:

July 21
Wednesday

1st ♏
☽ v/c 5:48 am

Color of the day: White
Incense of the day: Pine

Spell to Get a Better Job

To get a better paying job, light a red candle. Place your current paycheck stub and checkbook near the candle—one on the right and one on the left, not touching. Focus on the flame as an energy source. Take the paycheck stub in one hand and the checkbook in the other. As you imagine drawing energy from the candle, bring your hands together and see the energy transform the current paycheck stub to the amount you need to match your financial needs. Chant:

> Candle flame,
> energy being,
> bring to me
> the job of my dreaming.

Therese Francis

Notes:

July 22
Thursday
St. Mary Magdalene's Day

1st ♏
☉ → ♌ 7:50 am

☽ → ♎ 12:39 pm

Color of the day: Crimson
Incense of the day: Chrysanthemum

Lodestone Prosperity Spell

Obtain two lodestones, and paint them green to attract prosperity, money, or business success. Put the stones into a green drawstring bag with a silver coin, one small gold item, and some cinquefoil, cloves, and patchouli. Alternatively, you may use other money-drawing herbs such as tonka beans, ginger, or cedar. Secure the bag's contents with string, and consecrate it at the altar using a green candle. Carry the bag when you go out.

S. Y. Zenith

Notes:

Holiday lore: There are a number of myths concerning Mary Magdalene. In ancient Jerusalem, there was a temple with a triple tower representing the triple goddess Mari-Anna-Ishtar. After her life of sin, the "seven devils" exorcised from Mary Magdalene were believed to be the seven Maskim, spirits of the seven nether spheres born of the goddess Mari. One myth indicated that she lived for some time with the Virgin Mary at Ephesus before going to Marseilles, a town named after the sea-mother Mari. It was believed her cult was centered there. For thirty years she lived in a cave dwelling at St. Baume without eating or drinking. Each day, her sustenance was the sweet songs of the angels. A church was later built on the site, and wine-growers of the region offer votive candles to her for good harvests.

July 23
Friday

1st ♎

Color of the day: Coral
Incense of the day: Ginger

Draw a Lover Spell

As the Moon waxes in Libra, now is a wonderful time to cast a spell to attract a partner or a lover, if you don't already have one. Go to your altar and take a juicy apple and two red candles with you. Then light the candles in your altar and visual-ize the type of person you want to attract. Make this very clear, and set your desire firmly. Then cut the apple in half, and say:

> I cut an apple with my knife. Bring love into my life.

Eat both halves of the apple.

Jonathan Keyes

Notes:

July 24
Saturday

1st ♎
☽ v/c 5:54 pm
☽ → ♏ 7:08 pm
2nd Quarter 11:37 pm

Color of the day: Brown
Incense of the day: Violet

Lazy, hazy Days of Summer Spell

Summer is a season when we expect to have plentiful spare time. Unfortunately, the reality is often the opposite. People travel in summer, and we are then consumed with map-reading, the desperate search for a restroom, lost toys in the ocean, too much cotton candy, and often much more stress than the rest of the year. And as Saturday is the

traditional day of Saturn, planet of getting things done, today you might choose to go against tradition. Arrange for someone else to be responsible for the children today. Send them to a friend's or grandparents' house for a sleepover on Friday night. Don't use the alarm clock in the morning. Sleep until you wake up. Stay in your pajamas as long as you want. Put away the telephones; turn off the fax machine; don't log on to your e-mail. You are incommunicado for the day. You can watch all the TV you want. You can lie in a hammock and read a trashy novel. Even if you don't have a backyard, try stringing up a hammock in your home. You can have pizza for breakfast and popcorn for dinner. Think about everything, think about nothing, but make sure you are listening to yourself, and not all the white noise that surrounds us all the time. Luxuriate in a bath full of sweet-smelling oil. Order in a good meal. By Sunday morning, you will feel refreshed.

Cerridwen Iris Shea

Notes:

July 25
Sunday

2nd ♍

Color of the day: Yellow
Incense of the day: Coriander

Rise and Shine Smoothie Recipe

Make a magical smoothie to boost your health today, and take advantage of the abundance of the goddess. Almonds add clarity for the conscious mind, and a touch of protein to nourish the body and spirit. Vanilla and nutmeg attract love.

- ½ cup milk or soy milk
- ½ cup raw almonds
- 1 ripe banana or peach, peeled and/or pitted and sliced
- 1 Tbl. honey
- 2 Tbls. plain or vanilla yogurt
- ⅛ tsp. almond or vanilla extract
- 5 ice cubes
- Dash of nutmeg

Combine all of the ingredients in a blender, cover, and blend on high speed until smooth and frothy. As you blend your smoothie, set your intentions for good health and for vitality, saying: "The Goddess supports my well-being."

Karri Ann Allrich

Notes:

On the following morning, pour the water into a spray bottle or covered jar, allowing the stones to remain in the water if possible. Use the elixir to mist each room of your home, and visualize peace and harmony. You can add the rest of the water mixture to your bath water, or use it to anoint objects.

Ember

Notes:

July 26
Monday

2nd ♏
☽ v/c 6:48 am
☽ → ♐ 10:48 pm

Color of the day: White
Incense of the day: Peony

Moon Water Ritual for a Peaceful Home

Fill a glass bowl or jar with clean water. Place either a quartz crystal, moonstone, or both in the water. Add three drops each of rose and lavender oil, and set the water outside overnight in a place where the light of the waxing Moon can shine upon it. Say this blessing upon the water:

> Moonlight,
> bless this water,
> clean and pure.
> May it bring peace
> and simple joy
> to my home.

July 27
Tuesday

2nd ♐

Color of the day: Red
Incense of the day: Gardenia

Spell to Banish Troublesome Ghosts

Spirits, like anyone, can be come annoying at times. Poltergeists, especially, can create havoc in the home. In order to banish your troublesome ghosts, burn sage. This remedy comes from Native American tradition. Sage drives away unhappy ghosts but allows the pleasant ones to stay. When you feel an unnatural coldness on your skin, or just the creeps, ring bells or *tsingsha* cymbals, or blow a whistle. Spirits don't like high-pitched or discordant sounds. Put a broomstick over the transom each night, and a bottle of rum or vinegar at your back door. No ghost will venture past these. Don't bother calling an exorcist. This only makes matters worse, since most haunts love the attention.

Susan Sheppard

Notes:

front step or porch. Sweep away from your house toward the street, visualizing all negativity being swept in that direction. For soothing vibrations, place a rose quartz crystal in your living room or den. If you cook, recipes including lemon or basil will open the mind and help spark lively conversation. Houseplants and bouquets of fresh-cut flowers absorb negativity. In the guest bath, leave lavender-scented soaps or bubble bath. These ease tension and promote harmony. Soon, you'll gain a reputation for being the perfect host.

James Kambos

Notes:

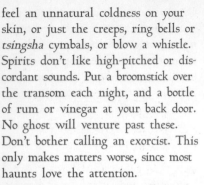

July 28
Wednesday

 2nd ♐
☽ v/c 11:06 am
☽ → ♑ 11:57 pm

Color of the day: Topaz
Incense of the day: Neroli

Be a Perfect host Spell

If you are going to have houseguests staying with you this summer, the following magical tips will help things go more smoothly. Using a broom you've blessed, on the morning before your guests arrive, sweep your

July 29
Thursday

2nd ♑
Color of the day: Turquoise
Incense of the day: Evergreen

Money Dust Spell

With Jupiter and the waxing Moon on your side today, now is the time to make Money Dust. With mortar and pestle mix ground cinnamon, patchouli, ginger, coriander, myrrh, and nutmeg. Stirring deosil (clockwise), crush any large particles until the mixture is a fine powder. Sing your favorite "money" song ("Money Makes the World Go Round," "Material Girl," etc.) or have it playing while you make the powder. When it is finely ground, use it to dust your checkbook, wallet, purse, bankbook, and any other money place. To spread the wealth and bring back more prosperity to yourself, give baggies of the dust to friends.

Denise Dumars

Notes:

or vanilla incense. Pour a bowl of water, and drop rose oil or rose petals in it. Create sacred space by walking clockwise three times around the bowl, and chanting or singing:

I walk in beauty.
I walk in love.
I walk in strength.
I walk in joy.

Return to gaze into the water. See your inner and outer beauty glowing from every pore in your skin. Your inner light shines through your eyes. As you splash the water over your face and neck, feel the beauty and passion within you. Holding the intent to live your life in beauty and strength, splash your face again.

Kristin Madden

Notes:

July 30
Friday

 2nd ♏
☽ v/c 7:21 am
☽ → ♒ 11:54 pm

Color of the day: Rose
Incense of the day: Parsley

Tension-Slip-Away Spell

Let the tensions of the week slip away as you light some sagebrush

July 31
Saturday

2nd ♒
Full Moon 2:05 pm

Color of the day: Gray
Incense of the day: Cedar

harvest of Aspiration Spell

The second Full Moon that falls within a solar calendar month is often referred to as a Blue Moon. This Moon is thought to be very strong in magic of prosperity and gain. Use berries to reflect on the harvest, both literal and metaphorical. Use grain or corn to reflect what you wish to harvest in the next year. Light a green candle behind the berries, and light a brown candle behind the grain or corn. Reflect on your accomplishments over the past year. Focus your reflections to the berries and the green candle. Project yourself into the year to come. What specific aspirations do you have for this next year? Write these aspirations down on paper. Focus the aspirations into the grain and the brown candle. Wrap the paper with some of the grain, and store it in a safe place. Take the berries and the remaining grain and place them on the ground. State these words: "Bountiful harvest, I reap from these seeds I sow."

Karen Follett

Notes:

Notes:

August

August is the eighth month of the year and named for Augustus Caesar. Its astrological sign is Leo, the lion (July 21–Aug 20), a fixed fire sign ruled by the Sun. August begins with Lammas, the celebration of the first harvest, especially the grain harvest of corn, rice, millet, rye, barley, oats, and wheat, brought in from the fields in sheaves. In the past, such grains were associated with gods and goddesses of death and resurrection—Tammuz in ancient Sumeria, Adonis in Babylon, Demeter in Greece, Ceres in Rome. Small figurines representing these goddesses were buried with the dead to ensure their resurrection into the afterlife. Baking bread is celebrated now, in all of its steps: grinding the grain, moistening the grain with water, shaping it into a loaf, and baking it. In some Mediterranean countries, women ritually sprout grain seed in dishes or pots to be given as offerings, either thrown in rivers or left at churches, to harvest gods. By midmonth, we begin to transition from the high heat of summer. The harvest is over and signs of the coming fall and winter begin to appear for the first time. Birds have begun to vanish from the trees, cooler air has moved in. The August Full Moon is called the Barley Moon, a time to contemplate the eternity of life evident in the grain of the fields.

August 1

Sunday

Lammas

 3rd ≈

☽ v/c 4:51 pm

Color of the day: Gold
Incense of the day: Poplar

Victory Day Spell

Lughnasadh, also spelled Lunasa, is the first day of the autumn on the modern Celtic calendar. The name means "the games of Lugh." Lugh is the Celtic god of the Sun and the harvest. He is called "the master of all the arts," and is prayed to for prosperity. Because of his skill and because he is the benefactor of one's prosperity, the Celts associated him with the Roman god Mercury. Like Mercury, Lugh is a god of magic. In Celtic myth, before the evil Fomorian earth-giants will relinquish the fruits of the soil, they have to be persuaded by the hero Lugh. In his heroic quest, Lugh, like many sacred heroes such as Christ and Buddha, dies and is reborn. This holiday commemorates his victory and his rebirth. The day is celebrated with horse races and athletic events and the baking and eating of bread—hence its Christian name Lammas, which means "loaf mass." As we eat this bread, we share in the power and health of Lugh. To participate in the holiday, bake round loaves of bread using pure whole wheat, and transform them into Lugh's talisman by inscribing the symbol of a wheel—a circle divided by a cross—on the top crust.

Robert Place

Notes:

Holiday lore: Lammas is a bitter-sweet agricultural holiday, mingling joy at the current high season's harvest with the knowledge that summer is soon at an end. Many cultures have "first fruit" rituals on this day—the Celt's version is called Lughnasadh; the Anglo-Saxon version called *hlafmasse*. In the Middle Ages, the holiday became set at August 1, taking its current form for the most part, with sheaves of wheat and corn blessed on this day.

August 2

Monday

3rd ≈

☽ → ♓ 12:34 am

Color of the day: Lavender
Incense of the day: Lavender

Purification Paste Spell

Sometimes when we touch certain objects, we can feel our hands being permeated with negative vibrations. The following hand-wash recipe will help eliminate such extraneous sensations from disturbing us. As the paste is made without synthetic substances, it can be used by anyone at home with sensitive skin. Ingredients include: 2 tablespoons olive oil, 1 tablespoon avocado oil, 1 tablespoon dried yarrow, 2 teaspoons dried sage, 1 teaspoon sandalwood powder, and a tiny bowl of raw sugar. Grind the yarrow and sage together, and add sandalwood powder to it. Combine the mixture with the oils, and add some sugar to form a paste. Store the paste in jars, making sure to label them. Whenever the need arises, rub some paste on your hands and rinse.

S. Y. Zenith

Notes:

August 3
Tuesday

3rd ♓

☽ v/c 10:58 pm

Color of the day: Black
Incense of the day: Ginger

Marie Laveau Energy and Protection Spell

It is a basic principal of magic that when we call upon our patron spirits for favors we must make some form of sacrifice. Voodoo queen Marie Laveau was often seen kneeling on the steps of St. Louis Cathedral in prayer with chili peppers in her mouth in order to find help in casting a particularly difficult spell. To make your own sacrifice in exchange for some helpful magic, take an object that you own. (The more precious to you, the better.) Bury or conceal it in your yard or near your front door. With broom or stick, circle the area and repeat these words:

> With this broom I do
> make,
> a blessed circle around
> my living space.
>
> No one can curse, vex or
> hate,
> the souls within this
> sacred place.

Spread loose chili pepper on the entrances to your home. Anyone who is not a true friend and tracks over the chili pepper spices will not return to your house.

Susan Sheppard

Notes:

people, but rather name your problems. For example, do not name a bubble with your boss's name, but rather, name your boss's refusal to give you a raise. Watch the bubbles until they pop—they always do—and imagine that problem disappearing with the bubble.

Magenta Griffith

Notes:

August 4
Wednesday

3rd ♓
☽ → ♈ 3:59 am

Color of the day: Yellow
Incense of the day: Coriander

Banish Trouble Bubble Spell

To banish trouble, get some bubble mixture and a bubble wand (a big bubble wand if you can find one). Blow bubbles for a little while without thinking about it. Try to relax a little. Then, blow a few bubbles more deliberately, and give each bubble a name relating to things that are going wrong in your life—debts, arguments and conflicts, various lackings. Be sure you name things you want to disappear. Do *not* name

August 5
Thursday

3rd ♈

Color of the day: Crimson
Incense of the day: Dill

Touch the Earth Ritual

As the fields of August begin to bring forth the bounty provided for us by the Goddess, it is now time to get in touch—literally—with the Earth. At sunset, respectfully approach a newly harvested field, and speak these words:

You, who have nurtured
our sacred seed,
and fulfill our every need.

You, who have are known
as Demeter and Ishtar,
who follow the seasons
by Sun and Moon and
star.

You, whom we call
Mother Earth,
please accept my deepest
thanks.

Now, kneel forward until your fore-head and palms touch the ground. Feel the life-force, and accept this power even as your own energy sinks deep into the soil. During this ritual, cast no spell, nor ask for anything. Simply touch the Earth, and give thanks.

James Kambos

Notes:

August 6
Friday

 3rd ♈

☽ v/c 9:59 am

☽ → ♉ 11:26 am

Color of the day: Purple
Incense of the day: Rose

A Spell for Peace

On this day in 1945, the first atom bomb fell on Hiroshima, dropped by an American military plane. More than 100,000 people were killed from the blast and subsequent radiation of that one bomb. A week later, World War II was over. We must all pray and work magic today in the hopes that human society will enjoy an everlasting peace, and no more such megabombs need be dropped. Buddhists float little boats down river to accompany souls who have departed from this realm. This spell becomes even more powerful if you can join with like-minded people in making these requests for peace. To start, make rafts of balsa wood and write your prayers for peace on the boats. Buy enough blue votive candles for there to be one candle for each of the boats you have made. Bring the boats to the river, light the candles on the shore, and then send the boats forth. To seal the spell, afterward write a letter for peace to your representative in

Congress, or join a political coalition for peace.

Lily Gardner

Notes:

 istorical fact: Today commemorates the day that atomic bomb Little Boy fell, in 1945, on the city of Hiroshima in Japan. In Japan, on this day, the people of Hiroshima celebrate a peace ceremony in memory of the dead. You may also take today to offer a silent prayer vigil, chanting: "Never again, never again."

August 7
Saturday

3rd ♉

4th Quarter 6:01 pm

Color of the day: Brown
Incense of the day: Patchouli

Reflection Spell

We often don't really "see" ourselves. If we did, we would know that each of us has faults and traits we would improve if we knew about them. This spell is to help us understand our true self—our deepest desires, feelings, hopes, dreams, fears, and characteristics. To reflect on our lives and seek answers to our questions, gather a mirror and a number of candles. Create a sacred space, and calm yourself. Set the mirror, or several mirrors, in a place where you can comfortably see your reflection. Light candles all around you, and extinguish all other light sources. Face yourself without looking away. Talk to your reflection as you would another person. Look within. Write in your journal about "who you are" and "who you want to be." Be honest. In time, as you reflect, you will begin to understand yourself and your traits more clearly. Take action if change is desired.

Ember

Notes:

August 8
Sunday
Dog Days

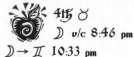 4th ♉
☽ v/c 8:46 pm
☽ → ♊ 10:33 pm

Color of the day: Amber
Incense of the day: Cinnamon

heal an Old Scar Spell

To heal an old scar, imagine the healing power of the Sun as you pour a handful of jojoba oil into your palm. Add one to two drops of organic *Helichrysum italicum* essential oil. Mix the old with with your finger. As you rub the oil into the scar tissue, clearly see the Sun's healing power enter your old injury and pour into the cells. This oil will irritate your eyes, so be sure to wash your hands before you do anything else. Do this every day for one week or until you notice the scar is fading.

Therese Francis

Notes:

August 9
Monday

4th ♉
Color of the day: White
Incense of the day: Maple

Dragon Day Spell

Today is the day to use dragon energy. Dragon energy is straightforward, so be careful for what you ask. You will receive it in the most direct way. Be very specific. Dragon logic is not human logic. Dragon moves from A to B, and simply removes anything in its way. For example: an acquaintance asked Dragon, without going into specifics, to change her living situation. As a result, a few days later there was a fire in her apartment building, and she was left without a place to live. That's a change, but it was not the one she wanted! Dragon energy is great for removing blocks, but only use it when you are determined to make a change. Using Dragon energy when you fear change will backfire on you. Pick something in your life that you wish to unblock. Find an image of a dragon that you feel connected to. Decorate your altar using bright colors and shiny, sparkly accessories. Cast a circle. Invite Dragon energy to join you in the ritual. Discuss the situation thoroughly with Dragon; consider the options, and request Dragon's help

in a way that will harm none. Ground and close the circle. You should feel energized at the end of the ritual. Dragon energy usually works quickly and in unexpected ways, so be aware of everything around you—as rapid change is on its way.

Cerridwen Iris Shea

Notes:

and a higher spiritual vibration to any intention. The flavor is strong—a little goes a long way. Marigolds contain the fire element, bringing courage, protection, sexuality, and health. Slightly musky and bitter, this flower pairs beautifully with garlic and spices. Nasturtiums invoke physical energy and protection. Their taste is a bit peppery, which makes them perfect for salads. Rose petals invite love and passion. Scatter these petals at will.

Karri Ann Allrich

Notes:

August 10
Tuesday

 4th ♊
☽ v/c 3:59 pm

Color of the day: Gray
Incense of the day: Juniper

Edible Blooms Spell

Certain flowers are edible as well as beautiful, and can add a magical accent to your salads, desserts, cold soups, and festive beverages. Choose blossoms that are pesticide-free. Rinse the flower off quickly, and dry it lightly before you add it to your dish. Garnish your dish with the flowers just before serving. Lavender buds bring love and luck,

August 11
Wednesday
Puck Fair

 4th ♊
☽ → ♋ 11:20 am

Color of the day: Topaz
Incense of the day: Sandalwood

Moon Magic Spell

With the Moon waning in Cancer, now is a good time to strengthen your core energy that is stored in your belly just two inches below your navel. This area is known as the *Dan Tian* in Chinese medicine and correlates to the solar plexus chakra. This area of the body is associated with the Moon and the sign of Cancer in medical astrology. Relax and rejuvenate this area of the body by taking a nice warm bath. Add essences such as jasmine and mugwort to the tub. While bathing, slowly rub your belly clockwise with a couple drops of these healing aromatic oils. Imagine the area being strengthened and deeply nourished. Say the words:

> My belly heals,
> my body is strong.
> I am at peace,
> my belly is calm.

Jonathan Keyes

Notes:

oliday lore: King Puck is a virile old goat who presides over the fair in Killorglin in Ireland. He watches the proceedings from a platform built in town, wearing a shiny gold crown and purple robes. Among the activities: gathering day, which includes a parade; fair day itself, and the buying and selling of livestock; and scattering day, when the goat is disrobed, dethroned, and sent back into the fields at sunset.

August 12
Thursday

 4th ♋

Color of the day: Green
Incense of the day: Carnation

Prosperity Cologne Spell

This cologne blend helps boost prosperity and money luck when you use it as a facial astringent or add it to bathwater. During quiet times when the ringing of the cash register is direly needed at places of business, it may be sprayed around the premises to help draw customers. Start by obtaining 1 cup chamomile flowers, 2 cups honeysuckle, 2 drops bergamot essential oil, 5 cups boiling water, and 2 tablespoons vodka. Fill a clean and sterilized stainless-steel container with the first three ingredients, and add boiling water. Leave the infusion to cool for one hour before adding the vodka. Cover the container with a white cotton cloth, and let the mixture cool down completely. Strain out the organic ingredients,

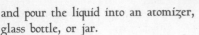

and pour the liquid into an atomizer, glass bottle, or jar.

S. Y. Zenith

Notes:

dead. Today, leave offerings of seasonal foods like bread, apple cider, garlic, and other root crops. Say this prayer:

> Goddess, watch over us
> in all your forms—
> bright face, dark face,
> and shadowed face.
>
> Accept our thanks for
> blessings received,
> and protect us during
> this harvest time.

Elizabeth Barrette

Notes:

August 13
Friday

 4th ♋

☽ v/c 6:17 am

☽ → ♌ 11:30 pm

Color of the day: Rose
Incense of the day: Thyme

Prayers Answered Spell

The ancient Romans dedicated this day to the goddesses Diana and Hecate. Women held processions to thank the goddesses for answering their prayers. The holiday was such a crucial one that the Christians later adopted it as the Assumption of Mary. This day also marks the beginning of harvest time, when a bad storm can still destroy most of the crop in the fields. It is a day of balance between life and death, hence the emphasis on female divinities who protect both the living and the

August 14
Saturday

4th ♌

Color of the day: Blue
Incense of the day: Lilac

Foxy Lady Spell

Today is the day of Inari, the elusive trickster goddess of Japan, also known as Fox Woman. Honor her sexy, playful side by placing rice cakes, red flowers, red candles, and fruit on your altar. Wear red and black tonight, and when you put on your makeup use Japanese rice powder. Before leaving the house, say the following:

> Inari, beautiful one,
> playful one,
> reside in me tonight.
>
> Inari, Fox Woman,
> I am quick and cunning
> and fun-loving like you.
>
> Bless me and keep me
> safe tonight,
> and I shall reward you
> with sweet oranges.

If you drink alcohol this evening, make it sake or plum wine. And be sure to enjoy yourself.

Denise Dumars

Notes:

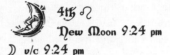

August 15
Sunday

4th ♌
New Moon 9:24 pm
☽ v/c 9:24 pm

Color of the day: Yellow
Incense of the day: Sage

Flame of Your Creation Spell

Generally, most of us would agree that a good idea is a good idea regardless of who thought of it. That is, we can all recall countless times when our friends and coworkers have flourished with ideas that were of our origin. And while they basked in success of our making, we say nothing about the ideas being "ours." We have the inner warmth of knowing that our inspiration led to the fulfillment of others. Or perhaps you have not felt exactly that way when your ideas have been taken without attribution. There are times when we want and deserve recognition for our hard work and for our creative input. To encourage this, light a red candle and place peppermint on a charcoal block, saying:

> Embers of creativity,
> spark into flame.
> Inspiration flourishes in
> my name.

Focus on creative energy flowing to and from you. Carry a small book to write down inspirations. Keep in mind that no idea is truly original. All ideas originate in the universal unconscious. Be humble. Also realize that ideas that flourish and ideas that crash will both bear your name. Push ego aside, and use good judgment when presenting your creative inspirations.

Karen Follett

Notes:

your candle flame dip and dart. If the fire appears to go out and spikes up again, you have likely made spiritual contact. Ask your spirits to reveal themselves. After contact, consider the words, thoughts, and pictures that surface in your mind. Examine such thoughts carefully. Telepathy is the usual way most spirits communicate with us.

Susan Sheppard

Notes:

August 16
Monday

1st ♌
☽ → ♍ 9:49 am

Color of the day: Silver
Incense of the day: Chrysanthemum

Spell to Draw Spirits

To draw beneficial spirits toward you, place an Ouija board in the center of your table for three nights, but don't use it. Later, get together with three spiritually inclined friends. Light a candle, hold hands, sit in a darkened room, and call on the spirits. Make up a name for your ghost. Ask: "Jack? Is that you?" If the spirit is not named Jack, he or she will then correct you. Watch

August 17
Tuesday

1st ♍

Color of the day: White
Incense of the day: Honeysuckle

Dispel-the-Evil-Eye Spell

Some people are born with the malignant ability to ruin the joy of others with a glance or stare. One of the most famous amulets against the evil eye is the Egyptian *udjat,* or Eye of Horus. Greeks, Lebanese, and the Turkish are known to wear glass pendants of white and blue eyes set in silver. Huichol Indians of modern

Mexico make eye amulets called *ojos de dios,* or "eyes of God," to protect homes, fields, and communities. A potent deterrent is to paint white and blue eyes on a piece of white cotton cloth or on a piece of cardboard and display these in the home. Smaller ones may be painted for carrying on your person.

S. Y. Zenith

Notes:

plant in your garden to protect your home. It is also said that a pot of Jupiter's Beard on your roof will keep your house in money. For a spell for safety, center yourself. Take a sprig of Jupiter's Beard and walk widdershins around the perimeter of your house or apartment, saying:

> Dear St. Helena,
> protect this home
> from fire and storm.

Lily Gardner

Notes:

August 18
Wednesday

 1st ♍
☽ v/c 3:15 am
☽ → ♎ 6.09 pm

Color of the day: Brown
Incense of the day: Eucalyptus

Jupiter's Beard Spell for Safety

St. Helena, whose feast day falls on August 18, is invoked against fire, wind, and lightning strike. Her plant is called Jupiter's Beard, or sometimes sengreen or houseleek. The custom is to hang the dry stalks of the plant from the ceiling, or better yet, to cultivate the

August 19
Thursday

1st ♎

Color of the day: Turquoise
Incense of the day: Geranium

Feast-and-Be-Merry Spell

In honor of the Roman festival Vinalia Rustica, this is a day to feast and drink good wine or grape juice. Put on a green tablecloth, and create an altar centerpiece with grapes and white candles. Carve symbols for money and prosperity into the sides of the candles. As you light them, see these energies flowing to you.

Visualize your bank account growing and never having to worry about money again. Before feasting, toast Dionysus and Bacchus. Give thanks to ancient Roman gods Pomona and Vertumnus, and ask for their blessings. Dig in, and fully enjoy your feast.

Kristin Madden

Notes:

bond with. Concentrate on your desire as you pull the sides together and wrap the pink cord around the top. Bind your spell as you tie the cord into three knots. Bury the amulet in a safe location in your garden, or with a potted plant.

Ember

Notes:

August 20
Friday

 1st ♎︎

☽ v/c 9:39 pm

Color of the day: Pink
Incense of the day: Sandalwood

Friendship Knot Amulet

To promote friendship, gather the following materials: pink cord, ribbon, or yarn; a small piece of green fabric, made of a natural fiber if possible; a chip of rose quartz, jade, or moonstone; one violet or an ivy leaf; some sandalwood, vanilla, or patchouli essential oil; and some moss. Wrap the items in the fabric, and sprinkle with five drops of the oil. As you assemble the amulet, think of a friend you wish to form a closer or deeper

August 21
Saturday

 1st ♎︎

☽ → ♏︎ 12:37 am

Color of the day: Gray
Incense of the day: Juniper

Consualia Spell

Consus is the Roman god of stored harvest, and Consualia is the day to celebrate his gifts. Go through your cupboard today, and make a list of what staple items are missing. Ask a blessing, and take a sacred trip to the grocery store. Stock up on items that can be stored—such as soups, canned goods, flour, sugar, rice, and pasta. When you return home, bless each item in the name of Consus as you put it away. Offer him a libation of beer. As you use your stores during winter, give thanks to Consus. Enjoy the abundance of your pantry. You will be surprised at how good everything tastes.

Cerridwen Iris Shea

Notes:

the mixture is used up. Then bathe or shower in cool water to wash off the mixture. Brew another cup of mint tea, chill it, and enjoy.

Magenta Griffith

Notes:

August 22
Sunday

1st ♏
☉ → ♍ 2:53 pm
☽ v/c 4:53 pm

Color of the day: Orange
Incense of the day: Clove

Mint to Cool Spell

I s it hot where you are today? If you live in the Northern Hemisphere, it probably is. Here is a recipe to help you cool off. Brew a cup of mint tea, and allow it to cool. Mix the tea with an equal amount of cool water in a shallow bowl. Do not add ice, and do not refrigerate the tea. Undress, and soak a clean washcloth in the diluted mint tea. Go to your tub or shower, and rub the washcloth up and down your body. Repeat until

August 23
Monday

1st ♏
☽ → ♐ 5:08 am
2nd Quarter 6:12 am

Color of the day: Ivory
Incense of the day: Frankincense

Worship the Sun Spell

A s the Sun begins to fade, now is a good time to bask in the Sun's rays and soak up some of the energy of summer. This energy can help nourish us and provides a storehouse of energy to help ward away depression in the coming fall and winter. On this Sagittarius Moon, go outside and take in the heat of the Sun for a short while. Lift your arms up to the Sun, and say:

healing Sun, strengthen me.
Let your currents of warmth
nourish my soul.

Let your rays bring me
inner joy and peace.
I give thanks for your
heat and light.

Jonathan Keyes

Notes:

obtain three sunflower
seeds, shiny and black.

Stuff these charms into a worn sock,
and say:

Gossip and lies, I hereby
block.
Tie the sock into a knot.
When the Moon begins
to wane,
bury it and let it rot.

James Kambos

Notes:

August 24
Tuesday

 2nd ♐

Color of the day: Scarlet
Incense of the day: Evergreen

Joe-Pye Spell to Stop Gossip

On certain lazy August afternoons
swallowtail butterflies drift among
the Joe-Pye weed flowerheads in my
garden. Wise herbalists once included
the leaves of Joe-Pye in spells calling
for protection against slanderous gossip. To do this, say these words:

If you have committed
no bad deed,
remove three leaves from
Joe-Pye weed.
If what is said about you
is untrue,
also collect a sprig of rue.
To further replace lies
with fact,

August 25
Wednesday

2nd ♐
☽ v/c 7:1 am
☽ → ♑ 7:46 am

Color of the day: White
Incense of the day: Cedar

Organizing Your Space Spell

Whether you work at home or
just have a small office area at
home, it is wise to periodically clear
your home workspace and organize.
Clutter jumbles the mind and spirit,
as well the physical space we inhabit.
Weed through old mail, catalogs, and

papers, and toss what you no longer need into a bag for recycling. Search your space with a keen eye, and remove anything that doesn't have a purpose. Dust and clean with intention. Choose three items that nurture your tri-part self: body, mind, and spirit. Perhaps a goddess statue (of Athena or another figure), some peppermint aromatherapy oil (for mental clarity), and a relaxing music CD. Afterward, say:

> I invite peace and calm into my space and into my life.

Karri Ann Allrich

Notes:

favorite hot drink (such as rosemary tea or hot cocoa), a blank sheet of paper, a favorite pen, pencil, or marker, a candle, and some incense (such as jasmine). These represent the four elements. Light the candle, and meditate on how fire contributes to your creative side. Then light the incense from the candle flame. Meditate on how air contributes to your creative side. Sip the tea. How does water contribute? Then take your pen and the blank paper in your hands. How does earth contribute? Now you are ready to ask these elements to contribute directly to your current project.

Therese Francis

Notes:

August 26
Thursday

2nd ♑
☽ v/c 10:58 pm

Color of the day: Purple
Incense of the day: Musk

Bring the Muse to a Blank Piece of Paper

aving trouble getting started on something? Gather together a

August 27
Friday

2nd ♑
☽ → ♒ 9:08 am

New Moon 12:26 pm

Color of the day: Coral
Incense of the day: Ylang-ylang

Love Apples Spell

Get an apple and a red candle, or an apple-shaped candle. Find an area where you can focus on your desire. With a knife, scratch your name and your desired's name on the skin. Core the apple. In the hole, lodge a red candle. Light the wick, and say:

> Apple of love,
> apple of bliss,
> feel my passion,
> feel my kiss.
>
> By Moon, by star,
> by wind, by blood,
> strong is our love.
> So mote it be.

Now allow your love to radiate outward. Feel your passion. If a tingling begins in your groin, let it glow. Snuff out the flame. Your spell is complete.

Susan Sheppard

Notes:

thunderheads that appear as if out of nowhere. Their awesome force wreaks havoc, but also brings needed rain. You can tap into this power for needed inspiration. When the sky darkens, go outdoors where you can feel the wind. Lift your palms to the storm and say:

> Lightning, fire in the sky,
> thunder, air rushes by.
> Rain, water falling down,
> hail, stones on the ground.
>
> Bring me passion,
> as this storm passes.
> By your power and flame,
> grant me all my aims.

Don't forget though: thunderstorms can spawn tornados, so stay alert.

Elizabeth Barrette

Notes:

August 28
Saturday

 2nd ♒

Color of the day: Indigo
Incense of the day: Pine

Summer Storms Spell

Late summer brings unpredictable weather, especially the wild

August 29
Sunday

 2nd ♍
☽ v/c 5:23 am
☽ → ♓ 10:33 am
Full Moon 10:22 pm

Color of the day: Amber
Incense of the day: Basil

Don't Worry, Focus on It Spell

My father always told me that worry was like "rocking in a rocking chair." It gives you something to do, yet in spite of the energy you expend, you don't get anywhere. Positive insight rarely comes to a worried, tense mind. Ideas and answers do come to a mind that is quiet and focused. With your hands held over a hematite, forefingers and thumbs touching to form a triangle, charge the hematite to ground tensions and worries. Hold a hematite in your projective hand, and say: "Worried energy is released from me." Focus your worries and tensions into the hematite. Visualize this energy becoming neutral and calm. Repeat the triangle gesture over the amethyst. Charge the amethyst with focused energies, and say: "In calm and focus, the answers will be." Feel the calm flow through the amethyst. Allow your mind to grow quiet. Be alert for any insight given either during this meditation, during sleep, or while you attend to other activities.

Karen Follett

Notes:

August 30
Monday

3rd ♓

Color of the day: Gray
Incense of the day: Myrrh

Family house Spirit Invocation

Use today's waning Moon energy to clear the home of unwanted, negative vibrations. Enlist the aid of your house spirit, called the *Domovoi* in Russian folklore. To obtain one, open the door and let your cat or a neighbor's cat walk in. A Domovoi will follow. No cat? Place milk and cookies near the open door. You won't see him—but don't worry, he's there. Once you have a Domovoi, ask him to guard and cleanse the home. For more protection, charge a lawn gnome, gargoyle statue, or similar guardian with his energy. Warning: the Domovoi doesn't like it if you go to bed without doing the dishes. And don't forget to leave him occasional snacks.

Denise Dumars

Notes:

August 31
Tuesday

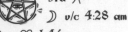 3rd ♓

☽ v/c 4:28 am

☽ → ♈ 1:46 pm

Color of the day: Black
Incense of the day: Sage

Sun Dance Spell for Strength

Choose several white and yellow candles, place them in a circle around your sacred space. Imagine dancing around a huge fire, and visualize its warmth on your skin. Choose your favorite music, or imagine music in your mind. You can play recorded music or use any hand-held instrument, such as a rattle. Focus on those parts of your body, mind, or spirit that feel weak or in need of energy. Concentrate on them as you dance, imagining the energy of the Sun flowing through you. Imagine your body glowing with sunlight. As you move, feel your body heat increase and your blood moving. Your strength has returned.

                                    Ember

Notes:

Notes:

September

September is the ninth month of the year. Its name is derived from the Latin word *septum*, which means "seventh," as it was the seventh month of the Roman calendar. Its astrological sign is Virgo, the maiden (Aug 21- Sept 20), a mutable earth sign ruled by Mercury. Though September afternoons are warm, the days quickly shorten. Meadow grasses dry up as birds and monarch butterflies migrate southward. Leaves begin to fall from trees and bushes now, and though most of the harvests have been taken in, clusters of grapes hang dark and heavy on the vine. The wine harvest is most important now; it is best to begin this process by pouring a ritual libation into the soil, and praying at an altar decorated with images of Bacchus and Dionysus. In ancient Germany, wine was considered sacred and placed into special stoneware jugs. Because wine is such a sacred fluid, the Full Moon of September was called the Wine Moon, though it is more commonly known as the Harvest Moon today. A ritual for this time involves dancing in a circle around some white wine in a silver cup with the Moon shining overhead. Corn, gourds, and squash play a part of the Autumnal Equinox celebrations, or Mabon. This celebration marks the time of the waning Sun, and the harvesting and storage of food for the coming winter.

September 1
Wednesday
Greek New Year's Day

 3rd ♈

Color of the day: Brown
Incense of the day: Maple

Pleasant in–Between Days Spell

In the pleasant days between summer and fall, the countryside blossoms with a series of harvest festivals and street fairs. At most of these, you can find the food of the goddess: funnel cake. Made from fluffy batter poured into a complex spiral shape and deep-fried to golden brown, then sprinkled with drifts of powdered sugar, this confection represents the extravagant bounty and festivity of the season. It expresses the sweet love of the goddess and of love of self. On your festival plate, funnel cake looks like a tiny spiral galaxy. And it's the ideal food for sharing—you can easily break off pieces to share with your friends today.

Elizabeth Barrette

Notes:

Holiday lore: Many Greeks, based on the agricultural traditions of the region, consider this their New Year's Day. This day marks the beginning of the sowing season, a time of promise and hope. On this day, people fashion wreaths of pomegranates, grapes, quinces, and garlic bulbs—all traditional symbols of abundance. Just before dawn on September 1, children submerge the wreaths in the ocean waters for luck. They carry seawater and pebbles home with them in small jars to serve as protection in the coming year. Tradition calls for exactly forty pebbles and water from exactly forty waves.

September 2
Thursday

 3rd ♈
☽ v/c 12:17 pm
☽ → ♉ 8:16 pm

Color of the day: Crimson
Incense of the day: Jasmine

Conserving Money Spell

Start up some conservation money-magic by setting a resolution not to spend unnecessarily and to save money for the future. Find a decorative box, and fit a mirror to the base with glue. Put coins, dollar bills, and a piece of valuable jewelry on top of the mirror in the box. Sprinkle dried basil over the contents. Close the lid and say the following:

> Money come, money go,
> Banish all money woes.
>
> This day forth, money hold,
> And security be manifold.

Make a regular habit of putting your spare cash in the box. Hide the box in a secure place. Each time the box is full, deposit the money in the bank and let it stay there.

S. Y. Zenith

Notes:

near you—this can be a squirrel, deer, raccoon, or opossum. Go outside and examine the areas where this animal lives. Then breathe deeply, and close your eyes. Start to imagine the shape and size of the animal—the way it moves its head and body, and the way it examines the world with scent and sight. If you want, begin to imitate its movements and its characteristics. Act like the animal. After a few minutes, open your eyes. This new-found awareness will help develop your connection to the animal world and to your own natural instincts and innate skills.

Jonathan Keyes

Notes:

September 3
Friday

 3rd ♉

Color of the day: Rose

Incense of the day: Almond

Animal Magic Spell

With the Moon in Taurus, now is a good time to connect to the animals and woodland creatures that live near you. Developing a relationship with the animal world expands and augments our sense of nature. To start, pick an animal that lives

September 4
Saturday

 3rd ♋

Color of the day: Blue

Incense of the day: Carnation

Weave a Bittersweet Spell

Come September, each warm afternoon is a small gift of grace, as we witness the first touches of gold, and the burnished beauty of the Crone's alchemy. It is the season for harvesting bittersweet vine laden with orange berries. Make a wreath for your door that evokes autumn's blessings. As you intertwine the vines, meditate on the year. Time affects us in its ever-winding wheel. The harvest season is a time of fruition, and as we look back upon our labors it is a good time to evaluate our spiritual path by asking:

What have I left unfinished?

What words need to be said?

have I nurtured my year's intentions?

have I honored Spirit this year?

have I lived in accordance with my convictions?

Blessed be these lessons you weave.

Karri Ann Allrich

Notes:

September 5
Sunday

3rd ♉

☽ v/c 2:56 am

☽ → ♊ 6:25 am

Color of the day: Yellow
Incense of the day: Coriander

Spell for Prosperity and Good Luck

Ganesh, the Hindu elephant-headed god, is celebrated on this day. Ganesh dispels ignorance and removes obstacles that keep us from our success. On your altar, set an image of Ganesh, an offering of flowers, incense, coins, a green candle anointed with patchouli, a cauldron, and a sheet of new parchment. Write on the parchment: "What blocks my success melts away. What blocks my prosperity melts away. What blocks my happiness melts away." Continue to write this prayer, being mindful of the words until you run out of space. When you are finished, say: "Lord Ganesh, remove what blocks me from my success. Lord Ganesh, bless me." Burn the prayer sheet and incense, bury the coin, and enjoy the flowers. Ganesh will bring you luck.

Lily Gardner

Notes:

September 6
Monday

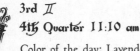

3rd ♊
4th Quarter 11:10 am

Color of the day: Lavender
Incense of the day: Rose

Getting a New Car Spell

Go to a toy store, and buy a toy version of the vehicle you are interested in obtaining. Focus your intention by standing before your altar and breathing deeply and slowly. Place the toy on your altar along with a dollar bill, any literature you have on the car, and something that represents "you" (such as an earring you wear often, or your favorite old ski hat). Have these items touching each other if possible. Stand before your altar for about five minutes every day for a week. See yourself in the vehicle of your choice. Take note of your sensations. How does it smell? What does it sound like? Do you feel excited? Liberated? After five minutes, say: "This or something better."

Therese Francis

Notes:

September 7
Tuesday

4th ♊
☽ v/c 2:08 pm
☽ → ♋ 6:50 pm

Color of the day: Red
Incense of the day: Musk

Rowan and Red Thread Spell

An old Scottish saying goes: "Rowan tree and red thread, put the Witches to their speed." "Witches" in this case refers to malevolent magic-workers who would do harm to people. The Rowan trees have small red berries on them in the fall. The rowan berry shows a five-pointed star—a pentagram—which is an ancient protection symbol and a modern symbol of Witchcraft. Traditionally, pieces of the rowan tree were carried for protection. Women would wear a necklace made of rowan berries strung on red thread. A protective amulet can be made from two Rowan twigs tied into a cross with red wool or thread.

Magenta Griffith

Notes:

September 8
Wednesday

 4th ☽

Color of the day: White
Incense of the day: Pine

Day of harvest Spell

Today is the birthday of the Russian harvest goddess, Berehynía. In her honor, make your own harvest incense. Combine two parts sweetgrass, one part each cedar, sage, juniper, and rosemary essential oils. Mix them together in a glass bottle. Or you may use the dry herbs and grind them together in a blender or bowl. Once your incense has been mixed, chant:

> Sacred herbs,
> Children of the land,
> Bring us the blessings of
> the harvest season.

Burn your incense on a charcoal disk, and wish Berehynía a very happy birthday.

Kristin Madden

Notes:

September 9
Thursday

4th ☽

Color of the day: Green
Incense of the day: Chrysanthemum

Tartan Money Spell

September means back-to-school or back-to-work after half-day Fridays, long weekends, and long vacations. For good luck, I always wore a tartan dress on the first day of school. The different colors symbolized the different elements woven together to create a whole. Since September is often a time of fresh starts, a fresh start for prosperity is often needed. You can try this prosperity spell using the good luck symbol of my childhood. Make a small pouch out of a piece of tartan. Use whatever tartan has meaning for you, either because it represents your clan or you simply like the colors. I tend to use one that is predominantly green, for prosperity. Put in a dollar coin, a whole nutmeg seed, and a sprig of rosemary in the bag. Bless and consecrate the bag in the name of your favorite prosperity deity, and carry it with you for three Moons. Be aware of new opportunities to manifest abundance. At the end of three months, throw the nutmeg seed and the rosemary into moving water. Put the coin and the bag in a safe place. You can use it as the basis for another tartan money spell next year, starting with two coins. You've already prospered.

Cerridwen Iris Shea

Notes:

September 10
Friday

 4th ♋
)) v/c 12:41 am

)) → ♌ 7:06 am

Color of the day: Pink
Incense of the day: Nutmeg

Make Me Beautiful Glamoury Spell

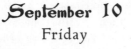or a dose of glamour, you will need a mirror, some glitter, and starlight. Glamoury is an ability Witches have to transform themselves into something else. This is where our word "glamour" originated. Glamoury is more than beauty though—it is the projection of allure and charisma. Glamoury demands attention, reverence, and awe. When all is quiet, say this into your mirror:

> Moon above,
> I want to change my love.

I need a little starlight
For my lover to see me right.
Starlight in my eyes,
Will make his love rise.
When my lover dreams of me,
It is only glamoury.
Beauty is as beauty does.
So mote it be.

Go outside. Blow your glitter in four directions. All eyes love you for you are beautiful.

Susan Sheppard

Notes:

September 11
Saturday

4th ♌
)) v/c 9:22 pm

Color of the day: Brown
Incense of the day: Jasmine

Day of Unity Ritual

Three times the wheel of the year has turned since America was attacked by terrorists. Three times the snows have fallen, and three times the flowers have bloomed. Three is a significant number, for it is the

number of unity—the result of the union between the male and female forces. It is a healing number, combining body, mind, and, of course, spirit. As we observe the third anniversary of this day, we can unite and complete the healing process. A tragedy of this magnitude should never be forgotten. But, it is now history and history can never be undone. Let us focus our healing energies on preventing a tragedy like this from occurring again. The key lies in affirming that we stand united in confronting prejudice and hatred. To do so, join me in performing this Unity Ritual. On your altar light one tall light blue candle. From this ritual candle flame, light seven white votive candles, representing the world's continents. Stand before them and say:

> Together we may be
> different, but as one we
> are united. Together we
> celebrate our differences
> for they make us special
> and unique. Never again
> will our differences create
> fear, prejudice, or hatred.

Take time to meditate as the candles burn down.

James Kambos

Notes:

September 12
Sunday

4th ♌
☽ → ♍ 5:16 pm

Color of the day: Orange
Incense of the day: Parsley

healing Breath Spell

Walk outside today, or open a window, so you can be in a place where the air is clean and clear. Prepare your sacred space by burning frankincense or myrrh—or a combination of both. Light a white candle, and circle it with gems that correspond with the Sun's glow. These include: amber, citrine, topaz, and pyrite. Face east and give thanks for the life-giving air. Concentrate on the miracle of breath. Imagine each time you inhale you are breathing in pure, golden, cleansing air, and when you exhale you are forcing impurities from your body. Draw in several deep breaths as you count to four, and fill your lungs to capacity. Hold the breath in for a four-count, and release it. Repeat and relax.

Ember

Notes:

September 13
Monday

4th ℳ

Color of the day: Silver
Incense of the day: Daffodil

Nephthys Moon Meditation

Today is Nephthys' day. She is the dark twin of Isis, and the night belongs to her. Light a black candle for her today, and scry in a dark mirror or in a piece of obsidian. Burn kyphi or lotus incense and wear either scent. Buy a black and gold *galabaya* from an online Egyptian goods store, and wear it whenever you honor Nephthys. Statues and paintings on papyrus of Nephthys and her son, Anubis, are easy to find as well. Pet a black dog today, sit by your altar, and sympathize with Nephthys' troubles—then tell her your troubles. Have a good cry if you need to. Take an Epsom salts bath before retiring.

Denise Dumars

Notes:

September 14
Tuesday

4th ℳ
New Moon 10:29 am
☽ v/c 8:55 pm

Color of the day: White
Incense of the day: Gardenia

Attracting Wellness Spell

The energy of this spell is intended to give a boost to your health and to be a palliative in the face of the upcoming "flu months." Light a green candle. Place a glass of water between you and the green candle. State these words: "Spirit guides, healers, and angels allow me to act as a channel for your healing rays. Energy on." Visualize a ray of energy entering your crown. Allow this ray to stream through your body with each breath. Visualize healing and balance being restored to your body. Use your intuition to indicate when the energy has reached its fullness within you. At the point of fullness, hold your hands over the water and visualize the ray stretching from your hands into the water. This action allows you to ground the ray's energy into the water. As this grounding occurs, the water also become "activated" with the healing properties of the energy. Thank the spirit guides, healers, and angels for their energy and say: "Energy off." Unless a doctor recommends you do not, drink at least eight glasses of activated water daily.

Karen Follett

Notes:

area to soothe frazzled nerves, draw harmony, and prevent overwhelming negative emotions. A tiny sprinkling of earth beneath the desk grounds energy and alleviates stress.

S. Y. Zenith

Notes:

September 15
Wednesday
Respect for the Aged Day

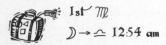 1st ♍

☽ → ♎ 12:54 am

Color of the day: Topaz
Incense of the day: Neroli

Balance Equilibrium Spell

Before facing the next hectic day of business or travel, prepare a balancing and grounding concoction at home a day in advance. This is beneficial for easing topsy-turvy nerves and anxiety. Mix one part bergamot essential oil, one part lavender oil, and one part pine oil in an atomizer containing spring water. Add a pinch of earth and a small hematite crystal to the bottle, and shake it. Before getting dressed, spray a fine mist over your body, your limbs, and the soles of your feet. The atomizer may be taken to work and sprayed around your desk and work

Holiday Lore: Keirou no Hi, or "Respect for the Aged Day," has been a national holiday in Japan since 1966. On this day, the Japanese show respect to elderly citizens, celebrate their longevity, and pray for their health. Although there are no traditional customs specifically associated with this day, cultural programs are usually held in various communities. School children draw pictures or make handicraft gifts for their grandparents and elderly family friends or neighbors. Some groups visit retirement or nursing homes to present gifts to senile residents.

September 16
Thursday
Mexican Independence Day – Rosh hashanah

 1st ♎︎

☽ v/c 9:31 pm

Color of the day: Gray
Incense of the day: Evergreen

New Day Spell

Rosh Hashanah is the Jewish New Year. On the Jewish calendar, today is the first day of the month Tishi in the year 5765 AM. The AM stands for *Anno Mundi*, "the year of the world." It is the year of the world because the Jewish calendar is calculated from what was believed to be the creation of the world, which occurred in the year 3761 B.C. of the Gregorian calendar. As with all days in the Jewish calendar, this day begins at sundown on the night before. This is the beginning of a ten-day period that commemorates the creation of the world. Today, a ram's horn, or *shofar,* is blown in the temple to call the people to a spiritual awakening. Over the next ten days, Jews are asked to review their behavior, atone for their sins, and renew their relationship with God. But on this day there is a feast and delicacies are eaten to assure luck through the New Year. The symbolic foods at

this meal include spiced apples, honey, and challah—a bread made of eggs, sugar, and wheat. The apples and the challah are dipped in honey before they are eaten. As this is done, one repeats the following magical invocation: "May it be Thy will, O Lord our God, to renew unto us a happy and pleasant new year."

Robert Place

Notes:

September 17
Friday

 1st ♎︎

☽ → ♏︎ 6:25 am

Color of the day: Purple
Incense of the day: Ginger

Transform–Emotions–into–Physical–Movement Spell

On this watery Scorpio Moon, now is a good time to make connections to the water element as it appears in the natural world. If you can, go to the nearest body of natural water. This may be a stream, a river, a waterfall, or the ocean. Take time to observe the rhythm and energy of the water in its natural setting. See how the energy of the water affects your body and emotions. In this place, make a prayer such as:

> healing waters,
> I honor your precious gifts.
> Teach me to understand my own flow and my depths.

Then sit and meditate, and allow messages to come to you.

Jonathan Keyes

Notes:

page. Write down dreams, stray thoughts, opinions of movies and TV shows you've seen. Sketch the tree outside your window or your cat as she sleeps. Most Witches keep a journal, called a *Book of Shadows*. In it, they records spells and everything else magical. It's a good idea to write down spells you try, and if or how well they worked.

Magenta Griffith

Notes:

September 18
Saturday

 1st ♏

Color of the day: Gray
Incense of the day: Violet

New Beginnings Spell

Today is a good day for new beginnings. If you have never kept a journal or diary, maybe this would be a good time to start. Get a blank book—one with lined paper is easier to write on, one without lines is better if you like to draw as well as write. Write your name on the first

September 19
Sunday

1st ♏
☽ v/c 8:24 am
☽ → ♐ 10:30 am

Color of the day: Amber
Incense of the day: Poplar

Eleusian Mysteries Spell

There is very little evidence regarding the specifics of the Eleusian mysteries. We only know they were performed in Greece to honor Demeter and Persephone, and that those who participated in them were sworn to secrecy. Theories abound about what these mysteries were. Perhaps they included drama, dance, the retelling of the legend of Demeter and Persephone, divination, sacred marriage, sacrifice, or rituals of initiation. No one knows for sure what could possibly inspire such awe and devotion that no one ever betrayed the secrets. Whatever the truth, today is perfect to begin creating your own set of Eleusian mysteries. Three important aspects of a holistic life are connection to divinity, knowledge of the self, and positive action to improve everything around you. Give yourself quiet time. Meditate with your journal. Write about your connection to divinity. Write about yourself honestly, taking care to balance the positive and the negative. And write about how you can make your corner of the world the best it can be. Take time for the next nine days to write about these three topics every day, even if only for a few moments. Then, begin developing rituals to fulfill the three aspects. By this time next year, you will have the foundation for your own mysteries. Take the time to perform them every year, as these are your personal mysteries. You don't ever have to reveal them to another person. After several years of practice, you may choose to teach them to your descendants. Or you can keep them secret forever. It is up to you.

Cerridwen Iris Shea

Notes:

September 20
Monday

 1st ♐

Color of the day: Ivory
Incense of the day: Peony

Family Concerns Spell

Monday concerns the home and family. Take care of yours today by checking the doors and windows. Light a candle, and pass it over every opening. Imagine your house sheathed in a cocoon of light that blocks out all harm. If the candle flame flickers a lot, it can indicate a drafty window or door that needs repair, but if the flame flickers and you don't feel any air movement, the "draft" is in your house wards instead of the boards. Sprinkle a pinch of salt across the sill, and strengthen your visualization of a protective barrier. Then say:

Love and kin,
Safe within.

harm and doubt,
Stay without.

Elizabeth Barrette

Notes:

May my every action be
made in honor and
respect.

Pour the water out onto the earth at
a special spot in your yard, in your
plants, or at your front and back doors.

Kristin Madden

Notes:

September 21
Tuesday

1st ♐
2nd Quarter 11:54 am
☽ v/c 12:19 pm
☽ → ♑ 1:35 pm

Color of the day: Black
Incense of the day: Pine

Water-Pouring Ritual

It is believed that this was a day of water-pouring rituals in the Eleusinian mysteries of ancient Greece. Ask for the blessings of water as you take your morning shower or bath. See the water become vibrant energy as it cleanses your body and energy field. Before going out for the day, crumble some tobacco into a bowl of water. Offer this sacred herb in thanks for all you have received, and ask the blessings of the tobacco spirit and the elements to guide and protect you in your steps. Then say:

September 22
Wednesday

Mabon – Fall Equinox

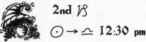

2nd ♑
☉ → ♎ 12:30 pm

Color of the day: Yellow
Incense of the day: Coriander

Fall Equinox Spell

Once again the Sun's path crosses the celestial equator, and the day and the night are now again of equal length. On the Gregorian calendar this is the first day of autumn, but on the modern Celtic calendar it is midautumn. This holiday is more commonly known by its Welsh name Mabon. Mabon means "divine youth." It is the name of a mythic hunter hero whose story is told at this time of year. At the beginning of time, Mabon was born to the mother goddess Modron. That we only know his mother and not his father attests to the matriarchal lineage of the early Celts. The equinox marks the time when Mabon was three nights old and stolen from his crib. For the next three months, the heroes Cai and Bedwyr will search for him and ask all manner of birds and beasts for help. But, according to legend, it is only the salmon who can give them direction. On Yule, the heroes retrieve the divine child by freeing him from a prison in Gloucester. Like Apollo, Mabon is a hunter with a bow and a musician with a harp. He is a Sun god. Mabon represents the Sun that is waning in strength during this quarter of the year and that will begin to return only after the solstice. The waning of the light is frightening and depressing, and it is necessary for our own sake to use magic at this time to help in the quest for Mabon. The strongest act of magic that one can do at this time is to participate in the celebrations of the yearly cycle. As one integrates the yearly cycle deep into one's unconscious, serenity and confidence are gained. This is the peace that comes from knowing and accepting that the light will return when it is time.

Robert Place

Notes:

September 23
Thursday

 2nd ♑
)) v/c 3:41 pm
)) → ♒ 4:10 pm

Color of the day: Purple
Incense of the day: Dill

Paint Brush Blessing

Take your new paint brushes and some rosemary oil. Anoint each brush's handle while dedicating it to beauty, clarity, inspiration, or any of other muses you are drawn to. Then dip the brush quickly into some clear water, again dedicating it to the muse of your choice. Dry the brushes with a soft, linen cloth, knowing that as you take care of your brushes they are inspired to express the muse you have called into them.

Therese Francis

Notes:

I deserve to be happy,
I give and receive love.
Your cycles flow through
me.
We are one.

Repeat the words until you know
they are true.

Ember

Notes:

September 24
Friday

2nd ≈

Color of the day: White
Incense of the day: Cedar

Invoking Venus Spell

The Sun enters Libra this time of year—a time of love, beauty, and harmony. To strengthen these aspects of your life, invoke the goddess Venus. Prepare a sacred space. Stand and raise your arms over your head as you gaze toward the sky. See Venus in your mind, imagine how she appears to you. Picture her face. Her hands are reaching down toward yours. Feel her presence, and chant:

Venus,
I invoke your power.
Your spirit grants me
love and beauty.

Bring peace and harmony
into my life.

September 25
Saturday
Yom Kippur

2nd ≈
☽ v/c 2:25 am
☽ → ♓ 6:55 pm

Color of the day: Blue
Incense of the day: Cedar

Penitence Spell

Yom Kippur is the last day of the ten-day period that began on Rosh Hashanah. It is also called the Day of Atonement, and is the most solemn and sacred festival of the Jewish calendar. During this period, one is asked to contemplate one's sins and seek reconciliation with God.

We forgive our friends for any transgressions now. By forgiving others, we are forgiven by others and by God. It is through our relationship with each other that we establish our relationship with God. The kindness we show to each other is kindness to God. As in all religions, compassion is the virtue that leads away from egotism and toward spiritual development. The Yom Kippur service begins on the evening before, and after a nighttime break is resumed at sunrise and continues to sundown. During this entire period Jews are asked to fast and pray. To fast one must abstain from all food, drink, and sexual activity. This is an ancient shamanic practice that allows one to diminish the physical world and experience the world of the spirit. These things are avoided not because they are evil, but simply because they must be diminished for our consciousness to shift focus to the spirit within.

Robert Place

Notes:

September 26
Sunday

2nd ♓

Color of the day: Gold
Incense of the day: Cinnamon

health and Longevity Invocation

Make a clean sweep of your living space today. Open windows and hang out rugs and blankets. Lay pillows in the sunshine—this is Mother Nature's disinfectant. Gather fresh air and sunny energy into your space. Burn rosemary sprigs for protection and longevity, and allow the smoke to cleanse the stagnant atmosphere. Stock your pantry with fresh herbs and spices. Plan for a time of study. Find some new books to spark your interest for the longer evenings ahead. Most importantly, go outdoors during the last golden rays of the Sun. Take a slow walk through falling leaves, and savor autumn's clean, crisp air. For a seasonal tonic, brew ginger tea with fresh ginger slices and honey, and say: "Blessed be my health."

Karri Ann Allrich

Notes:

September 27
Monday

2nd ♓

☽ v/c 9:12 pm

☽ → ♈ 10:57 pm

Color of the day: Gray
Incense of the day: Lavender

An Autumn Planting Meditation

Spring flowering bulbs, which are planted in the Fall, hold the secrets of life, death, and reincarnation. As you plan your Spring garden, reading this meditation aloud will put you in the proper frame of mind:

When leaves of russet
begin to fly,
And wild geese sing
their mournful cry,
When the grasses are
bleached white as bone,
And the Earth is barren
as a stone,
When a lone zinnia raises
its head,
Kneel down before this
flower bed
And plant bulbs which
bloom in the Spring.

Good fortune this will
bring,
As will these holy words:
Eternal cycle of birth,
death, and rebirth,
I return these bulbs to
Mother Earth.

Now, when the dark season obscures the Sun, You will be glad for what you have done.

James Kambos

Notes:

September 28
Tuesday

2nd ♈

Full Moon 9:09 am

Color of the day: Maroon
Incense of the day: Juniper

Balance of Light and Shadow Spell

One of the main concepts in witchcraft is that of the duality of the universe. Nothing is purely good or purely bad. All aspects reflect the duality of nature. People bear these aspects of duality. We have the "light" traits (kindness, intellect, generosity) that we readily acknowledge and present to others. We also have our "dark" side as well. These are the traits (such as jealousy, anger, and greed) that we hold from public view and many times neglect to acknowledge. Again, nothing is purely good or bad. With that in mind, we can think of our dark traits as a power that balances our lives and promote positive change. Jealousy can be a motivator to strive for better. Anger can be the motivator to change or prevent bad situations. Light a black and a white candle, and say:

> Goddess of darkness,
> Goddess of light,
> Balance of duality I
> accept as my right.

Focus on your traits, both in the light and dark realms. Focus on the positive messages that both have for you.

Karen Follett

Notes:

Michaelmas customs are entwined with old harvest customs, so a feast is definitely called for on this day. Goose is the traditional entree. A fruity white called "Saint Michael's Love" is served today. Carrots are also considered lucky both to eat or to make into charms. To make them into a charm, wrap three carrots in a bunch with red thread. If you find forked carrots, they are especially lucky. Say:

> Cleft, fruitful, fruitful,
> fruitful,
> Joy of carrots pass upon
> me.
> Michael the brave
> endowing me,
> Bride the fair aiding me.

Lily Gardner

Notes:

September 29
Wednesday

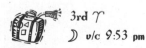 3rd ♈
☽ v/c 9:53 pm

Color of the day: Brown
Incense of the day: Sandalwood

Blessings for Good Health and Fortune through the Winter

September 29th is Michaelmas Day honoring the archangel Michael.

September 30
Thursday

 3rd ♈
☽ → ♉ 5:24 am

Color of the day: White
Incense of the day: Carnation

Lakshmi Prosperity Ritual

A prosperity ritual honoring the Hindu goddess Lakshmi is an appropriate seasonal ritual. To do this, obtain an image of her—this may include pictures, statues, or jewelry—and place it on your altar with red candles, red flowers, and coins. Offer her some prosperity or other Indian incense. Listen to the recording "Lady of Prosperity" by Joni Abbatecola or any other Hindu devotional recording. Close your eyes, and visualize yourself floating on the river in a boat made of a giant red lotus. Lakshmi is with you. She wears a red-beaded sari edged in gold. Where will she take you? What gift will you give her, and what wisdom will she impart to you? Let your imagination flow, listen to her words, and bask in her abundance.

Denise Dumars

Notes:

Notes:

October

October is the tenth month of the year, its name derived from the Latin word *octo*, meaning "eight," as it was the eighth month of the Roman calendar. Its astrological sign is Libra, the scales (Sept 21–Oct 20), a cardinal air sign ruled by Venus. Colors are everywhere now, as trees burst into masses of red, orange, and yellow leaves. Our bodies begin to change in metabolism at this time of year, and our consciousness shifts from an active mental state to a more psychically receptive state appropriate to the dark half of the year. The biggest celebration of October, and one of the most magical nights of the year, is Samhain (or Halloween, which is used interchangeably today). It is a time to decorate with signs symbolizing the outward manifestation of inward changes. Gourds and pumpkins decorate the porch or stoop; bundles of dried cornstalks sit by the front steps. As the day nears, the pumpkins change to jack-o'-lanterns that stare from the windows. Blood is common in Halloween costumes, and the Full Moon of October is known as the Blood Moon. Samhain is a celebration of death and is marked by several traditions—such as the Dumb Supper, in which dinner is served with places set for the dead; and the Samhain Circle, in which the living attempt to contact the dead to gain spiritual knowledge.

October 1
Friday
The Godless Month

3rd ☿

Color of the day: Pink
Incense of the day: Ylang-ylang

Reconciliation Chili Spell

Ease hurt feelings and soothe loved ones with some simple kitchen witchery—namely, this quick and easy reconciliation chili. Serve with cornbread spiced with cinnamon.

- 2 tablespoons olive oil
- 1 yellow onion, peeled and diced
- 4 garlic cloves, minced
- 1 pound ground beef or turkey
- 1 one-pound can each: black, white, and kidney beans, drained, rinsed
- 1 28-ounce can crushed tomatoes
- 1 teaspoon chopped rosemary leaves
- Pinches of: clove, nutmeg, cayenne pepper, chili powder
- Salt, to taste

Heat the oil in a soup pot, and saute onion and garlic in the oil for seven minutes. Add the meat, and brown well. Add the beans, tomatoes, and seasonings. Stir with intention for reconciliation. Cover and simmer on low heat for 45 minutes. Serve with love.

Karri Ann Allrich

Notes:

Holiday lore: According to Shinto belief, during the month of October the gods gather to hold their annual convention. All of the *kami* converge on the great temple of Isumo in western Honshu, and there they relax, compare notes on crucial god business, and make decisions about humankind. At the end of this month, all over Japan, people make visits to their local Shinto shrines to welcome the regular resident gods back home. But until then, all through the month, the gods are missing—as a Japanese poet once wrote:

The god is absent;
the dead leaves are piling up,
and all is deserted.

October 2
Saturday

 3rd ♉
☽ v/c 12:34 pm
☽ → ♊ 2:55 pm

Color of the day: Indigo
Incense of the day: Patchouli

World Peace Spell

In honor of the birth of Mahatma Mohandas Gandhi, born on this date in 1869, place a globe or picture of the Earth in the center of a table. Sprinkle some vervain around the globe. Light three candles. A green candle is lit for the Earth. Focus your intentions. Express the hope that all beings on this planet know healing. A pink candle is lit for love. Express the hope that all beings on this planet love and feel loved. A blue candle is lit for enlightenment. May all beings on this planet radiate peace and harmony. Meditate on the globe or picture. See love permeate all things and heal all wounds. Visualize a world that is peaceful and celebrates harmonious diversity.

Kristin Madden

Notes:

October 3
Sunday

3rd ♊
Color of the day: Orange
Incense of the day: Sage

Revitalize Auric Shield Spell

This ritual may be performed to purify and strengthen your auric shield. Outline a pentagram on the floor with chalk or salt. Make the pentagram large enough to accomodate you sitting in the middle on a stool. Gather five mirrors, and place each at the five points of the pentagram. Put a tea light candle on top of each mirror. Light sage incense, and place a bowl of water infused with rosemary along with a sprig of the herb in the center of the pentagram. Sit on the stool, pray to your personal deities, and begin to meditate. Listen to the rhythms of the universe, and clear your mind of all thoughts. Slow down your breathing, and gently keep your mind from wandering to any place other than here. Once you have passed some time in this manner, thank the deities, then take the rosemary sprig and pass it around your body three times. Dip the sprig in the infusion, and sprinkle the water from your head to your feet. When you have finished this ritual, pause to thank your divinities for your renewed strength.

Extinguish the candles, and remove traces of the pentagram.

S. Y. Zenith

Notes:

Lord, make me an instrument of your peace.
Where there is hatred,
let me sow love;
where there is injury,
pardon;
where there is doubt,
faith;
where there is despair,
hope;
where there is darkness,
light;
and where there is
sadness, joy.

Magenta Griffith

Notes:

October 4
Monday

3rd ♊
☽ v/c 6:28 am

Color of the day: Silver
Incense of the day: Maple

Man of Peace Spell

In the Roman Catholic tradition, this is the feast day of St. Francis of Assisi, the most nature-oriented of all the saints. The patron saint of animals, he is often pictured surrounded by various birds and beasts. He was said to have preached a sermon to birds. In the prayers he speaks of Brother Sun, Sister Moon, and Mother Earth. He is best known for these words:

October 5
Tuesday

3rd ♊
☽ → ♋ 2:54 am

Color of the day: Black
Incense of the day: Honeysuckle

Festival of the Old Woman Spell

Lithuanians celebrate October 5 as the Festival of the Old Woman. They make an old woman doll out of the last sheaves of grain from the harvest. The doll is kept safe through the winter so as to keep the spirit of the grain alive until replanting in the spring. What spirit do you need to sustain through the winter? Make a doll from bits of your garden, driftwood from the beach where you spend your summer, or maybe a cord from your sail. Decorate it with ribbons and flowers, and store it safely through the winter.

Lily Gardner

Notes:

Grape Harvest Spell

The harvest begun at Lammas continues through Samhain. Today is a day to celebrate the grape harvest. You don't need to get drunk and turn into a Manaed to celebrate this harvest. Red wine often substitutes for blood in ritual, and blood equals life. Perform libations today with red wine, giving thanks for your life. Look back on your year, and give thanks for all the progress you've made, for where you are on your journey, and for what comes ahead. You can perform libations in your yard, or, if you don't have a yard, use a special pot of earth kept for ritual work. Treat yourself to a bottle of wine you've never tried. If you don't drink alcohol, substitute grape juice or an actual bunch of grapes. Dance, sing, and go out for a luxurious dinner with friends. Let today be about thanks and joy. Let that joy carry you into your future.

Cerridwen Iris Shea

Notes:

October 6
Wednesday
Yom Kippur

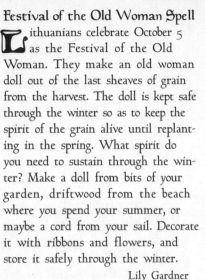

3rd ♋
4th Quarter 6:12 am

Color of the day: Yellow
Incense of the day: Eucalyptus

October 7
Thursday

 4th ♋

♌ v/c 8:13 am

♌ → ♌ 3:23 pm

Color of the day: Turquoise
Incense of the day: Geranium

Ritual to Refresh

Thursday is the day of jovial, generous Jupiter. The traditional color today is purple, and the elements are air and fire. So, wear purple, ring bells, light fires (both literal and figurative, as long as you are not harming anyone or anything), and do something jolly and completely out of the ordinary today. Find a recording of *The Planets* by Gustav Holst, and in particular listen to the "Jupiter" movement. The Moon is waning, so this is also a good time to refresh yourself and to rid your life of unwanted clutter and bad habits. That is, you should take the time to make room for success and good fortune. Begin by listing what you wish to be rid of. List things such as careless spending, harmful habits, ungrateful friends, or overwhelming debt. Purple has long been associated with royalty and magic, so use purple ink or purple paper in writing down your list. Cut each item into a strip. Burn each one in a safe container.

Ember

Notes:

October 8
Friday

 4th ♌

Color of the day: Coral
Incense of the day: Almond

Bring Your True Love to You Spell

Crush a handful of pomegranate seeds, and steep them in hot water for three minutes. Strain out the berries. Allow the tea to cool to a drinkable temperature. Drink this in front of a fire in three swallows while concentrating on the traits of the person you want in your life.

Therese Francis

Notes:

October 9
Saturday

 4th ♌
　　☽ v/c 6:42 am

Color of the day: Blue
Incense of the day: Lilac

Worth the Wait Spell

Think about the future today,
That is, make some plans that
take a long time to fulfill. After all,
autumn is the time for planting
spring bulbs like crocus, tulips, and
daffodils. You do a lot of work and
you don't see the results for months,
but it's certainly worth the wait.
These bulbs flower when you most
need the burst of color, and so will
your plants flower just when you
most need them to. As you dig into
the chilly October earth, recite this
prayer:

> I work today—
> not for tomorrow,
> but for a time to come.

> I work for hope—
> and not for sorrow,
> though every year brings
> some.

> Lady of the Earth,
> accept these hours—
> the best I have to give.

> Lord of the Sun,
> turn them to flowers—

in spring when all
dreams live.

Elizabeth Barrette

Notes:

October 10
Sunday

 4th ♌
　　☽ → ♍ 2:00 am

Color of the day: Gold
Incense of the day: Clove

Stone Magic Spell

During this earthy Virgo Moon,
try creating a magical connection
to a stone or rock that you have in
your home. First cleanse yourself by
bathing and putting on fresh clothes.
Then take your special stone to
your altar, and admire its beauty
and power. Remember where you
were bought or found it. Then smudge
the stone with cedar or sage smoke.
While smudging, give thanks for
having the stone in your life, then
hold it in your hand and feel its

powers. Some stones may be heating and stimulating, others may be grounding and centering. Honor your stone's powers, and say:

> Precious stone, I give thanks for your healing power. Please help to strengthen and nourish me and all others in this home.

Then place the stone in a special place on your altar or in your home. Use the stone in rituals and ceremonies.

Jonathan Keyes

Notes:

go of any lingering encumbrances. As Luna's energy wanes, perform an egg spell to draw the negative out of your life. This spell is especially appropriate for relationship or self-esteem issues. After dark, gather a black candle, an egg, a magic marker, and clove of garlic. Light the candle, and visualize a circle of safety surrounding you. Hold the egg in your dominant hand, and focus on what you need to get rid of. Holding the marker in your non-dominant hand, write upon the egg the words or symbols that convey your intention. Infuse the egg with your projection. Bury the egg beneath a thorn bush along with a garlic clove.

Karri Ann Allrich

Notes:

October 11
Monday
Columbus Day (observed)

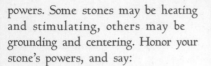 4th ♏

Color of the day: Ivory
Incense of the day: Chrysanthemum

Waning Moon Spell

Before the New Moon, it is wise to finish up old business and let

October 12
Tuesday

 4th ♏

☽ v/c 3:32 am
☽ → ♎ 9:32 am

Color of the day: Red
Incense of the day: Evergreen

Three Goddesses Devotion

Around this time of year is celebrated Navrati, the nine-day festival of the Hindu goddesses. You should plan to celebrate Durga the warrior goddess for the first three days, then Lakshmi the prosperity goddess, and finally Sarisvati, the goddess of knowledge and creative arts. Chant each goddess's name. Bow to each in turn, and wear lotus oil and burn incense and pink, red, or lavender candles. These goddesses may be approached to ask for peace, abundance, protection, success, and creativity. Each one may be addressed with the greeting: "Jai Ma." As a devotion, give up meat, alcohol, and tobacco for the nine days of Navrati.

Denise Dumars

Notes:

October 13
Wednesday

 4th ♎
New Moon 10:48 pm

Color of the day: Brown
Incense of the day: Cedar

Radiating Your Beauty Spell

Within the face of every person lies the beauty of divine creation. This is not the mask that is defined as beauty by the cosmetic companies and beauty magazines. This is the beauty that exists in all the layers of our being. Occasionally we just need to be reminded of this beauty so we can allow its radiance to surface from our souls and shine for the world to see. Sit before a mirror so you can see your entire face in the reflection. Light a pink candle between you and the mirror. Gaze into your own eyes. Focus on your beauty. Focus on your physical, mental, emotional, and spiritual attributes. Visualize a beautiful radiant energy swirling around you. Allow this energy into your soul. Allow the energy to begin to surface from your soul and go into your aura. Visualize your own inner beauty becoming evident to all. State these words:

> I am birthed from the
> Goddess,
> beautiful and divine.
>
> Let the beauty of my soul
> radiate and shine.

Visualize this flow surrounding and blending with your aura. Ground any excess energy. Allow yourself to meditate on the traits of beauty that you possess. Never let yourself forget the truth of the maxim: "Beauty is more than skin deep."

Karen Follett

Notes:

I seek, I ask,
I make my plan.
I draw good fortune
wherever I am.

On a piece of paper, write down your wish. Read the note before placing it inside an envelope, but don't seal it. Extinguish the fire. For the next seven days, light the candle and read the note. Imagine ways to achieve your wish. Each day, remove a penny until they are gone. Leave your note under the candle for one week. If you do not get your wish shortly, repeat the spell until you are well on your way to getting what you want. This spell works best when the Moon is in Scorpio.

Susan Sheppard

Notes:

October 14
Thursday

 1st ♎

☽ v/c 10:22 am

☽ → ♏ 2:10 pm

Color of the day: Purple
Incense of the day: Musk

The Good Luck You Need Spell

For good luck, find seven new pennies and a dark-red candle. Arrange the pennies in a circle on your altar area. You can also use a place where you keep sacred objects or special things. Put the candle in the center. Light it and say:

By flame, by star,
by dark of night,
I draw good luck
when the time is right.

October 15
Friday

Ramadan begins

 1st ♏

Color of the day: Rose
Incense of the day: Nutmeg

Ramadan Ritual

This is the first day of the most sacred period of the Islamic religion. It is the first day of the holy month of fasting and atonement patterned after the Jewish Yom Kippur. The need to observe this month is one of the Five Pillars of Islam. For this month, one is asked to abstain from all food, drink, and sexual activity on each day from sunup till sundown. In the evening there is a meal with family and friends, and one is encouraged to strengthen the bonds of friendship. During this month, Mohammed received his revelation. While walking in the wilderness near Mecca, the angel Gabriel came to him and showed him a book. Mohammed could not read. So, Gabriel read the book to him and helped him memorize it over the next ten days. This book was the Koran. During this month it is said that God determines the fate of the world for the next year. Although the Islamic New Year was already celebrated in February, this holiday fits the pattern of a new year's celebration. To understand this more fully, reread the spell on January 1. In the time between years there is always the threat that chaos will take over. Magic rituals are needed therefore to protect one from chaos and to reinstate order. The Chinese perceive the threat as coming from without and use fireworks for protection. In the Jewish and Islamic tradition, the threat is perceived as coming from within, and introspection is stressed.

Robert Place

Notes:

October 16
Saturday

 1st ♏

☽ v/c 11:43 am

☽ → ♐ 4:58 pm

Color of the day: Black
Incense of the day: Juniper

Past Life Mirror Visualization

In a darkened chamber, light a virgin white candle. Place the candle so your reflection is illuminated in the magic mirror. Gaze at the mirror as you say:

> Mirror, mirror,
> who was I?
> Was I royalty,
> or a simple field hand?

Was I an artist with
easel and paint?
Was I a farmer
working the land?

Mirror, mirror,
black as coal,
let me see the face I
should know.

As you look into this magic glass,
your own image will begin to form.
When you detect a mist or haze of
any sort, keep your vigil. Do not avert
your gaze. As the glass begins to
clear, your face will appear. Be calm,
and push aside all feelings of dread.
You and your former self will now
be eternally bound. Gaze for no more
than fifteen minutes initially, even
if no visions appear. To stop, simply
look away and snuff out the candle.
Give thanks. Keep a journal and
record anything you may have seen.
Pay attention to your dreams as well.

James Kambos

Notes:

October 17
Sunday

1st ♐

Color of the day: Yellow
Incense of the day: Basil

Winter Divination Lore

Folklore tells us that it will
be a long and hard winter if:
woolly caterpillars are more black
than brown; squirrels gather and bury
their nuts early; trees produce an
abundance of nuts; the leaves fall late;
apple skins are tough; cornhusks are
thick; onion skins are thick; birds
migrate early; fruit trees bloom in
the fall; or the breastbone of a fresh-
cooked turkey is dark purple. Begin
your own preparations for winter
by cleaning out closets and packing
away warm-weather clothing. Sit in
meditation, and decide what aspects
of self you are ready to handle this
winter. Ask for the guidance and
the protection of your gods as you
begin to explore your shadow side.

Kristin Madden

Notes:

October 18
Monday

1st ♐
☽ v/c 11:46 am
☽ → ♑ 7:07 pm

Color of the day: Gray
Incense of the day: Frankincense

Ritual for a Fuller head of hair

At sunrise during a waxing Moon, wash your hair and then rinse it with rosemary (if you have dark hair) or chamomile (if you have red or blond hair). Make a hair rinse by steeping the herb in hot water for five to ten minutes, then straining and cooling the infusion. Get your hair cut before sunset.

Therese Francis

Notes:

Sacred Sexuality Blessing

To Pagans, sexuality is a sacred part of life. To honor this part of life, honor your body and your partner's by blessing each other with the magical oil of your choice, and by placing birth control and prophylactic items on the altar before their use. Pass these too through incense smoke to charge them with power. Ask the gods to honor you as you practice responsible sex. All sex that is performed "in perfect love and perfect trust" is sacred. For remember, as it says in the Charge of the Goddess: "All acts of love and pleasure are my rituals."

Denise Dumars

Notes:

October 19
Tuesday

1st ♑

Color of the day: Maroon
Incense of the day: Sage

October 20
Wednesday

1st ♑
2nd Quarter 5:59 pm
☽ v/c 5:59 pm
☽ → ♒ 9:38 pm

Color of the day: White
Incense of the day: Maple

Page 205

Angel-of-Dreams Assistance Spell

Are you, or is someone you care about, planning to fly soon? Take advantage of today's energy to make a safe-travel spell. Wednesday is ruled by Mercury, the planet and god of travel. Cut out a bookmark-sized piece of heavy paper, and write on it:

> Mercury of the silver wings,
> messenger of divine words,
> open the sky, part the clouds,
> and keep me safe from all fell things.

Then cover the words with a mini-collage using pictures of birds, clouds, wings, feathers, airplanes, chariots, and so on. Use this as the bookmark in your in-flight reading material.

Elizabeth Barrette

Notes:

October 21
Thursday

2nd ≈

Color of the day: Green
Incense of the day: Jasmine

Pumpkin Carving Ritual

Samhain is only ten days away, and so it is time to start decorating. I love decorating for this day. You would, if you visited, find bats, Witches, skeletons, scarecrows, and ghosts peeking out of every pot, pan, bowl, closet, drawer, and bookshelf in the house. One of my favorite traditions at this time of year is to carve pumpkins. Sometimes I carve one large pumpkin. But more often, I will carve three smaller pumpkins, each with a different expression. Plenty of Halloween books, magazines, and articles offer ideas for carving methods and creative designs. I like to turn my carving into a ritual. I gather all my carving tools, my pumpkins, and my ritual tools. I cast a circle and ask angels of creativity for inspiration. Sometimes, I have designs worked out on paper ahead of time. Most often, I take the advice of sculptors: They let what is inside the stone or clay come out. In other words, I let the spirit of the pumpkin express itself. It's not easy, as words are more natural to me than artwork. But it is always rewarding. The innards become pumpkin pies or pumpkin cookies. Some of the seeds are toasted, and some of the seeds are given as offerings to the spirit of pumpkin and to the angels. Every year's pumpkins are different, because the spirit of each pumpkin is unique. Each pumpkin is a living being. The merry expressions lit by candlelight fill my home with joy and blessings.

Cerridwen Iris Shea

Notes:

Two in one,
bound yet free,
let our spirits
joined be!

Cook the vegetable, and feed it to each other, if you wish. Or you can make it part of your household altar or shrine for a while, then bury it your backyard, or someplace special to both of you.

Magenta Griffith

Notes:

October 22
Friday

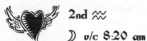 2nd ≈

☽ v/c 8:20 am

☉ → ♏ 9:49 pm

Color of the day: Purple
Incense of the day: Ginger

Double Vegetable Love Spell

This requires a double vegetable—such as two mushrooms growing together, or two carrots, or two potatoes. It's just a matter of luck, and waiting, until you find this at the grocery store. Once you have found a double vegetable, cast the following love spell. You and your partner should hold one part of the double vegetable and recite:

October 23
Saturday
Swallows depart

 2nd ≈

☽ → ♓ 1:13 am

Color of the day: Brown
Incense of the day: Pine

Ritual to Release Anger

Obtain a black stone, a handful of flowers, and some big sturdy leaves from a plant. Take them to your room and close the door. Hold the stone with both hands. Take several deep breaths and release feelings of frustration, resentment, jealousy, anger, and hatred into the stone. Cry, rant, rave, and feel the stone absorbing these energies. When you feel better and regain composure, use some glue to make a platter with the leaves. Arrange the flowers on the leaf-platter, and place the black stone in the middle. Take the platter to a stream, river, or to the sea, and set it afloat. Say a few words of thanks to the gods of the water. Begin your homeward journey, and do not look back.

S. Y. Zenith

Notes:

ore for an October day: Maples are among the most stunning trees in nature, often very brightly orange and red. In October, trees are in their full glory and natural beauty (as the green of chlorophyll fades from tree leaves, only the natural color of the leaves remains).

Cadmium-colored sumac gathers on roadsides and riverbanks, and provides contrast to the still-green grass and clear blue skies. The first fires have now been kindled inside to fight the coming chill at night, and days suddenly seem very short. Quilts have been pulled from cupboards to warm cold beds; our bodies begin to change in metabolism at this time of year, and our consciousness shifts from an actively mental state to a psychically receptive state appropriate to the dark half of the year. This is the time of the apple harvest; and apples fill fruit bowls or are stored in the root cellar. The house is scented with applesauce laced with cinnamon. Apples have always been magically important—playing a key role in the "wassailing" ceremonies meant to ensure a bountiful harvest in the coming year. Wassail was traditionally made with hard cider heated with spices and fruit—and a ritual imbibing of this drink was likely performed at Halloween and Samhain, and at Yule. Candy apples are a modern treat celebrating the magic of the apple harvest—these treats are eaten often at Halloween even today. Bobbing for apples, too, has a long tradition as a celebratory ritual. Apples have ancient associations with healing (thus the phrase "An apple a day . . ."), and were said to be useful for curing warts. This may be because the interior of an apple, if sliced horizontally, reveals a five-pointed star. The final harvest of the year is the hazelnut harvest; these nuts are gathered in wickerwork baskets to cure until they can be stored properly. The hazel tree was long sacred, and is symbolic of wisdom, secret knowledge, and divination. Forked hazel rods are useful for dowsing for sources of water or underground minerals, and hazel is a traditional wood for magical wands.

October 24
Sunday
United Nations Day

2nd ♓

Color of the day: Amber
Incense of the day: Coriander

Channel the Sun's healing Energy Spell

If you need healing for an ailment of your own, or know someone else who needs healing energy, this can help both of you simultaneously. Start by facing east. Greet the Sun at sunrise, if possible. Raise your arms as though embracing the light. Feel it entering your fingertips and coursing through your arms, torso, legs, and your entire body. Mentally direct the energy to those places within you that you feel need healing. When you are filled, point your arms in the direction of someone in need, no matter how far away

they are. Picture his or her face in your mind and imagine that same light, with its healing blessings, flowing to your friend until he or she is filled with healing energy. Visualize your friend glowing with health.

Ember

Notes:

October 25
Monday

2nd ♓
☽ v/c 1.17 am
☽ → ♈ 6:24 am

Color of the day: Lavender
Incense of the day: Myrrh

Magical Apple Doll Spell

In Appalachia there is a charming folk art custom of making apple dolls. These dolls lend themselves to many magical uses. A few nights before an autumn Full Moon, peel a red apple, then carve a face into it. As you do this concentrate on your magical intent. It may be used as a protective house talisman, or as a love charm. Hang the apple by a wire to dry for about three weeks, and don't disturb it or the enchantment will be lost. The face will take on its own characteristics as it dries. Use as a poppet, or attach the apple to a stick and dress it with scraps of cloth to create a folk doll. Keep the doll to protect your home, or release the spell at Yule by burning the doll in a holiday fire.

James Kambos

Notes:

successful. Whatever your aim is, spend some time today thinking about why you are doing it and what the outcome will be. Then find a special red stone such as garnet, ruby, or carnelian that you can wear as a necklace or put in your pocket for the next few weeks. At night, light a red candle and briefly warm the stone over the flame. Visualize your project and your intentions, and state them out loud. Then ask for permission from the rock to store your intentions and to remind you of the path you have chosen.

Jonathan Keyes

Notes:

October 26
Tuesday

2nd ♈

Color of the day: White
Incense of the day: Musk

Intending Path Spell

With the Moon waxing in Aries, now is a good time to set your intention to start any new projects or tasks. Good intentions are the foundation for helping a project to be

October 27
Wednesday

2nd ♈
☽ v/c 8:24 am
☽ → ♉ 1:37 pm
Full Moon 11:07 pm

Color of the day: Topaz
Incense of the day: Neroli

Craft Ancestors Devotion

The precarious freedom that we have to practice our spirituality has been earned by the sweat and the blood of those who have walked this path before us. At this time of the year, we generally honor the ancestors of our blood. This working will focus on honoring the ancestors of our soul—those who blazed the path of witchcraft. Select an object that represents your connection to the elders of the craft. Light both a red and a black candle, and say:

> Across the veil, your
> torch burns bright,
> goddesses shining
> through darkest night.
> honored ancestors of my
> soul and heart,
> tell me the wisdom of
> your art.
> In privilege, I walk the
> path you made.
> As you pass the torch,
> I tend its flame.

Meditate on the lives of those who have gone before. Honor the object that represents your craft ancestor.

Karen Follett

Notes:

October 28
Thursday

3rd ♉

Color of the day: Crimson
Incense of the day: Carnation

Love Divination

For centuries, seekers of love have invoked the apostles Simon and Jude on October 28. This spell requires a red candle anointed with the herb mimosa, a knife, and a perfect red apple. Center and light the candle. Carefully peel the apple so the peel comes off in one strip. Turn deosil three times with the peel in your right hand, and say:

> St. Simon and St. Jude,
> I must intrude.
> Without delay,
> tell me today
> the first letter of my
> true love's name.

Drop the peel over your left shoulder, and it will form the initial of your future spouse's last name.

Lily Gardner

Notes:

October 29
Friday
Lost–in–the–Dark Bells

 3rd ♉
)) v/c 5:50 pm

)) → ♊ 11:11 pm

Color of the day: Pink
Incense of the day: Parsley

Love in "Vein" Spell

On this countdown to Halloween Friday, give yourself an evening of vampire romance. If staying at home tonight, rent a Dracula movie starring a sexy actor, buy a bottle of vampire wine from Romania, or curl up with a good vampire novel or erotic horror story. Write romantic poems to your favorite vampire in scented red ink, and dine by candlelight. If going out, dress accordingly, and go to a goth nightclub or Halloween party. Be a vamp. Be as sexy or as scary as you wanna be. For the really adventurous, take a stroll through a cemetery at night with your favorite werewolf.

Denise Dumars

Notes:

Holiday lore: Many villages in the English countryside share the tradition of "lost-in-the-dark bells." Legend tells of a person lost in the dark or fog, and heading for disaster, who at the last moment was guided to safety by the sound of church bells. The lucky and grateful survivor always leaves money in his or her will for the preservation of the bells. This day commemorates one particular such case, a man named Pecket in the village of Kidderminster, in Worcestershire, who was saved from plummeting over a ravine by the bells of the local church of St. Mary's. In honor of this event, the bells still ring every October 29.

October 30
Saturday

 3rd ♊
Color of the day: Gray
Incense of the day: Lavender

Eve of Samhain Spell to Connect with the Spirit World

Get a white candle, matches, and a mirror for this spell. At dusk, go to a haunted area or a place you feel the spirits are especially powerful. Make contact by walking about and allowing your mind to roam. Light your white candle, and stare into it saying:

Clear as midnight,
the spirits are bright.
Ghostly curiosity
brings you to me.

As a form takes shape,
I am not asleep.
Spirit awake,
take your shape.

Let the candle flicker. Glance into the mirror, and look past your shoulder. Do you see mists or lighted balls in the reflection? This is how ghosts typically appear. Return to the area on the next three nights. Take some pictures. At home, place your mirror facedown. Mirrors trap spirits. Some spirits will track you as you search for their reflections. If you want your ghost to leave, just say so. Follow this up by putting a broom over your transom and burning sage.

Susan Sheppard

Notes:

October 31
Sunday
halloween – Samhain – Daylight Saving Time ends 2 am

 3rd ♊
☽ v/c 8:21 pm

Color of the day: Gold
Incense of the day: Poplar

Druid Reading for Samhain

The celebrations on the eve of All Souls Day, called Halloween, stem from the Celtic New Year celebration called Samhain. When the Sun goes down on this eve, there is a time between the old year and the creation of the new. Specifically, this occurs at sunrise. In this twilight of the years, the veil between this world and the world of the spirit is thin. It is a time when ghosts and spirits can interact with the living, and a time when divination is most effective. This is a sacred time when all warriors were to keep their swords sheathed. Samhain literally means "end of the summer." This day marked the last harvest of the summer, and so it is a harvest celebration. But, because there were only three months in the ancient Celtic calendar, and no autumn, it is also the beginning of the winter death that will lead to next year's regeneration. On this night, the lord of death reigns, and the Celts protect themselves from this threat with bonfires and animal sacrifice. Animal sacrifice is closely associated with divination. In most ancient cultures, the remains of the sacrificed animal were examined to discover the will of the gods and to predict the future. The Druid priests would take advantage of this auspicious time to look into the events of the upcoming year—at least up until Beltane, which marked the year's midpoint. Although predicting the future is not necessarily the best use of the tarot, this is a good time to try reading the future. You can do this by laying out three cards for each of the six months from Samhain to Beltane (you should have eighteen total cards). Read each set of three cards as a story that will pertain to that month.

Robert Place

Notes:

Notes:

November

November is the eleventh month of the year, its name derived from the Latin word *novem*, meaning "nine," as it was the ninth month of the Roman calendar. Its astrological sign is Scorpio, the scorpion (Oct 21-Nov 20), a fixed water sign ruled by Pluto. The golden and ruddy leaves of October now lie brown on the ground, and bare tree branches stand out against a bleak gray sky. It is cold outside, and dark, and home hearths glow now with warmth. This is the time of year for psychic, as opposed to physical, activity, and for quiet. Use candles of various magical colors inscribed with runes for magical purposes at this time. It is a good time for nurturing your shamanistic instincts, or for consulting a shaman. As the first snows begin to dust the ground, there are many indoor chores to be done. Celebrate your circle of fire now, knowing that the dark months of the year are what lie ahead. Be thankful for the warmth of your oven, bulging with turkey, pheasant, mincemeat and pumpkin pie. The main holiday of November, Thanksgiving, was originally designed to celebrate the first harvest of Indian corn by the Pilgrims in 1621. The original holiday was not much different from ours today—a large feast, games and contests, with all the community gathered around to look forward to winter months.

November 1
Monday
Day of the Dead – All Saints' Day

 3rd ♊

☽→♋ 9:53 am

Color of the day: Silver
Incense of the day: Rose

Burying Spell

Perform a burying spell and lay to rest an old hurt, a dead relationship, or an outgrown habit. Choose a symbol that embodies the aspect of your life that you need to let go of—a cigarette for example can represent an obsolete love affair, out-of-date expectations, or your poor self-image. Hold the symbol in your hands and tell it goodbye. Wrap it up in paper and string, using an appropriate color—red for anger, hurt, or old passions; black for banishing and symbolic death; yellow for healing an old wound; purple for spiritual concerns. Find a quiet location and dig a hole. Bury the symbol, cover with earth, and dust your hands off three times, saying: "I've wrapped it up, it's dead and buried. Farewell and good riddance!"

Karri Ann Allrich

Notes:

Holiday lore: The time between sundown on Samhain to sundown today, the Day of the Dead, was considered a transition time, or "thin place," in Celtic lore. It was a time between the worlds where deep insights could pass more easily to those open to them. Through the portals could also pass beings of wisdom, of play, and of fun. And while in time these beings took on a feeling of otherness and evil, as our modern relationship between the realms has been muddled, today can be a day to tap into the magic and wonder of other worlds.

November 2
Tuesday
All Souls Day – Election Day

 3rd ♋

Color of the day: Black
Incense of the day: Gardenia

Banish an Adversary Spell

To be rid of someone who harasses you incessantly, dress a white or red candle with olive oil. Clear away all flammable items, and place a heat-proof dish on the altar. Take a square piece of brown paper and write the name of the adversary on it. Underneath the person's name, write your wish that this person fade out of your life totally. Dab some pine essential oil on the four corners of the paper and also upon the person's name. Cross out your adversary's name nine times with a pencil. Set the brown paper alight from the candle flame, and put it in the heatproof dish. Allow the paper to burn completely. Wrap up the remains, and bury them in the earth.

S. Y. Zenith

Notes:

ℌoliday Lore: All Souls Day, or the "Day of the Dead," is an official holiday of the Catholic calendar following All Saints Day. November 2 is traditionally attributed to St. Odilo, the fifth abbot of Cluny. The day was intended to honor the faithfully departed with offerings and masses that would assist their souls' transit successfully from purgatory to heaven. It is believed that the Aztecs had an important role in the development of this tradition, though their history is complex with varied interpretations. In one interpretation,

for example, when a person dies the soul is said to pass through nine realms before arriving at Mictlan, the place of the dead. Once there, according to the Aztecs, the soul awaits transformation, or its next destiny.

ℕovember 3
Wednesday

3rd ♋

☽ v/c 9:00 pm

☽ → ♌ 10:32 pm

Color of the day: Yellow
Incense of the day: Coriander

A hunter's Moon Feast Spell

𝕀n Belgium, this is the Feast Day of St. Hubert, the patron saint of hunters. Today kicks off the hunting season. This is appropriate since in some cultures November's Full Moon is known as the Hunter's Moon, a critical time when meat was prepared for winter use. As the frosts darken the fields, and the November wind whistles down the chimney, why not invite friends for a hunter's feast or potluck? Before your guests arrive, mix a pinch each of ground walnuts, nutmeg, and sage. Sprinkle this on your front doorstep and in each kitchen corner while saying:

> Protect this home and
> those within
> from winter's grief

so we may savor this
feast.

Serve foods such as meat, bread,
white and sweet potatoes, and wine.
For dessert, serve gingerbread or
apple pie.

James Kambos

Notes:

November 4
Thursday
Mischief Night

3rd ♌

Color of the day: Turquoise
Incense of the day: Sandalwood

Thor's Day Spell

On this Thor's Day, honor the
god and his wife Sif by pouring
libations in their honor. Beer or mead,
either alcoholic or nonalcoholic, are
good offerings. Pour a bit out onto
the earth first before drinking, and say:

hail Thor,
son of the Earth Mother,
strong and noble keeper
of thunder,
guide and protect us in
the coming winter.
As we love and honor you
let us find strength and
wisdom within us.
hail Thor!

hail Sif,
great golden-haired god-
dess of the ripening
grain,
patroness of harvest's
wealth,
bless us with prosperity
and creativity.
As we love and honor
you,
may we find beauty and
grace within us.
hail Sif!

Kristin Madden

Notes:

November 5
Friday

3rd ♌
4th Quarter 12:53 am

Color of the day: White
Incense of the day: Dill

Knock Down Roadblocks Spell

Do you feel like you can't get past a particular roadblock in your life? Try this tarot spell today. Read the cards as you normally would, then pick at least two cards from this reading that represent your obstacle. Place them on your altar in a row. Light a red candle on the far side of the obstacle to represent your goal. Meditate for a while on the challenge of getting from here to there. Then say: "These problems are no more than paper in the wind!" Blow the cards out of the way, being careful not to blow out the candle at the same time. Finish the spell by saying: "Nothing stands between my goal and me. As I will, so mote it be!"

Elizabeth Barrette

Notes:

November 6
Saturday

4th ♌
☽ v/c 3:45 am
☽ → ♍ 10:00 am

Color of the day: Indigo
Incense of the day: Jasmine

Break-the-habit Spell

To break a bad habit, get an old plate—one that is chipped or cracked or otherwise unusable. If you don't have one, go to a garage sale or Salvation Army store, and buy one for a quarter. Write on the plate in magic marker the name of the habit you wish to break—for instance, "smoking cigarettes," "overeating," "swearing," or "being unkind." Put the plate in a place where you will see it every day, and for a week or so focus your attention on the habit and the plate. Then, on a Saturday, or a day that rules the nature of the habit (see page 258 for more details), take the plate somewhere outside with a paved surface, such as a driveway or sidewalk. Bring along a broom and dustpan. Focus all your attention on the habit. Say aloud: "I break my habit of . . ." and name the habit. Then smash the plate as hard as you can with a hammer. Be sure to clean up all the fragments afterward, and dispose of them in a garbage can far

away from your home if it is at all possible.

Magenta Griffith

Notes:

the your licorice ice tea. Note: Children should have not have fennel tea unless it is diluted to not more than one-eighth cup of tea to one cup water.

Therese Francis

Notes:

November 7
Sunday

 4℞ ♏

Color of the day: Orange
Incense of the day: Clove

End Your Overeating Spell

Tis the season now for overeating, especially of sweets. To assist your efforts to battle this, keep fennel tea handy. Add about a quarter teaspoon of fennel herb to a coffee mug. If you really like the taste of licorice, add a small amount of anise herb, too. Boil some water, and pour it hot over the the herb(s). Let the herbs steep for two to three minutes, then strain them out. Let the tea cool, and then refrigerate. When you need some relief from gas or upset stomach, drink about a quarter cup of

November 8
Monday

4℞ ♏

☽ v/c 1:32 pm
☽ → ♎ 6:23 pm

Color of the day: Ivory
Incense of the day: Peony

Honor Your Patron Spirits Ritual

As you progress in your magical workings, you connect more strongly with certain deities than you do with others. One or more of these will become your patron spirits. These are the deities you will work with and frequently feel aligned to. Today is the day to honor these spirits. Spend the whole day personifying the best qualities in your patron deities. Be cheerful, forgiving, strong, and kind in every situation. Look for the joy in everything that happens today, even if it is a stretch. Tonight, when you have quiet time, set up your altar. Take a ritual bath or shower. Cast a circle, and perform a ritual with your patron spirits. Don't write it up ahead of time. Invite them into the circle, and let the ritual be spontaneous. Thank them for the support they've given you. Thank them for the lessons given during the past year, even the difficult ones. Let the way you feel today influence the way you live your life tomorrow and beyond.

Cerridwen Iris Shea

Notes:

Night of Nicnevin Spell

Nicnevin, the Scottish crone goddess, rides the skies tonight and tomorrow night between the hours of nine and ten. Can you hear her? Her calls sounds like the wild call of geese. Tonight is a very dangerous time to be caught outside. If she or a member of her fairy troop sees you on the road, you're likely to be swept up and forced to join the "Wild Host," as it's called. Before dark, sprinkle sea salt around the perimeter of your property, and say:

> Mother goddess,
> keep me safe this night
> and next,
> and mine own this night
> and next.

At nine o'clock light a gray candle in Nicnevin's honor.

Lily Gardner

Notes:

November 9
Tuesday

4ħ ☌

Color of the day: Red
Incense of the day: Ginger

November 10
Wednesday

 4ᵗʰ ♎︎

☽ v/c 11:02 pm

☽ → ♏︎ 11:05 pm

Color of the day: White
Incense of the day: Eucalyptus

Some Ghost-hunting Tips

As winds turn cold, and darkness grows deep, you may wish to try ghost hunting. For this, get a candle lantern, a camera (preferably digital), a flashlight, and dark clothing. Go to an old graveyard after dark. Light your lantern, and whisper:

By the spirit of fire and
water,
I call you down.
By earth and wind,
you come to me.
By the authority of the
rocks and the trees,
we mingle together.

Spirits, I know you.
Spirits, I see you.
Make your presence
known to me!

Once you hear any sort of rustling sounds, start taking pictures like mad. Before leaving, thank the spirits. Do not take anything away from the cemetery unless you plan to replace it. Download your images at home. If you get circles or balls of light, these are called ghost orbs. You may have captured the image of a real ghost.

Susan Sheppard

Notes:

November 11
Thursday
Veterans Day

4ᵗʰ ♏︎

Color of the day: Green
Incense of the day: Chrysanthemum

Memorial Prayer

Today we honor war veterans. Find an object symbolic of someone you wish to remember, and place it on your altar as an offering of thanks for those who have fought for freedom. Spend a few minutes today reading about history, watch a documentary program, or visit a memorial site and speak these words, either out loud or to yourself:

> Today we honor those
> who have fought and
> those who have fallen.
>
> Life holds many battles.
> Lend us their strength,
> grant us their courage.

Ember

Notes:

istorical lore: Veterans Day commemorates the armistice that ended the Great War in 1918. Oddly enough, this war ended on this day, November 11, at 11 am (the 11th hour of the 11th day of the 11th month). Though Congress changed Veterans Day to another date in October at one point during this century, in 1968 they returned the holiday to November 11, where it stands today. The number 11 is significant. In numerology, it is one of the master numbers that cannot be reduced. The number 11 life path has the connotation of illumination and is associated with spiritual awareness

and idealism—particularly regarding humanity. It makes sense then that this collection of 11s commemorates the end of an event that was hoped to be the War to End All Wars. Unfortunately, it wasn't the last such great war, but we can at least set aside this day to ruminate on notions of peace to humankind.

November 12
Friday

4th ♏
New Moon 9:27 am
☽ v/c 8:34 pm

Color of the day: Coral
Incense of the day: Thyme

The Power Within Spell

orrespondences, incantations, and the like are wonderful adjuncts to the art of magic. But all magic begins and ends with the practitioner. The magical practitioner is the one who charges the universal energy that creates magic. The mere act of reciting words at a particular phase of the Moon does little to influence outcome. This working is not one of attracting power to you. Rather, your power has to come from within. This working therefore is one of inner growth, as you learn what power you possess and how to recognize any blocks to that power. Sit in a relaxed position. State the intent of gaining wisdom regarding your personal power. Beginning with the root, focus a stream of energy to each chakra. Focus on the emotional aspect of the chakra—on the feelings and on any blocks or negative messaging clogging these power centers. Here is a list of associations to each of the seven chakras:

Root chakra: "I am."
Belly: Creation and pleasure.
Solar Plexus: Ability to manifest.
Heart: Emotions an perceptions; also, this is the link between the mundane and spiritual planes.
Throat: Speaking the truth.
Brow: Perceptions of the future.
Crown: Connections to a higher self.

Listen to the messages from your higher self. Ground any excess energy. Journal your perceptions.

Karen Follett

Notes:

November 13
Saturday

1st ♏
☽ → ♐ 12:56 am

Color of the day: Blue
Incense of the day: Violet

Energizing Spell

As the Moon waxes in Sagittarius today, now is a great time to energize and strengthen your creative impulses. This can be especially helpful for people who are lagging in energy or feel stuck and weighted down by the mundane aspects of life. To perform this spell, find a place where you can light a small fire. This may be your stove, your hearth, or in a campfire outside. Take a few pieces of kindling and add a few drops of juniper or cedar essential oil to the wood. At sunset, light the fire, and say these words:

> healing fire,
> I give thanks for your
> heat and light.
> Please help energize my
> spirit and increase my
> creativity.

Jonathan Keyes

Notes:

November 14
Sunday

1st ♐

☽ v/c 10:58 am

Color of the day: Amber
Incense of the day: Sage

herbal Cleansing Spell

Aromatic herbs do more than smell good. Most of them can be used to disinfect and clean, both physically and psychically. Take a handful of rosemary, peppermint, or lavender leaves, and add them to some boiling water. Remove the water from the heat, and let it steep for ten minutes. Strain, and use while hot to wash ceramic, tile, and walls. Pour the cooled leftovers into a spray bottle for quick cleanups.

Therese Francis

Notes:

November 15
Monday

 1st ♐

☽ → ♑ 1:33 am

Color of the day: White
Incense of the day: Lavender

honoring St. Expedite Spell

My favorite saint is St. Expedite, who is especially popular in New Orleans. St. Expedite is the one to invoke when you need help in a hurry. His day is Thursday, his color is yellow, and he is magically associated with the raven. Of course, if you keep getting into trouble and need help out of it because you refuse to learn from your mistakes, you will simply find the karmic return coming quicker and quicker each time you blow it. Ask for intervention from St. Expedite only when you've earned it. I like to keep a yellow jar candle with St. Expedite's image pasted on to it. When I need help, I light the candle, explain the situation, and ask him to guide me to the solution. If I want to give the energy an extra boost, I burn a magenta candle along with the yellow. I extinguish the candle at the end of the conversation, and I let the magenta candle burn out. Once I receive the assistance, I light the yellow candle again and say thank you. Then, I look for a way to pay it forward by performing a kindness for a stranger. It could be as simple as helping a mother get her stroller up the subway stairs or helping someone across the street. The important thing is that the help is genuine, and it is offered freely and without any expectations. I see something that needs to be done, I do it, and I continue on, without asking for anything in return. This keeps the energy flowing.

Cerridwen Iris Shea

Notes:

strain with coffee filter paper, and let stand for another week. Strain again, and pour into glass bottles for use.

S. Y. Zenith

Notes:

November 16
Tuesday

1st ♑
☽ v/c 10:07 pm

Color of the day: Gray
Incense of the day: Poplar

Toiletry Vinegar Protection Spell

Toiletry vinegar has protective qualities and can also be applied as a skin astringent or poured into the bath. Gather one cup each of dried thyme, dried sage, dried lavender, dried angelica, and dried marigold. Add to two cups cider vinegar along with eight drops of rose essential oil. Put the dried herbs in a large stainless-steel container. Bring the vinegar to a boil, and pour it over the herbs and rose oil. Leave the contents to cool for thirty minutes before pouring it into a jar with a lid. Let the contents stand for two weeks. Give it a good shake each day. After two weeks,

November 17
Wednesday

1st ♑
☽ → ♒ 2:39 am

Color of the day: Brown
Incense of the day: Cedar

Shadow Work Ritual

With its dark watery depths, Scorpio energy stirs our intuition and intensifies hidden desires. This is familiar territory to our descending goddess, Persephone, whose annual surrender to the underworld hones her insight with hard-won wisdom. Let us enter shadow territory with grace and clarity, and call upon the goddess Persephone to guide us through Scorpio's secretive undercurrents. As Carl Jung wrote: "That which remains unconscious comes to us as fate." We collectively struggle now to understand current events and to incorporate the abrupt alteration to our view of the world, so we should ponder Jung's wise words. May we also take the opportunity offered by the Sun's pass through Scorpio to meditate upon our own shadow. By owning our own dark side we help heal the world.

Karri Ann Allrich

Notes:

else is likely to pick it up. Tack the greenery over your front and back doors. The purity of the greenery will keep negative influences at bay for the holidays.

Susan Sheppard

Notes:

November 18
Thursday

 1st ♒

Color of the day: Purple
Incense of the day: Evergreen

Spell to Banish Anger

Get a black stone today (quartz crystal works well) and some winter greenery such as pine, holly, evergreen, or hemlock. Place the black stone to your forehead, and focus your negative emotions into it. Concentrate on the anger or negativity leaving your body, mind, and spirit. Take the stone and throw it in the nearest body of water, where no one

November 19
Friday

 1st ♒
2nd Quarter 12:50 am

☽ v/c 12:50 am
☽ → ♓ 5:38 am

Color of the day: Pink
Incense of the day: Sandalwood

Water Blessing for Greater Love and Understanding

Gather a bowl of water and some mugwort today. As you sprinkle the water with mugwort, consider a relationship in your life that has been tense or uncomfortable. See the other person in your mind's eye, and gaze into the water, chanting:

Blessed water, open the way to greater love and understanding today.

For now and future days to come, bless us and make us one.

Visualize the two of you in harmony. Feel your heart opening and healed. Open your mind to any images or insights that come up as you gaze into the water. Focus on anything that will contribute to greater understanding, and make a plan to manifest that.

Kristin Madden

Notes:

as a spell for change. For this, you need marshmallows and chocolate chips. Give each marshmallow chocolate chip eyes, nose, and mouth. Name each decorated marshmallow with a quality you want to personify, such as kindness, tolerance, unconditional love, the ability to accept compliments, etc. You can toast the marshmallows over a campfire, in the fireplace, or at the sacred Hibachi. There may be a way to toast them in the microwave, but I haven't figured it out. As you eat each marshmallow, visualize the desired trait entering your body. Then start taking the steps needed to make it come true.

Cerridwen Iris Shea

Notes:

November 20
Saturday

2nd ♓

Color of the day: Black
Incense of the day: Patchouli

Toasty Ghosty Spell

Many people have fond memories of making s'mores at the campfire. I use a variation on this experience

November 21
Sunday

2nd ♓
☽ v/c 10:35 am
☽ → ♈ 11:11 am
☉ → ♐ 6:22 pm

Color of the day: Yellow
Incense of the day: Clove

Creativity Spell

This is a day for inventions. On this day in 1783, the French physicians Jean-Francois Pilatre de Rozier and Francois Laurent, the marquis d'Arlandes, made the first untethered hot-air balloon flight, flying five and a half miles over Paris in about twenty-five minutes. Also, in 1877 on this day, Edison invented the phonograph, the first device to record sound. In 1969, the first link for the ARPANET was connected; the ARPANET later evolved into the Internet. This is an auspicious day for trying out new things, new technology, and new ideas. So make an effort to shake yourself out of your ruts.

Magenta Griffith

Notes:

Lull Yourself Ritual

Everyone has a hard time falling asleep occasionally. Here is a spell for restful sleep. Begin by playing quiet music for a few minutes, and then go to bed. Imagine yourself as a beach of pristine sand, and sleep as the tide comes in to cover you. Say this rhyme:

> Soft as sea on sand,
> soft as mother's love,
> soft as moonlight above,
> soft as the loving hand.
>
> Sleep, gentle healer of
> flesh and mind,
> come and restore what
> the day has drained.
> Fill the long night till the
> Moon wanes,
> then flee with dawn,
> leaving peace behind.

Elizabeth Barrette

Notes:

November 22
Monday

 2nd ♈

Color of the day: Lavender
Incense of the day: Maple

November 23
Tuesday

2nd ♈

☽ v/c 1:47 pm

☽ → ♉ 7:16 pm

Color of the day: White
Incense of the day: Pine

Get Ready for Relatives Ritual

Before leaving to be with family for the holiday, take some time to energize and center yourself. Stand before your household altar with your feet shoulder-width apart and knees relaxed, arms loose at your side. As you breathe in, raise your arms in front of you, keeping the rest of your body relaxed. See the air enter your body, moving your arms upward to the height of your shoulders. Simultaneously see a ball of protective light rise up from the ground, encircling you. Allow the energy to continue over your head and down your back. As you exhale, slowly lower your arms as you envision the energy circle complete itself and return to the earth.

Therese Francis

Notes:

November 24
Wednesday

2nd ♉

Color of the day: Topaz
Incense of the day: Neroli

Spell for an Easy Winter

Many of us in northern climes dread the winter with its cold and snowstorms, the accompanying illnesses and the loss of light. November 24 is a traditional day to pray to the mother goddess in her aspects of light and birth. Decorate your altar with red cloth, red candles, and your favorite image of the mother goddess, preferably one that shows her pregnant. It is customary to have libations. Say:

Mother, I beseech thee,
protect me from illness
and storm,
from pain and depression,
from now to the time of
the quickening,
when you wake from
winter's slumber.

Blessed be.

Lily Gardner

Notes:

November 25
Thursday
Thanksgiving

 2nd ☿
☽ v/c 11:37 pm

Color of the day: Crimson
Incense of the day: Dill

No More hardship Meditation

As we have seen, harvest festivals and feasts are common in ancient cultures. When the Pilgrims of Plymouth held the first American Thanksgiving in 1621, they were celebrating a harvest feast like those they knew back in England. The Pilgrims landed at Plymouth Rock in Massachusetts on December 11, 1620. Because it was the beginning of winter, forty-six of the 102 people who made the Mayflower voyage died in the first year. In the autumn of 1621, thanks to the help of native tribes, the Pilgrims had a bountiful harvest and invited ninety-one of their new friends to the first Thanksgiving. This first American harvest festival probably consisted of wild fowl, venison, boiled pumpkin, corn bread, fish, lobster, clams, dried fruit, berries, and plums. All provisions that had been brought from England had long since been used up, and all of the food was supplied by the new land. This story of hardship and eventual reward illustrates our dependence on

Mother Earth and the necessity of working with the cycles of nature. The celebration of the various holidays throughout the year stem from magical practices designed to show gratitude to the Earth and to help us find our place in her cycles. The story of Thanksgiving demonstrates the power of friendship between cultures. Thanksgiving was not held regularly in Plymouth until 1676. By then, the colonists had forgotten their debt to their native friends and were instead celebrating military victory over "heathen savages." Today Thanksgiving honors the land and the contribution Native Americans have made to our culture.

Robert Place

Notes:

November 26
Friday

 2nd ☿
☽ → ♊ 5:25 am
Full Moon 3:07 pm

Color of the day: Purple
Incense of the day: Ylang-ylang

Fast Cash Spell

The Full Moon of Taurus is a potent time for prosperity magic. This spell is designed to reveal to you any sources of money. But it will be up to you to take advantage of any opportunities brought to light. Start by lighting a green candle. Burn five-finger grass on a charcoal burner. Write the amount of money that you want on a small strip of paper, and anoint the paper with some patchouli oil. Focus your intent on the candle flame. Visualize that the money is in your possession. As you feel the energy build, state these words:

> Universal energy,
> moving fast,
> opportunities come to me,
> as this spell is cast.

Carefully light the paper in the flame of the candle, and allow it to burn on the charcoal with the five-finger grass. Visualize the energy of the herb and paper carrying your intent to the universe. Quiet your mind, ground any excess energy, and listen for any messages of opportunity that will be presented to you.

Karen Follett

Notes:

November 27
Saturday

3rd ♊

Color of the day: Brown
Incense of the day: Lilac

Magic of Birds Spell

With the Moon in Gemini, now is a good time to do some bird magic. First choose a bird—such as a swallow, hawk, robin, cardinal, and so on—that you have always liked. Then search out books and study the bird's characteristics, its features, and its habits. If you can, find pictures or a feather of this bird and make a special altar devoted to it. Light some yellow or light-blue candles, and sit in simple meditation while visualizing images of the bird—how it moves, flies, eats, and so on. Invite the bird into your heart. What are its spiritual qualities and its essential message? Give thanks when you are finished.

Jonathan Keyes

Notes:

November 28
Sunday

 3rd ♊

☽ v/c 10:04 am

☽ → ♋ 5:10 pm

Color of the day: Gold
Incense of the day: Basil

Warmth and Wellness Ritual

During the winter months, it's important to remember the healing Sun is still with us. At this time of year, fire is a perfect symbol of the Sun's warmth. Sit before a fire in a fireplace, or surround yourself with red and yellow candles. Bask in the warm glow, contemplating the wellness of your body and spirit. Think of one thing you can do just for you—to pamper yourself and be well—and do it as soon as possible, saying:

> Warmth of Sun
> shine for me.
> I deserve your presence,
> and I celebrate life.

Ember

Notes:

November 29
Monday

3rd ♋

Color of the day: Gray
Incense of the day: Frankincense

Night of Shadow's Spell

Throw another log on the fire, and lock the door. On this night, according to the old ways, the most magical events occurred. It was the night to practice divination, to seek omens in shadows and candle wax, and to watch out for vampires walking the planet. On this eve, when mystery lurks in every shadow, conjure your future with smoke. In your cauldron burn both stem and leaf of wormwood, marigold, and dried rosemary. Let the scents mingle and rise before you as you utter no word, nor make a sound. Watch the smoke; it is here that your future will reveal itself. If you hear a knock during the night, don't answer the door until you hear a second knock. Vampires only knock once.

James Kambos

Notes:

November 30
Tuesday

3rd ♋
☽ v/c 11:28 pm

Color of the day: Maroon
Incense of the day: Juniper

Worry Stone Spell

Comfort a loved one with a thoughtful gift—a blessed worry stone to keep in their pocket. Take a leisurely walk by a river bank, pond, or ocean beach, and ask the land spirits to lend you a stone. Let your intuition guide you to a smooth, pleasing stone that sits well in the palm of your hand. Wash it in the water, and thank the spirits for their gift. Leave a natural gift of birdseed, nuts, or acorns nearby. If possible, set the stone out in moonlight for three days. Anoint the stone with a drop of oil to enhance your intention. Rosemary, peppermint, or bergamot are all appropriate. Give your gift during the waxing Moon, and bless the receiver with love.

Karri Ann Allrich

Notes:

Notes:

December

December is the twelfth month of the year, its name derived from the Latin word *decem*, meaning "ten," as it was the tenth month of the Roman calendar. Its astrological sign is Sagittarius, the archer (Nov 21–Dec 20), a mutable fire sign ruled by Jupiter. This month is buried under blankets of snow. In the evenings, holiday lights twinkle for the Yule season. Back porches are stacked with firewood. Ovens bake confections for serving around a decorated table. Sweets have a particularly ancient history at this time; they are made and eaten to ensure that one has "sweetness" in the coming year. The Full Moon of December is the Oak Moon. It is a time when the waxing Sun overcomes the waning Sun, and days begin to grow longer again. In some Pagan traditions, this struggle is symbolized by the Oak King overcoming the Holly King; rebirth triumphing over death. It is no coincidence that Christians chose this month to celebrate the birth of Jesus. The Winter Solstice is a solar festival and is celebrated with fire in the form of the Yule log. New Year's Eve is another important celebration during December. The old dying year is symbolized at this time by an old man with a long white beard carrying a scythe. The new year is seen appropriately as a newborn child.

December 1
Wednesday

 3rd ♋

☽ → ♌ 5:50 am

Color of the day: Yellow
Incense of the day: Coriander

Travel Divination

If there is an upcoming trip that you feel uneasy about, perform this simple divination using a bowl of water and a stone. When you are alone, place the bowl of water on a table and sit in front of it. Ask whether you should undertake the journey. Be very specific in your wording. Meditate for a few minutes, and request your spirit guides to be present with you. Drop the stone into the bowl of water, and pay keen attention to the ripples created. An even number of ripples means the answer to your query is "yes." An odd number indicates "no." Thank your spirit guides, and pour the water down the sink. Wash the stone, and store it in a pouch.

S. Y. Zenith

Notes:

December 2
Thursday

3rd ♌

Color of the day: Green
Incense of the day: Carnation

A Simple Work Spell

Emile Zola wrote: "The artist is worth nothing without the gift, but the gift is worth nothing without work." The Japanese hold a festival for tailors called the Festival of Broken Needles. A shrine is built from the broken needles that tailors save through the year. This is intended as an offering and reminder of the work the needles have performed through the course of the past twelve months. In honor of this festival, ask yourself now: What are your broken needles? What tools, seldom acknowledged, do you rely on throughout your year? One you have decided, build a shrine to your patron god or goddess with symbols of the tools that helped you strive and succeed this past year. Burn an orange candle to represent the harvest, and reflect carefully on this last year's labors. Burn a brown candle for new endeavors. What do you wish to accomplish for the upcoming year? Ask your god or goddess for blessings.

Lily Gardner

Notes:

December 3
Friday

 3rd ♌

☽ v/c 9:52 am

☽ → ♍ 6:00 pm

Color of the day: Pink
Incense of the day: Nutmeg

holiday Card Spell

In this day and age, many people say they "don't have time" to write holiday cards. But is this really true? It doesn't take much to reconnect with friends and acquaintances during the holiday season. I believe maintaining and strengthening the connection at this time of year is part of the rebirth of the light, and this rebirth is what the Yuletide season is all about. Sure, sometimes it's difficult to find time to sit down and write the cards and notes. But it can be made easier if you make a ritual out of this task. For instance, buy boxes of cards all year round, and stock up on stamps. Make sure you have plenty of pens in whatever colors you like. Go through your Rolodex and make a list of people you plan to send cards. Over a period of several days, set aside one or two hours a day to begin working on this task. Gather your materials together, and cast a circle. Bless the cards, asking that your words be those of truth and joy, reflecting the spirit of the season. And write. When you are finished writing, leave the stack of stamped cards on your altar overnight. Charge the cards with positive energy before you send them out into the world. When you receive cards, fasten them to ribbons and hang them around the doorways of your home. They will give you joy every time you look at them, and you will appreciate the wonderful people in your life.

Cerridwen Iris Shea

Notes:

December 4
Saturday

 3rd ♏
4th Quarter 7:53 pm

Color of the day: Blue
Incense of the day: Pine

Cleansing Bath Spell

For a deep cleansing to chase winter blues or to get rid of a cold, mix one and a half cups each of sea salt and baking soda in a tub full of the hottest water you can stand. Soak for thirty minutes, and towel yourself dry. Take a regular bath about eight hours later. As an alternative cleansing bath, fill the tub with hot water, and add one pint of apple cider vinegar. Soak for thirty minutes and towel dry.

Therese Francis

Notes:

December 5
Sunday

 4th ♏
☽ v/c 9:28 pm

Color of the day: Orange
Incense of the day: Parsley

Centering Spell

Before the holiday crush, center yourself with this simple and powerful spell. Find a quiet space and gather a white or silver candle, a glass bowl of spring water, a smooth stone, and a spoonful of salt. Light the candle, and concentrate on the flame. Hold the stone in your palm. Feel its weight, and its solidity. This stone represents your core truth—the unchangeable, timeless, and solid aspect of your core being. Identify this aspect and name it. Place the stone into the water. Breathe. Hold the salt in your hand, and let it slip through your fingers into the water, saying:

This life and time,
ever changing.
Goddess, may I recognize
my truth
and center my life on it.

As time changes me,
may I remain timeless,
fluid, and honorable.

Karri Ann Allrich

Notes:

December 6
Monday

 4th ♏

☽ → ♎ 3:46 am

Color of the day: White
Incense of the day: Myrrh

Anti-Insomnia Spell

Get a cup of warm milk, some chamomile tea, or another sleep-inducing warm drink. Sit down in your most comfortable space. Make the sign of a spiral from the outer edge inward over the cup, and recite:

> All is well,
> moonlight beams.
> Sleep arrives
> with pleasant dreams.

Drink the warm drink slowly, taking at least five minutes. Think about pleasant things while you drink it. Listen to calming music, or look at something beautiful. Then go to bed immediately. Once you are in bed, continue to think only pleasant, restful thoughts. Do this every night for a week—even if it doesn't work well the first night or two.

Magenta Griffith

Notes:

December 7
Tuesday
Burning the Devil

4th ♎

Color of the day: Black
Incense of the day: Honeysuckle

Task Balancing Spell

We are all in a constant state of flux and disequilibrium. The Libra Moon can help teach us how to flow in the midst of an ever-changing world. We need to learn how not to get stuck and to go with the stream. For this spell, draw a large circle on a piece of paper. Then make segments of various sizes to indicate all the activities you are currently involved in. Perhaps work will get a big segment, and your personal relationships will get another fairly large segment. Continue to divide up the page into segments representing eating, sleeping, alone time, creative projects, and so on. When you are done, see if there are any areas of your life that are not getting enough attention, and if other areas are taking too much attention. Then take a new piece of paper, redraw the circle, and reapportion the segments to the fit your vision of the way you would like to live your life. You can then choose to bring balance to your life with a prayer of intention:

Goddess, help bring
balance into all areas of
my life.
So be it.

Jonathan Keyes

Notes:

Holiday lore: Cultures around the
world have shared throughout
history a penchant for the ritual
burning of scapegoats, enemies, and
devils. There is something primal
about the roar of a large bonfire and
its ability to bring purging light to a
community. Today is such a day in
the highland towns of Guatemala.
Men dress in devil costumes through
the season before Christmas, and children playfully chase the men through
the streets. On December 7, people
light bonfires in front of their homes,
and into the fires they toss garbage
and other debris to purify their lives.
At night, fireworks fill the air.

December 8
Wednesday
hanukkah begins

4th ♎

☽ v/c 3:41 am

☽ → ♏ 9:43 am

Color of the day: Topaz
Incense of the day: Sandalwood

Remember Our Inner Self Spell
Hanukkah is an eight-day celebration of religious freedom. It
commemorates the victory of the Jewish
people over a foreign king that
attempted to force them to worship
according to his religion. After the
Jews restored their own temple, they
found only one jug of oil for the
holy lamp. The jug should have lasted
only one day, but miraculously it
lasted for eight. On this day, light a
special candle in a place of honor
in your home. Reflect upon the religion you practice, and be thankful
that you are free to do so. Give thanks
to all those who made this freedom
possible. Consider how you can
spread tolerance for all religions and
contribute to world harmony.

Kristin Madden

Notes:

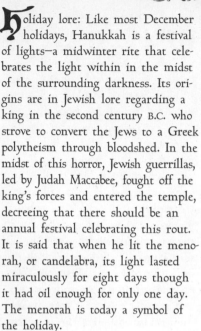

oliday lore: Like most December holidays, Hanukkah is a festival of lights—a midwinter rite that celebrates the light within in the midst of the surrounding darkness. Its origins are in Jewish lore regarding a king in the second century B.C. who strove to convert the Jews to a Greek polytheism through bloodshed. In the midst of this horror, Jewish guerrillas, led by Judah Maccabee, fought off the king's forces and entered the temple, decreeing that there should be an annual festival celebrating this rout. It is said that when he lit the menorah, or candelabra, its light lasted miraculously for eight days though it had oil enough for only one day. The menorah is today a symbol of the holiday.

Keep the cloves on your person. As soon as you see your potential love, strike up a conversation. Pass a slice of orange to this person as you eat. If the person accepts the slice, this is a genuine love interest. If he or she refuses the orange slice, the spell will be harder to achieve. Light an orange candle every night for seven days. Keep cloves in your pocket until your lover decides whether or not to pursue the love affair.

Susan Sheppard

Notes:

December 9
Thursday

 4th ♏

Color of the day: Turquoise
Incense of the day: Geranium

Spell to Attract a Lover

ou will need cloves, a cinnamon stick, and an orange for this spell. Hold the orange under your armpit to warm it. Rub the cloves over the orange. Insert the cinnamon stick inside. Wrap the orange in plastic, and put it in your bag or in the trunk of your car.

December 10
Friday

 4th ♏
☽ v/c 6:03 am

☽ → ♐ 11:54 am

Color of the day: Rose
Incense of the day: Ginger

Demeter Chthonia Devotion

s winter nears, Demeter goes under-ground to search for her

daughter Persephone. This aspect of the grain goddess is sometimes called Black Demeter. She has a fearsome visage and snaky hair. On her journey to the underworld, she brings gifts to the departed from their living relations. Honor your departed loved ones today by placing on your altar such astral gifts as "hell money," which is available in Asian stores and is burned for the dead. Decorate the altar with pomegranates and poppies to let Persephone know that she is not forgotten and that Demeter is coming to visit. If you wish, "become" Demeter by wearing a black veil, and sit at your altar to relay messages from survivors to their departed loved ones.

Denise Dumars

Notes:

December 11
Saturday

 4th ♐

🌑 New Moon 8:29 pm

☽ v/c 11:03 pm

Color of the day: Indigo
Incense of the day: Lavender

Your Lucky Day Spell

Who couldn't use a little luck every now and then? Whether you want general "all around" luck, or luck in a particular area of your life, this spell will allow luck to manifest in your presence. Light a green candle and any other candle to represent how you want luck to manifest (your career might be represented by a gold candle, and your relationship by a red one). Crumple an oak leaf, and combine it with another herb associated with the area of life where you want luck to manifest. Place the leaf and herb on a charcoal block. Place an acorn on your altar. Focus your intent, and transfer it to the acorn. Take a moment to visualize the idea that opportunities have presented themselves and that you are taking full advantage of them. Say these words:

> Energies of good fortune
> yield my way.
> Doors of opportunity are
> opening today.

Pass the acorn through the aura of the flame, and through the smoke of the herbs. Meditate on any universal messages that are being presented to you. Luck does occasionally appear blatantly as "found cash," but generally luck presents itself as a less obvious, "one time" opportunity. So be alert for your lucky breaks.

Karen Follett

Notes:

With peaceful heart
I now can sup.

Be sure to eat a hearty dinner.

Lily Gardner

Notes:

December 12
Sunday

 1st ♐
☽ → ♑ 11:42 am

Color of the day: Yellow
Incense of the day: Poplar

A Supper Spell to Cure Anxieties

Tonight, it is very unlucky to go to bed supperless. It was said that those who fasted on December 12 would be swept up by fairies and find themselves on a rooftop or in the uppermost branches of a tree. These people were never the same even after they recovered from their fright. For this spell, your altar is your dining table. Cover your altar with a red cloth, and burn silver candles. Write your fears on a sheet of silver paper. Burn the paper in your fireplace or cauldron, and say:

> What I fear,
> I now burn up.

December 13
Monday

 1st ♑

Color of the day: Silver
Incense of the day: Rose

Solar Lucina Devotion

Swedish people honor the Sun goddess Lucina, also known as St. Lucy, today. Girls dress in white gowns and wear garlands crowned with candles. They wake up their families with songs and a special breakfast. For this celebration, the Swedes make *lussekatter*, scrumptious saffron buns shaped in symbolic S-curves, figure-eights, and cats. The name of the bread itself means "light cats" and may refer to the magical cats who pulled the chariot of Freya, another northern goddess. Celebrate today by baking lussekatter yourself (you can find the recipe online or in ethnic cookbooks), and by honoring the girls in your family. Look for the Sun in the winter sky, and greet her as well. Burn a white candle on your altar for Lucina, who brings back the light.

Elizabeth Barrette

Notes:

being enclosed in a protective shield of white light as you prepare the amulet. Light the candle, and place the amulet nearby. Focus on the energy of the burning candle, and infuse the amulet with power. Allow the candle to burn completely, and carry the amulet with you for protection. Speak his charm when you need extra protection:

> Mars, breathe your fire
> into these stones and herbs.
> Wrap me in the warmth
> of your protection.
> Shield me from harm.

Ember

Notes:

December 14
Tuesday

 1st ♑
☽ v/c 6:43 am
☽ → ♒ 11:10 am

Color of the day: Red
Incense of the day: Evergreen

Martian Shield to Keep from harm

For this spell, you need the following materials: red cloth and ribbon; any combination of carnelian, bloodstone, ruby, garnet, jasper, and obsidian; a pinch of dried thyme; rose thorns; patchouli oil; and a red or white candle. Carve the protection symbol of your choice into the candle, and anoint it with oil. Combine the stones, herbs, and thorns, and wrap them in the cloth. Visualize

December 15
Wednesday

1st ♒
Color of the day: Brown
Incense of the day: Eucalyptus

A Basic Kitchen Blessing

In ancient Rome, Consus, the god of the stored-up harvest, was honored on this day. This

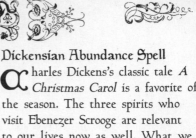

ancient idea of setting aside the harvest lives on in rural America, where the "blizzard pantry" is taken quite seriously. Jams, jellies, and canned vegetables are "put by" for winter use. Extra necessities are also stockpiled in case of severe weather. As the Earth rests now, take just a moment to bless your own kitchen. With a drop of olive oil, trace a holy symbol such as a cross, on a cupboard or pantry door. Here and there drop some whole cloves on the shelves. Cloves purify, and they also deter ants. Then, take time to donate to a food bank. Also, stock up on pet food and bird seed.

James Kambos

Notes:

December 16
Thursday

 1st ♈ ♒
꙳ 🌙 v/c 3:33 am
🌙 → ♓ 1:24 pm

Color of the day: Purple
Incense of the day: Musk

Dickensian Abundance Spell

Charles Dickens's classic tale *A Christmas Carol* is a favorite of the season. The three spirits who visit Ebenezer Scrooge are relevant to our lives now as well. What we put out comes back at least three times. In this season, where the idea of plenty is in sharp contrast to the paucity of those less fortunate, it is our responsibility to answer to the spirits of the season. To answer the Ghost of Christmas Past, contact someone with whom you lost touch over the years. It could be an old friend, a relative, or a former teacher. Send them a card or letter, with photographs, to catch up on missed time. If it is someone with whom you have quarreled, try to work it out and make a fresh start. To answer the Ghost of Christmas Present, take a bag or basket of food to your local food bank, so that those without will be assured a good meal during this holiday season. Volunteer for a few hours if you can. Bake a plum pudding for your friends, hiding a coin inside for luck (be sure to warn them, so no one breaks a tooth). Bake cookies, and take them in to work. Offer to shop for a sick or elderly neighbor. To answer the Ghost of Christmas Future, make a contribution to a children's charity. Better yet, find a way to volunteer some time over the next few months. Our children are the future. May the joy of the season be upon you.

Cerridwen Iris Shea

Notes:

Strain the mixture with a fine cotton cloth before adding the other ingredients to the container. Seal and shake well. Pour the contents into an atomizer or airtight bottle.

S. Y. Zenith

Notes:

December 17
Friday
Saturnalia

 1st ♓

Color of the day: White
Incense of the day: Almond

Essence of Romance Spell

This fragrant essence may be used as cologne to draw romance, or it may be presented to a lover in a heart-shaped bottle. It may also be added to facial rinses or to your bathwater. Ingredients include two handfuls red or pink rose petals, one handful of dried lavender, one cup vodka, two tablespoons orange blossom water, six drops jasmine oil, two tablespoons rosewater, and five tablespoons spring water. Pour the vodka over the rose petals and lavender in a glass container. Cover, and let the mixture stand for three days.

Holiday lore: Saturnalia was the Roman midwinter celebration of the solstice, and the greatest of the Roman festivals. It was traditional to decorate halls with laurels, green trees, lamps, and candles. These symbols of life and light were intended to dispel the darkness of the season of cold. The festival began with the cry of "Io Saturnalia!" Young pigs were sacrificed at the temple of Saturn and then were served the next day. Masters gave slaves the day off and waited on them for dinner. Merrymaking followed, as wine flowed and horseplay commenced. Dice were used to select one diner as the honorary "Saturnalian King." Merrymakers obeyed absurd commands to dance, sing, and perform ridiculous feats. It was also a tradition to carry gifts

of clay dolls and symbolic candles
on the person to give to friends met
on the streets.

December 18
Saturday

 1st ♓
2nd Quarter 11:40 am
☽ v/c 11:40 am
☽ → ♈ 4:52 pm

Color of the day: Brown
Incense of the day: Coriander

Solar Birthday Cake Spell

Winter Solstice is almost upon
us, and festivities abound. Yet
those celebrating birthdays around
Yule and Christmas often feel neg
lected. Winter holidays take center
stage, and birthdays may get lost in
the shuffle. If someone in your family has a birthday at this time of
year, be sure and make it special this
year. Bake a solar birthday cake,
and share the joy of the solstice
season. Sunny orange or lemon cake
topped with lemony yellow frosting
is a perfect way to celebrate the Sun's
rebirth. Cover the frosted cake with
tiny white candles, and decorate the
table with evergreens and oranges.
Brew up a pot of tea with cinnamon
sticks, orange slices, and cloves, and
offer tarot readings. The solstice
itself is a birthday party, after all.

Karri Ann Allrich

Notes:

December 19
Sunday

 2nd ♈
Color of the day: Amber
Incense of the day: Cinnamon

Energy Boost Spell

Yule is a perfect time to contact
the ghosts of ancestors or the
spirits that inhabit your home. You
can make contact through an old-
fashioned table tipping, a Spiritualist
technique that I learned from my
aunt. To start, locate a sturdy wooden
table. Arrange four "believers" around
the table. Each person should place
their palms flat on the table and
chant: "Up table, up! Up table, up!"
At this point, you may hear creaking
or other such noises. One side of
the table should rise up and crash back
down. (Watch your table hop across
the room!) After the table is energized, ask questions: "Are there spirits
in this house?" and so on. If you hear
two taps, this means "yes." One tap
means "no." If the spirits are willing,

ask if there is someone they wish to communicate with? Or ask: "Did we know you in life, spirit?" This should be a fun, energizing ritual before Yule. Unlike using the Ouija board, table tipping is safe for children when adults are present.

Susan Sheppard

Notes:

blessed with wisdom and balance today. Allow the experience to unfold as it will, trusting that you will learn what you need to in time. When you feel you have received what you will in this meditation, thank the Moon for its blessings, and go about your day.

Kristin Madden

Notes:

December 20
Monday

2nd ♈

Color of the day: Ivory
Incense of the day: Peony

Soothing Light of the Moon Spell

With the waxing Moon in Aries today, it would be beneficial to work with calming, centered energy. Take a few moments to breathe deeply, and imagine you are standing beneath a waxing Moon. Feel the cool light of the Moon on your body as it begins to sink into your skin, filling your being. Give thanks for the presence of the Moon and its energy. Then ask that you might be

December 21
Tuesday

Yule – Winter Solstice

 2nd ♈
☽ v/c 12:16 am
☽ → ♉ 12:52 am
☉ → ♑ 7:42 am

Color of the day: Gray
Incense of the day: Sage

Bring Back the Sun Spell

The Winter Solstice is the longest night of the year. The Sun has reached its weakest point, but on this night it will be reborn and begin its growth to the long days of summer.

All the holidays of December are connected to this event. The Celts call this day Alban Arthuan. The name *Yule* is Germanic. At this time of the year many people become depressed. Often this is blamed on the fact that the celebrations fail to meet their expectations. But people have always become depressed at this time of the year because of the lack of sunlight and the seeming death of all of nature. To ancient peoples this fear was personified as an attack of elves and ghostly spirits, similar to the beliefs surrounding Halloween. This is obvious when one studies the customs of the Shetland and Orkney Islands in the far north of Scotland. This was one of the last places in Europe to become Christian, therefore their customs are closer to the ancient past. Here, this holiday was called Yule into the twentieth century. On the actual solstice, these islands see only six hours of daylight. Their Yule lasts from December 20 to January 13. During this period, defense from the spirits of the dead becomes paramount. The house and barn are decorated with amulets in the form of straw crosses. Sheaves of corn are placed on the roof; round cakes are baked with the solar cross inscribed on them, and plenty of ale is brewed. Drinking ale is so important that there is a fine for anyone who abstains. During this period all work except the most necessary stops,

and the nights are spent singing and dancing. In this way, the danger and the depression are staved off by joy. We often hear that we decorate our homes with evergreens because they are a symbol of life everlasting in this season of frost. This is true, but holly is also an amulet that captures evil on its barbs before it can enter the house. In the West, one must realize that it is natural to become depressed at this time of year. Just accept it, and make use of the ancient amulets and rituals designed to help bring back the Sun.

Robert Place

Notes:

Holiday lore: The Yule season is a festival of lights, and a solar festival, and is celebrated by fire in the form of the Yule log—a log decorated with fir needles, yew needles, birch branches, holly sprigs, and trailing vines of ivy. Back porches are stacked with firewood for burning, and the air is scented with pine and wood smoke. When the Yule log has burned out, save a piece for use as a powerful amulet of protection through the new year. Now is a good time to light your oven for baking bread and confections to serve around a decorated table; sweets have a particularly ancient history at this time. They are made and eaten to ensure that one would have "sweetness" in the coming year. Along these lines, mistletoe hangs over doorways to ensure a year of love. Kissing under the mistletoe is a tradition that comes down from the Druids, who considered the plant sacred. They gathered mistletoe from the high branches of sacred oak with golden sickles. It is no coincidence that Christians chose this month to celebrate the birth of their savior Jesus. Now is the time when the waxing Sun overcomes the waning Sun, and days finally begin to grow longer again. In some Pagan traditions, this struggle is symbolized by the Oak King overcoming the Holly King—that is, rebirth once again triumphing over death. And so the holly tree has come to be seen as a symbol of the season. It is used in many Yuletide decorations. For instance, wreaths are made of holly, the circle of which symbolized the wheel of the year—and the completed cycle. (*Yule* means "wheel" in old Anglo-Saxon.)

December 22
Wednesday

2nd ♌

Color of the day: White
Incense of the day: Cedar

Get Ready for a Performance Review Spell

To get the most out of a dreaded "performance review" at work, take a quiet moment one day before your review. This should be exactly twenty-four hours before the review's scheduled time, if possible. Put on the clothes you intend to wear for the review. Sit relaxed in a chair, and close your eyes for a few quiet moments. Remember all the things you've done—all of your accomplishments—since your last review. Ask yourself, which of these things will you bring with you to the interview as positive reasons for a raise, promotion, or whatever you intend for this current review? Write the reasons down on a piece of paper, fold the paper, and place it in your pocket. Just before your interview, find a quiet spot and quickly review your list. Return the list to your pocket (or inside a sock, or other hidden place, if you don't have pockets). Feel the energy of these positive items flow into your body, giving you confidence during the review.

Therese Francis

Notes:

to have a supply of blessed water on hand.

Magenta Griffith

Notes:

December 23
Thursday

 2nd ♉
)) v/c 8:41 am

)) → ♊ 11:32 am

Color of the day: Crimson
Incense of the day: Vanilla

Moon Water Spell

After sunset tonight, when the Moon is up, take a bottle or other container you can close, and fill it full of water, preferably from a well or other natural source. You can use bottled spring water if there is no safe natural source of water nearby. Put the open container of water outside, and set it where the light of the Moon will shine on it. Ask the Goddess to bless the water with her light. Leave the container there as long as the Moon is up, then close the container carefully. Keep it to use in all rituals and spells that require water. You can do this every month at the Full Moon

December 24
Friday

 2nd ♊

Color of the day: Coral
Incense of the day: Dill

Spell for Christmas Eve

On Christmas eve, you can reconnect with some of the Pagan imagery associated with this time of year. Santa Claus is really a red-robed shaman who works with reindeer medicine and can fly through the night. He brings gifts by sneaking through your chimney in the middle of the night, but his true gift is the gift of transformation, of bringing love and cheer to a time of darkness and coldness. Honor Santa by leaving a few cookies out on a plate tonight. If you have a chimney, leave them near the hearth. You can also honor Santa by giving magical gifts that honor each one of your loved ones.

Gifts that matter are gifts that come from the heart, and that bring love, joy, and healing. When you are wrapping your gifts, intend the best for the recipient, and say a small prayer:

> Goddess, bless this gift I give. May it bring joy and love to my loved one.

Jonathan Keyes

Notes:

December 25
Saturday
Christmas

2nd ♊

☽ v/c 8:30 am

☽ → ♋ 11:38 pm

Color of the day: Blue
Incense of the day: Violet

Christmas Magical Lore

The feast celebrating the birth of Christ was not always celebrated on this day. Originally the church celebrated Christmas on the day of Epiphany, January 6. In A.D. 336,

after Christianity had conquered Rome, the holiday was moved to December to coincide with the Festival of the Unconquered Sun. In this way, Christ was identified with the Sun god, the god of light. Other aspects of the holiday are derived from the Roman Saturnalia. The Saturnalia was a Winter Solstice festival dedicated to Saturn, the god of agriculture. It lasted from December 17 to 23. During this period there was a sacrifice at the temple of Saturn followed by a public feast. All work stopped; servants and slaves were freed from their chores. There was public gambling, merriment, and gift-giving presided over by a mock king. The midnight mass, the feast, and the giving of presents at Christmas are derived from the Saturnalia. The most popular presents during the Saturnalia were small figures made of wax or clay that represented the gods. Likewise today, we decorate our homes with small figures that represent the mythic beings that are associated with this season: Santa Claus, snowmen, reindeer, and elves. The Christmas tree can be traced to the myth of Yggdrasill, the Germanic world tree. The holly and the Yule log derive from the Germanic solstice celebration, and the tradition of mistletoe comes form the Celtic holiday. The creche was added by St. Francis. During this holiday everyone participates in magic.

Robert Place

Notes:

of nourishing energy. Visualize this energy touching your crown and flowing into your body. Feel this energy warm and regenerate you with every breath. Allow the energy to reach through you, trailing off into the earth, grounding any excess or unwanted energy. Allow the energy to continue its flow until you feel it is no longer necessary. Thank your higher self for this rejuvenation. Spend the rest of the evening participating in activities that you enjoy.

Karen Follett

Notes:

December 26
Sunday
Kwanzaa begins

2nd ♋
Full Moon 10:06 am

Color of the day: Gold
Incense of the day: Sage

Nourishing Energy Spell
The days are growing longer, but the air is still cold and the ground barren. Beneath the soil, the mother is nourishing the seeds that will become next spring's flowers. The growing Sun is introducing warmth and light to nourish these tender infants of the next growing season. As the universe nourishes the seeds of spring, focus these energies to nourish your inner seeds. Light a white candle. Burn your favorite incense, and relax in a comfortable position. Relax your body, and quiet your mind. Ask your higher self to open to rays

December 27
Monday

3rd ♋
Color of the day: Lavender
Incense of the day: Chrysanthemum

First Day of Kwanzaa Spell
Today is the second day of Kwanzaa, the African-American cultural holiday. Kwanzaa comes from the Swahili phrase "Matunda ya kwanza," which means "first

fruits." It is based on the many harvest festivals of Africa. Kwanzaa is not a religious festival; rather, it is a cultural holiday that seeks to unite all African-Americans and provide them a sense of identity with their African heritage. Family unity is the holiday's main focal points. The number seven features prominently in Kwanzaa. There are seven principles of Kwanzaa, and seven candles are displayed during the holiday. Although Kwanzaa is a secular holiday, this would be a good time to honor the seven African powers: Obatala, Oshun, Ellegua, Chango, Oggun, Orunla, and Yemaya. Candles for each of these deities can be found at *botanicas*. The colors of Kwanzaa—red, black, and green—are appropriate for these deities as well. Burn the candles for the five days of Kwanzaa, and ask these gods and goddesses to protect your family and friends. Offer spring water, hard candies, and African violet incense. If you work with the powers, research ways to incorporate the principles of Kwanzaa with their worship.

Denise Dumars

Notes:

December 28
Tuesday

3rd ♋
☽ v/c 2:34 am
☽ → ♌ 12:14 pm

Color of the day: White
Incense of the day: Gardenia

Good Fortune Coin Cake

When I was a child, as each year drew to a close my Greek grandmother would follow an ancient Byzantine custom of baking a "coin cake." To make such a coin cake, drop a blessed coin into the batter prior to baking your cake. When the cake is cut, whomever receives the coin has good luck during the coming year. Be sure to sterilize your coin beforehand by placing it in boiling water for one minute; you may also wish to wrap it in aluminum foil before adding it to the batter. Tell everyone before you serve the cake that they may find a coin—no one should be surprised. Slice the cake in this manner: The first piece is for the home; the next for the head of house. Thereafter, slices are passed from oldest to youngest.

James Kambos

Notes:

December 29
Wednesday

3rd ♌

Color of the day: Topaz
Incense of the day: Neroli

Travel Protection Spell

To protect yourself during holiday travels, collect a white votive candle, a pinch each of dried basil, lilac, and sage, and any combination of tiger's-eye, moonstone, amethyst, malachite, or turquoise. Carve the protection symbol of your choice into the candle, while visualizing a safe journey. Place the candle in a heat-proof container, and sprinkle the herbs around the candle. Place the stones on the outside of the container. Light the candle and chant:

> Great spirit, keep me safe
> by land or sky or sea.
> Safe journey, safe return.
> So mote it be.

Allow the candle to burn completely, and then carry the stones with you when you travel.

Ember

Notes:

December 30
Thursday

3rd ♌
☽ v/c 9:54 am

Color of the day: Green
Incense of the day: Chrysanthemum

State of the Budget Spell

Jupiter rules Thursday and all matters of money and responsibility. With Yule's expenses now past, you can focus a clear eye on your financial situation for the previous year and the one to come. This spell is extra helpful if you make New Year's resolutions about money. Set your altar with four candles: red for funds going out; black for funds coming in; green for prosperity; and brown for security. As you light them, say:

> All in balance and trust,
> going forth as it must.
> Let all debts be duly paid,
> and successes be made.
> Jove see us through the year.

Meditate on the state of your budget; see if you have any insights. Leave the candles to burn out naturally.

Elizabeth Barrette

Notes:

December 31
Friday
New Year's Eve

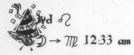

2nd ♌

☽ → ♍ 12:33 am

Color of the day: Purple
Incense of the day: Nutmeg

Noise-Warding Ritual

Once again, the old world is dissolving into chaos as the new one is born. As in the Saturnalia, work is put aside today, and things not normally permissible are now permitted. During the Saturnalia in Rome, slaves were permitted to give orders to their masters. Like the Chinese, we must make as much noise as possible at this moment of great change to ward off danger. Instead of fireworks, use New Year's noisemakers that are made just for this occasion. Celebrate the holiday with friends. At the stroke of midnight, kiss the one closest to you for luck throughout the year.

Robert Place

Notes:

A Guide to Witches' Spell-A-Day Icons

 New Moon Spells

 Full Moon Spells

 New Year's Eve, Day

 Jewish Holidays

 Imbolc

 Samhain, Halloween

 Valentine's Day

 Thanksgiving

 Ostara, Easter

 Yule, Christmas

 April Fool's Day

 Sunday Health Spells

 Earth Day

 Monday Home Spells

 Beltane

 Tuesday Protection Spells

 Mother's Day

 Wednesday Travel Spells

 Father's Day

 Thursday Money Spells

 Litha

 Friday Love Spells

 Lammas

 Saturday Grab Bag

 Mabon

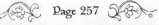

Daily Magical Influences

Each day is ruled by a planet that possesses specific magical influences:

Monday (Moon): peace, healing, caring, psychic awareness, and purification.

Tuesday (Mars): passion, sex, courage, aggression, and protection.

Wednesday (Mercury): conscious mind, study, travel, divination, and wisdom.

Thursday (Jupiter): expansion, money, prosperity, and generosity.

Friday (Venus): love, friendship, reconciliation, and beauty.

Saturday (Saturn): longevity, exorcism, endings, homes, and houses.

Sunday (Sun): healing, spirituality, success, strength, and protection.

Lunar Phases

The lunar phase is important in determining best times for magic. Times are Eastern Standard Time.

The waxing Moon (from the New Moon to the Full Moon) is the ideal time for magic to draw things toward you.

The Full Moon is the time of greatest power.

The waning Moon (from the Full Moon to the New Moon) is a time for study, meditation, and little magical work (except magic designed to banish harmful energies).

Astrological Symbols

The Sun	☉	Aries	♈
The Moon	☽	Taurus	♉
Mercury	☿	Gemini	♊
Venus	♀	Cancer	♋
Mars	♂	Leo	♌
Jupiter	♃	Virgo	♍
Saturn	♄	Libra	♎
Uranus	♅	Scorpio	♏
Neptune	♆	Sagittarius	♐
Pluto	♇	Capricorn	♑
		Aquarius	♒
		Pisces	♓

The Moon's Sign

The Moon's sign is a traditional consideration for astrologers. The Moon continuously moves through each sign in the zodiac, from Aries to Pisces. The Moon influences the sign it inhabits, creating different energies that affect our daily lives.

Aries: Good for starting things, but lacks staying power. Things occur rapidly, but quickly pass. People tend to be argumentative and assertive.

Taurus: Things begun now do last, tend to increase in value, and become hard to alter. Brings out an appreciation for beauty and sensory experience.

Gemini: Things begun now are easily changed by outside influence. Time for shortcuts, communications, games, and fun.

Cancer: Stimulates emotional rapport between people. Pinpoints need, supports growth and nurturance. Tend to domestic concerns.

Leo: Draws emphasis to the self, to central ideas or institutions, away from connections with others and emotional needs. People tend to be melodramatic.

Virgo: Favors accomplishment of details and commands from higher up. Focus on health, hygiene, and daily schedules.

Libra: Favors cooperation, compromise, social activities, beautification of surroundings, balance, and partnership.

Scorpio: Increases awareness of psychic power. Precipitates psychic crises and ends connections thoroughly. People tend to brood and become secretive under this Moon sign.

Sagittarius: Encourages flights of imagination and confidence. This Moon sign is adventurous, philosophical, and athletic. Favors expansion and growth.

Capricorn: Develops strong structure. Focus on traditions, responsibilities, and obligations. A good time to set boundaries and rules.

Aquarius: Rebellious energy. Time to break habits and make abrupt change. Personal freedom and individuality is the focus.

Pisces: The focus is on dreaming, nostalgia, intuition, and psychic impressions. A good time for spiritual or philanthropic activities.

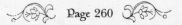

Glossary of Magical Terms

Altar: a low table that holds magical tools as a focus for spell workings.

Athame: a ritual knife used to direct personal power during workings or to symbolically draw diagrams in a spell. It is rarely, if ever, used for actual physical cutting.

Aura: an invisible energy field surrounding a person. The aura can change color depending upon the state of the individual.

Balefire: a fire lit for magical purposes, usually outdoors.

Casting a circle: the process of drawing a circle around oneself to seal out unfriendly influences and raise magical power. It is the first step in a spell.

Censer: an incense burner. Traditionally, a censer is a metal container, filled with incense, that is swung on the end of a chain.

Censing: the process of burning incense to spiritually cleanse an object.

Centering yourself: to prepare for a magical rite by calming and centering all of your personal energy.

Chakra: one of the seven centers of spiritual energy in the human body, according to the philosophy of yoga.

Charging: to infuse an object with magical power.

Circle of protection: a circle cast to protect oneself from unfriendly influences.

Crystals: quartz or other stones that store cleansing or protective energies.

Deosil: clockwise movement, symbolic of life and positive energies.

Deva: a divine being according to Hindu beliefs; a devil or evil spirit according to Zoroastrianism.

Direct/Retrograde: refers to the motions of the planets when seen from the Earth. A planet is "direct" when it appears to be moving forward from the point of view of a person on the Earth. It is "retrograde" when it appears to be moving backward.

Dowsing: to use a divining rod to search for a thing, usually water or minerals.

Dowsing pendulum: a long cord with a coin or gem at one end. The pattern of its swing is used to predict the future.

Dryad: a tree spirit or forest guardian.

Fey: an archaic term for a magical spirit or a fairylike being.

Gris-gris: a small bag containing charms, herbs, stones, and other items to draw energy, luck, love, or prosperity to the wearer.

Mantra: a sacred chant used in Hindu tradition to embody the divinity invoked; it is said to possess deep magical power.

Needfire: a ceremonial fire kindled at dawn on major Wiccan holidays. It was traditionally used to light all other household fires.

Pentagram: a symbolically protective five-pointed star with one point upward.

Power hand: the dominant hand, the hand used most often.

Scry: to predict the future by gazing at or into an object such as a crystal ball or pool of water.

Second sight: the psychic power or ability to forsee the future.

Sigil: a personal seal or symbol.

Smudge/Smudge stick: to spiritually cleanse an object by waving incense over and around it. A smudge stick is a bundle of several incense sticks.

Wand: a stick or rod used for casting circles and as a focus for magical power.

Widdershins: counterclockwise movement, symbolic of negative magical purposes, and sometimes used to disperse negative energies.

Norse Runes

Feoh: money, wealth	ᛙ	Eoh: resilience, endurance ᛃ
Ur: strength, physicality	ᚾ	Peordh: change, evolution ᛣ
Thorn: destruction, power	ᚦ	Eolh: luck, protection ᛉ
Os: wisdom, insight	ᚠ	Sigil: success, honor ᛋ
Rad: travel, change	ᚱ	Tyr: courage, victory, justice ᛏ
Ken: energy, creativity, change	ᚲ	Beorc: healing, renewal ᛒ
Gyfu: gift, sacrifice	ᚷ	Eh: journeys, work ᛖ
Wynn: joy, harmony	ᚹ	Mann: man, self, intelligence ᛗ
Haegl: union, completion	ᚻ	Lagu: healing, protection, life ᛚ
Nyd: need, deliverance	ᚾ	Ing: fertility, energy ᛝ
Is: ice, barrenness	ᛁ	Daeg: opportunity, change ᛞ
Jera: bounty, fruition, reward	ᛇ	Ethel: land, prosperity, power ᛟ

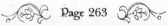

Call for Submissions

We are looking for magical daily lore for next year's *Witches' Spell–A–Day Almanac*. If you have lore or history to share about a day or holiday, we'd like to hear about it.

Writers: Daily lore pieces should be 100 to 150 words long, and focus on the folklore, historical information, or trivia particular to a calendar day or holiday. We are looking for unique and interesting lore that is timely, revealing, and intriguing.

Submissions should be sent to: annualssubmissions@llewellyn.com

or

Witches' Spell-A-Day Submissions
Llewellyn Worldwide
P.O. Box 64383
St. Paul, MN 55164

(Please include your address, phone number, and e-mail address if applicable.)

If you are under the age of 18, you will need parental permission to have your writing published. We are unable to return any submissions. Writers and artists whose submissions are chosen for publication will be published in the 2005 edition of the *Witches' Spell-A-Day Almanac* and will receive a free copy of the book.